COLLECTING, RESTORING AND RIDING

Classic Motor Cycles

A thorough guide to the best in the
fascinating field of old motor bikes.

COLLECTING, RESTORING AND RIDING

Classic
Motor Cycles

TIM HOLMES & REBEKKA SMITH

Patrick Stephens, Wellingborough

First published in 1986

British Library Cataloguing in Publication Data

Holmes Tim
    Collecting, restoring and riding classic
    motorcycles.
    1. Motorcycles
    I. Title   II. Smith, Rebekka
    629.2'275   TL440

    ISBN 0-85059-782-X

*Patrick Stephens Limited is part of the Thorsons Publishing
Group*

Photoset in 10 on 11 pt Palacio by MJL Typesetting
Ltd, Hitchin, Herts. Printed in Great Britain on 115
gms Vol 13 Claire Super Offset, and bound, by The
Garden City Press, Letchworth, Herts, for the
publishers, Patrick Stephens Limited, Denington
Estate, Wellingborough, Northants, NN8 2QD,
England.

Contents

The good old days when a BSA B31 was part of every well-dressed young man's wardrobe. A popular post-war bike.

unfairly, sometimes perceived as being slightly aloof and aristocratic (and its Pioneer Register is by definition highly selective), the VMCC is open to everyone and always welcomes new members. Both have performed invaluable services for people interested in old machines. They have laid a solid foundation of practical wisdom, information, dating practice and regular use (especially regular use), and the best tribute that can be paid to either is to join whichever is most appropriate to your interests.

In addition to these two 'root stocks', there is the network of single-make clubs, some of which are quite venerable, like the London Douglas MCC, and others which have started up with the increasing interest and specialization to be found. On top of this, there has been a burgeoning of locally-based clubs catering for British or classic (or both) bikes, so the owner of an old machine can be sure of as much support as he or she could possibly wish for.

Is there a particular type of person attracted to old motor cycles? A visit to almost any classic show or event will answer that—with a resounding 'NO!'. There are not many places where one could see a biking outlaw rubbing shoulders with a tweeded member of the squirearchy, but the Manchester Classic Bike Show is one of them. The Bristol Classic Motorcycle Show is another, and the scenario is repeated at most of the major gatherings. The Pioneer Run, an annual outing from Epsom to Brighton organized by the Sunbeam MCC, always attracts a huge following

Two veterans—a 1910 Precision 3½ hp and a 1913 Premier 2¼ hp.

of motor cyclists of all shapes, sizes, socio-economic groups, cults and interests. It's a pretty universal addiction.

So, if there is no particular type, is there a common reason? Scratch a classic motor cyclist and you could find an ecologist, a nostalgic person, a practical person, a bigot or a status seeker. The reasons for wanting to join in are as varied as the people involved. Do some of these look a little unlikely? They will all stand examination.

The ecological aspect of owning an old bike is that we can imagine—even if it is not quite true—that we are recycling a manufactured product. In fact, where the old artefact is a prime-use vehicle there are grounds for this belief, but when it is used as a leisure-time vehicle the argument does not really stand up. However, it is better that something which has absorbed a considerable amount of energy in its manufacture, and which represents a specific amount of non-renewable resources, is treated with respect rather than be abandoned. A manufactured product which is not used, either for its prime purpose or to provide raw materials for further use, represents a squandering of resources which our planet cannot afford—so let's keep the old bangers going!

It is worth remembering at this point the cottage industries which the classic revival has engendered. When *Classic Bike* magazine began in 1979 there were few specialists and only a sketchy network of engineers or machining shops willing to undertake work on such antiques. Nowadays there is a strong selection of small businesses catering for the needs of the movement, and whether one requires a simple machining job or a complex casting done to pattern, a firm can be found to do it. One of the strongest arguments for actually using old bikes is the trade it encourages in parts and services. Not only does this ensure a continuing supply of the components which regularly wear out, it also fosters employment, which in this day and age is an achievement of some merit.

Another 'ecologically' based reason for enjoying old motor cycles is the pleasure to be gained from dropping out of the conspiracy of planned obsolescence. Whether it's new bikes or cars or washing machines, all products are designed to become unfashionable—if not totally worn out—after a relatively short period. Our current industrial system demands that this is so, for there must always be buyers to keep the factories in business, and there are a limited number of consumers. It can be intensely frustrating, however, to have to abandon an otherwise serviceable product for lack of one part which is no longer available. In their day, the old motor cycle manufacturers were as guilty of this as anyone else, but by deliberately buying something which is hopelessly out of date one subverts the normal scheme of things. This can afford a certain satisfaction, even if in all other of life's aspects one is in the hands of the manufacturer.

And there's another reason: the control it gives you. You choose the jolly thing, and it's up to you to make it go or keep it going. You've got to find out all about it, find the things you need and find out how and where they fit. In

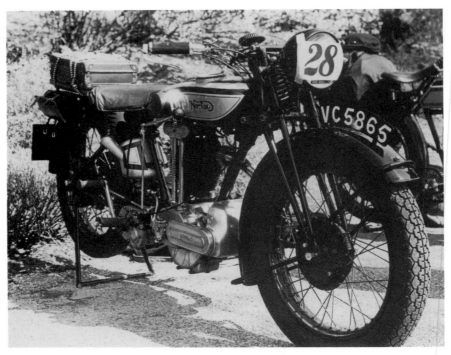

Above *A Norton Model 14 from the vintage period.*

Below *Post-vintage machines, like this 1934 AJS V-twin, are generally better equipped to cope with modern traffic.*

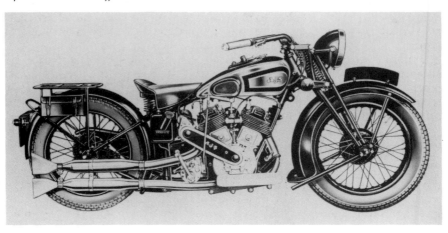

a time when more and more is being taken out of the consumer's hands, an old motor cycle offers a whole host of problems which the average person can both understand and do something about. Motor cyclists by tradition enjoy maintaining (or just fiddling with) their machines, but most modern bikes offer little scope for this, either through complexity or the need for special tools. In addition, it is often easier, quicker and cheaper to buy parts for an obsolete British bike than for a current—or three-year-old—Japanese model. This probably sounds like another of those motor cycling myths, but it has been found to be so in many, many cases. Workshop manuals are generally available in photocopy form, and magazines such as *Classic Mechanics* offer serious technical advice on working on your old bike.

Not unconnected with the two reasons above is nostalgia, plain and simple. Nostalgia for a particular make or model, or nostalgia for a period when things were simpler or the world seemed younger. Many of those entering the classic fold are 'Born Again' bikers who either had a bike in their youth or longed for a specific model but could never afford it. Now, with better paid jobs, more spare cash and—perhaps—the dream machine less expensive in relative terms, they can afford to indulge their youthful desires. Others again are happy to buy any kind of machine from the period they remember with fondness and will be as happy with a cheap two-stroke utility model as with a four-stroke roadburner. Or perhaps they'll get both, eventually.

The choices made are very personal, and any machine chosen is as validly a classic as any other. There is no hard and fast definition of a 'classic' motor cycle. Veteran, thanks to the VMCC, is defined as a model made before 31 December 1914; vintage, a model made between then and 31 December 1930; post-vintage, between then and 31 December 1945; post-war anything after that, up to 1960 (at present). Classic means all of those and more, and if you happen to think that a particular model from 1963 or '69 or '75 fits the bill, there is no one to gainsay you. In general usage, as a loose definition, the term is applied to models of the '50s and '60s, but almost any bike qualifies—indeed, there are some current machines which enthusiasts would pick out as future, if not instant, classics.

If there is no hard and fast definition, classic status being imparted by subjective decision, neither are there any national boundaries. A good many people would admit only British bikes to the classic pantheon; others would allow any machine made within Europe and America; an increasing number would select Japanese bikes. As those who choose the classics get younger, so the selection of models they grew up with will change. The history of motor cycling, like any other branch of the discipline, does not stand still.

There is one class of classic motor cyclist so far omitted, to whom none of the above has much relevance, and that is the seeker of status. A look at magazines dealing solely with modern bikes soon reveals that they are looking more and more towards the classic end of the market. This has more

Foreign classics, like the Ducati, are an accepted part of the scene and attract much admiration.

to do with trying to boost their falling circulation figures than a true appreciation of the old machines, but it also emphasizes the fashionable element of the scene. Just as the magazines do, so some of the readers will want to follow the classic trend and, again, just as the same kind of person must have the latest superbike, so the most classic of classics will be demanded. There is a reason why BSA Gold Stars and Vincent twins fetch such high prices, and it is not entirely due to their intrinsic worth. They command exceedingly high prices in America, Australia and Japan (where anything old sells like hot cakes) but there are also a lot of poseurs over here who want to be seen on the best. Having mentioned these people—and it is not implied that all Vincent and Gold Star owners fall into this category—we can now ignore them again!

Deciding which category you fit into is not important; deciding what kind of motor cycle you want is very important. There are a number of factors to be taken into consideration by the would-be classic motor cyclist, not the least of which is what you can afford. Think first of all about what you want the bike for once you've got it. Chapter 12 offers some more specific advice

Even Japanese makes can be found at the classic shows, and the Vintage Japanese Club is growing fast.

on the options open to active riders, but before considering them, think more generally.

Will you be using the machine every day? Every week or month? Or just once a year? Will you be covering long distances, perhaps with a passenger? Do you need a dead reliable vehicle with a good spares back-up, or can you afford to have something unusual which, if it does go wrong, may be out of service for some time?

If you have any previous knowledge of a particular make or model, it may be a good idea to choose what you already know; it will at least save that initial 'getting acquainted' period, and you should have some idea of how the bike is performing.

An absolute beginner would be sensible to choose a common post-war machine, such as the AJS or Matchless 350 cc single, a Triumph or BSA twin, or one of the BSA 350 or 500 cc singles. These are random examples—they all have their own problems and pitfalls, but there is a good body of knowledge about them and a multitude of reliable sources of spare parts. Almost all of the major post-war makes have specialist spares dealers and clued-up

Above *There's nothing new about liking old motor cycles—veteran meets post-war during a day out in 1948. The post-war Douglas was brand new then: the 3½ hp model was 35 years old.*

Below *A first-time buyer would probably avoid an unusual machine like this Riley.*

owners' clubs, but not all models are equally well catered for. If you are disposed to undertake a little fieldwork, a visit to one of the larger classic shows will open a wealth of free advice to you, as the people on one-make clubstands can always be relied on to give you the lowdown.

If you already have a certain grounding in the ways of old motor cycles, or are a little more adventurous, the post-vintage period offers a good number of possible purchases. By this time, bikes had become quite convenient and reliable, and features such as the brakes—so useful in modern traffic—tend to be quite advanced. In addition, many machines designed in the post-vintage period carried on into the post-war period, either because the model was felt to have stood the test of time or because manufacturers had no opportunity, or no resources, to develop new ones. A post-vintage bike offers an excellent compromise between the esoteric nature of a true vintage motor cycle (well, some of them) and the reliability and ease of ownership of a post-war model.

Straddling the two periods are the ex-WD machines. There is, it must be said, a body of riders devoted to such machines and they will go to some pains to ensure that both their bikes and their persons are turned out as accurately as possible, even down to correct serial numbers on the tank. It has even been whispered, and let us whisper it now, that some real cranks go so far as to put real, working examples of rifles or sub-machine guns into the bike-mounted holster. That kind of illegal foolishness apart (and there are only one or two such people), WD-aficionados have, probably quite unfairly, been stereotyped as wearing trench coats or despatch rider macs in all weathers, having a fondness for strong drink and doing a lot of hard riding. This should not dissuade you from buying a bike: such people are harmless and will give you any amount of help and encouragement.

Dedicated or experienced classicists will go for a vintage—or perhaps veteran— model, and will need no advice on their choices. However, it should not be assumed that all of the older machines are beyond the ken of a tyro. They are, on the whole, simple to understand, certain models have very good spares back-up (usually those made in some numbers like the Triumph or the Douglas) and the VMCC was formed for the very purpose of helping its members to keep vintage machines going; likewise the Sunbeam MCC.

Then again, general guidlines apart, consider the drawbacks of owning an old motor cycle. In the first place it is an expense, and it may represent a considerable capital outlay. Like any machine it will consume further amounts of money in spare parts (which, if they are not available will cost quite a lot to have made), will take up a deal of your spare time in maintenance, and could in certain circumstances prove a total waste of money. That is the black side of the operation, and it is unlikely to influence anyone keen on the idea.

So, you still want an old bike, or you want to augment the one (or several) you already have. You know roughly what period, what type, perhaps even

Shows have played their part in popularizing the classics. This display embraces a rare Hagg and Wilkinson, and the more mundane Francis-Barnett and James two-strokes.

what make and model, but there is still a basic choice to be made. Do you want to use the bike straight away or do you want to restore it first?

For many people an intrinsic part of the enjoyment of having a classic bike lies in the actual process of restoration. It can indeed be satisfying to take an old heap and transform it into a gleaming beauty. On the other hand, many people want to be able to jump straight on their purchase—even if it looks a bit shabby—and ride it away. Naturally the state in which you are willing to accept your choice of machine will be reflected in its price. It can also be off-putting, and this really is worth bearing in mind, to have to put a lot of work into a motor cycle before you are able to take it for a spin down the road. If you are thinking of a purchase, now is the time to decide: ride or restore?

Now is also the time to decide on a budget, a realistic budget, of both time and money. The following chapters offer guidelines on the factors affecting cost, and these should be studied before attempting to set any kind of figure on the project. There is one rule that applies to all situations: it always costs much more, and it always takes much longer, than you think. This is not intended to put you off, far from it, but to try to ensure that your bike does not become another 'uncompleted project' in the small ads of the motor cycling press.

Chapter 2

Buying your bargain

It is worth stressing again that the choice of which old motor cycle you will buy should have some basis in rational decision. Nothing is easier to waste than money (not even time), and a bad old bike will be one of the greatest wastes of money ever, especially if you get absolutely no enjoyment out of the thing. Enjoyment, let us remind ourselves, is the goal that we hope our old wheels will take us to. Nothing will give you less enjoyment than a horrible old dog of a bike which you stand no chance of getting into reasonable shape—so don't buy the first one that comes along. This is a common mistake brought on by over-enthusiasm, over-estimation of your abilities and skill, and the fear that there may not be another one offered for sale for ages. This is never true; or even if there is not another cycle of the exact model which you have set your heart on, there will be another model. With a slight adjustment of your list of desirable features you may come up with an alternative choice—or choices. It is always a good idea to have more than one, for you will soon learn to love a sound second or third choice, whereas you will quickly grow to hate a problem-riddled favourite.

The list of desirable features mentioned above should start with yourself. Experienced classic motor cyclists will have a pretty clear idea of what they can or cannot tackle, but the novice will have to make a serious estimation of his or her ability and knowledge. When doing this it is always tempting to think that you will be able to do a bit more than you really can. Often this takes the form of promising yourself that you'll spend at least one hour every evening in the workshop, and you'll make time for it by not watching 'Coronation Street', or by giving up playing Scrabble. The brutal truth is that most people do not easily break old habits, and your estimate should be made in the light of what you normally do, and not what you could do if . . .

The best judge of your ability is yourself. We are all guilty of deceiving ourselves from time to time, but this is one occasion when you must be honest. You should decide whether you want something to ride straight away or something to restore but remember also that although a restorable heap may be cheaper than a complete machine which is up and running, the cost of restoring anything is at least twice what you think it's going to be.

With all that in mind, where do you start looking for a suitable machine?

An obvious beginning is in your circle of friends and acquaintances, particularly if they are motor cyclists. It is surprising just how often someone knows someone else who's got this old bike for sale. If you belong to a club, that's another good place, as is work. Word of mouth is often the speediest way of promulgating your requirements.

The next best place, and perhaps the richest concentrated hunting ground, is the small ad. *Motor Cycle News, Classic Bike,* and *The Classic Motor Cycle* are good places to look, as is the VMCC's journal, which members receive free—another good reason for joining. Small ads are also good sources of spares. Whatever you are buying, however, you should remember that you are buying from a private individual (if it's a trade ad the fact should be disclosed) and there is no legal redress should you be sold a pup. Although it would be nice to pretend that we are all altruistic enthusiasts, the fact is that where there is money to be made, there will be rogues and sharks out to make it. Having said that, by far the most small ads will have been placed by genuine people.

When you are looking to buy from a small ad it is a good idea to act quickly, because they are an incredibly good and fast way of selling things. *Motor Cycle News,* for example, is published on a Wednesday; leave replying to an advert until the weekend and, if it's a popular machine, the chances are that it will have been sold. So buy the paper or magazine, scan the classified columns and get on the phone right away. Make a firm appointment to see the bike as soon as you can, ensure the seller has your name and phone number (just in case anything should happen which would render your visit pointless), and make sure that you turn up when you've said you will. Good manners and sound business work both ways, and the seller may have put off a firm sale to honour a promise to you.

A word here to sellers, too. Make a note of everyone's name and phone number so that you can contact them all if a sale falls through or you are unlucky enough to get a time waster. And, above all, do not let anyone ride off to test your bike unless you have some valuable possession of theirs (like cash, not a cheque). It is horrible to have to advise people not to trust one another, but one of the oldest tricks in the book is for a solo test ride to be extended into a driving away for good. Even without the registration document a bike can be a valuable prize of spare parts to sell. It is, as always, a very small number of people who would do this, but it only has to happen to you once!

If you don't find anything in the small ads, the next place to look is at the advertisements from dealers and specialists. These may take the form of a full page, complete with photographs of the motor cycles in question, or a simple list of models and prices tucked into a two-inch box. The size and style of the advert does not necessarily tell you anything about the dealer other than that some of them can afford to buy a bigger space to proclaim their wares.

Buying from a shop you have all the legal advantages that the Trade

Descriptions Act and the Sale of Goods Act can offer. Essentially, the former states that goods must accord with their description; thus if you are sold a BSA which is described as a Gold Star and you subsequently discover it to be a B31 with clip-ons, you can claim your money back from the vendor. The Sale of Goods Act states that goods must be fit for the purpose for which they are sold, which means that if you buy something as a runner and it turns out to be a mechanical disaster you can again claim your money back. Both laws also apply to spare parts or, indeed, anything else you buy from a trader.

Naturally there are disadvantages to buying from a dealer, the main one being that you will probably pay more than you would in a private transaction. There is also the possibility of buying from a shady or dishonest business, but all magazines and newspapers try to take care to ensure that the firms which advertise in their pages do give the customer a fair service. Both of the classic monthlies are staffed by enthusiasts who do not want to see anybody ripped off.

On the whole, though, a classic specialist will offer a good choice of bikes in one place, so you can see and compare them, and will have a reputation to maintain. Some will undertake to find a particular machine if you are after something very rare. There may not be an equivalent of Pride and Clarke

An auction can be a good place to buy a motor cycle, but you don't always know what you're getting.

Doing your 'homework' will help you determine originality and completeness.

nowadays but a visit to one of the larger specialists will leave you with plenty to think about.

If you have picked up a copy of *The Classic Motor Cycle* to peruse, you will undoubtedly have noticed a column called *Wheelin' n' Dealin'*, which contains reports from various auctions. It is not without significance that the major auction houses, like Sotheby's and Phillips, regularly conduct auctions of classic motor cycles. Not only does it demonstrate that there is money to be made at it, but it also indicates that the collecting of such vehicles is recognized as a legitimate pursuit. *Wheelin' n' Dealin'* reports on the prices fetched by the machines sold off (and on those which do not sell, which can be just as interesting!), and can serve to give you a good idea of a fair price to pay at auction.

Major auctions are generally advertised in the classic magazines, but Sotheby's, Phillips and Onslow's (a new house) will undoubtedly keep you informed if you so wish. There are also local and regional motor cycle auctions, and both the Manchester and Bristol shows have an auction. Check your local papers for events such as these.

Buying at auction can be a good way of getting a bargain, but it has its pitfalls. In the first place you are buying as seen. If you are lucky you might get to hear the engine running, but the chances of having a test spin are remote. There is no redress if you bid for and get what turns out to be a wreck, so it is important to be sure of what you are seeking. A second opinion can be of great assistance, especially if you don't quite trust your own judgement. The idea that an auctioneer will regard you as having made a bid if you so much as blink at the wrong moment is a myth, but it is very easy to get carried away in the heat of the moment, and end up paying over the odds. That's great for the seller, of course, and for the auctioneer who has his percentage to think of, but it's not much good for you. Set a top limit and *stick to it*. Some auctioneers also charge a buyer's premium, which seems rather unfair, so ask about this beforehand.

People who like a gamble should also consider purchasing a bike from an autojumble. Invaluable though they are as sources of spares and paraphernalia, autojumbles cannot really be recommended, *per se*, as sources of complete motor cycles. There is no slight intended to the well-known and respected businesses which regularly attend such events with a selection of machines, they will be obvious as such, but there are others which appear like the mayfly, spread their wares for a summer's day and just as rapidly disappear. In their wake they may well leave bemused owners of mix'n'match two-wheelers—it is surprising how many parts of how many makes are nearly interchangeable.

So, how do you avoid paying too much for a worthless collection of scrap metal? The answer lies in thorough research—doing your homework, as one professional restorer puts it. The best way to check prices is, yet again, to read the small ads. By collating the asking prices of likely machines you will soon gain a clear idea of what is acceptable in the market place.

Judging what a dealer will ask can be done the same way, but assessing private sales first of all will give you a clear picture of the trade mark-up. The more you know, the less you'll have the wool pulled over your eyes—but remember this: all the prices are asking prices. It does not mean that the seller seriously expects to get that much. We don't haggle much over here, but it is worth offering a lower price and getting as good a deal as you can. A thing, motor cycle or otherwise, is only worth what you think it's worth (this is, of course, a gross simplification, but this is not the book in which to discuss theories of value and it will serve very well!). There are two factors which affect the value of a bike more than any others: completeness and originality. You can assess both by doing that homework, and very often one will follow from the other.

Originality, in the sense of a bike being in the same trim and having the same colour scheme and fitting as when it left the factory, may not feature high in the list of requirements, if it appears at all, but it will affect the asking price. If you're going to pay for it, you might as well make sure you've got it. Checking will mean that you have to select a particular model (or models) beforehand, or that the seller is not in a hurry, thus giving you time to collect your facts. This is not always likely.

Unless you know an expert, you will have to consult books and photographs (or in the case of VMCC members, the relevant marque expert). A good place to start would be the VMCC library, which holds

Looking for advice? A one-make club is a good place to ask.

numerous photographs and articles, copies of which are available at a price. Likewise the East Midlands Allied Press archive, which as it consists of the records of *The Motor Cycle* and *Motor Cycling* since their respective beginnings early in the century, should in theory be able to supply a copy of every picture and a photocopy of every article which has ever appeared in those journals. Due to various human failings this is not always so in practice, but it is well worth making an enquiry.

The library of the National Motor Museum at Beaulieu is another good source, while the National Motorcycle Museum has an excellent selection of machines for you to examine in the metal. Other museums are interesting or useful to visit for similar reasons.

There are more books on motor cycles, especially detailed marque histories, in bookshops and public libraries now than ever before. They are all worth looking at, and can provide invaluable information, as can the magazines devoted to the classic scene. One-make clubs are always willing to help (though you may need to be a member) and specialist clubs like the Classic Racing MCC or Pre-65 Motocross Club are founded on enthusiasm and a willingness to help out.

In short, there is a great deal of information available from a great many sources, and discovering the details of your chosen model, if it is a reasonably common one, does not present an immense obstacle. With some you could even check out the frame and engine numbers to make sure they left the factory in the same year.

Originality though, is not the be all and end all. In many cases it might be more important to get a bike which simply fits together and works. The requirement here is for a complete machine, and whilst researching a model will equip you to determine whether everything is present and correct, you may not want to undertake such detailed homework. If you are an old-time motor cyclist returning to the fold, you should be able to determine the state of completeness of your potential purchase, especially if you refresh your memory with a quick dip into a magazine, book, museum or rally. A novice would be well advised to take a knowledgeable friend.

When it comes to looking the bike over, the golden rule is to take your time. Check it over. Is it all there? Does it run? Ask to hear it, and, if the owner makes a feeble excuse, be on your guard. If you have attended a couple of classic or vintage rallies, the sound of a sweet-running motor should be familiar to you—any engine which makes grinding or knocking noises should be treated with suspicion.

Have a good look at the state of the tyres and the chain (or belt). Are they worn or scuffed? Is the chain well-adjusted and lubricated, or slack and rusty? These things may not mean much in themselves (although replacing a tyre is a heavy expense) but they indicate what kind of a life the bike has had.

Check the state of the forks by grasping them firmly at the bottom and pushing or pulling them; test girder forks for side play too. Test wheel bearings by holding the rim with your hands diametrically opposite each other and try to rock the wheel on its spindle. Excessive play is easily felt, but watch out that you are not rocking the whole fork instead of just the wheel.

Turn the handlebars from side to side and feel for roughness or notchiness. If any is found, the steering head bearings will probably have to be replaced, not a big job but a nuisance. Also check these bearings by grasping both fork legs just below the bottom fork yoke and trying to rock the forks laterally on the main spindle or stem; there should be little or no play.

Check the rear wheel bearings and, if the machine is so equipped, the swinging arm (which is really a fork) by trying to rock it, too, on its spindle. When performing these checks it is a good idea to have the help of a friend (especially one who has done this before) as one person can do the rocking while the other feels for play. Also check rear hydraulic suspension units (on post-war machines, on the whole) by bouncing them. They should move downwards rapidly but come back to the fully extended position more slowly. If they just bounce straight back up, the damping has been lost, and they will have to be replaced.

On bikes equipped with plunger suspension (ie, spring units attached to the rear frame rails and offering limited movement to the wheel spindle) do

Above *Check the bike thoroughly, including tyres...*

Below *...and front forks (telescopic or girder).*

Above *On link-type suspension, check all the joints.*

Below *Are the wheels in line and the frame true?*

Are the spokes tensioned—it's an MoT failure if they aren't.

your best to check that the mechanism is not worn, because they are all dependent on regular greasing, which may well have been neglected.

Items which seem fairly unimportant, like control cables and electrical wiring, can often tell you a lot about the general condition of a machine. Stiff controls with frayed cables and ragged wiring held together with insulating tape generally indicate a lack of attention, while smoothly operating brake and clutch levers and a neat electrical system show a sensible concern for what are very important parts of a motor cycle. A failure in either system could be annoying or it could be fatal.

Is the owner at all knowledgeable about the machine? Again, this is not to say that all owners must know everything about the make and model in order to be good, but it may indicate that the duties of ownership have been taken seriously, which is to the buyer's benefit. Having done your homework on a particular machine will at least enable you to discover something about the seller's interest in the motor cycle—and remember, even a novice may know more than some dealers.

Something which has not yet been touched on, and something about which it is impossible to know anything is the dreaded 'basket case'. This term is used to indicate a machine which has been stripped and put into various baskets, boxes, bags or bundles—or at least it should mean that. In practice what it generally indicates is that someone is trying to sell a load of parts which may or may not all come from one make, and which may or may not contain all the items required to assemble a complete machine. In all transactions the thing to remember is 'Let the buyer beware', but when contemplating a basket case this saying must be either adhered to strictly or completely forgotten. Unless you are a fanatical expert on one model it is very unlikely that you would be able to detect whether you are buying a complete bike or, indeed, if all the parts came from the same factory. On the

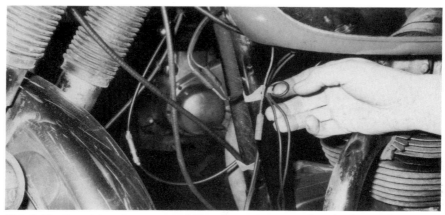

Details like the wiring give you a good idea of a previous owner's attitude to maintenance.

other hand, they are usually cheap, and may provide, if nothing else, a valuable source of miscellaneous spares. However, if you want something that you'll be able to ride fairly quickly, don't go for a dismembered motor cycle. Remember too that a lot of knowledge is gained by stripping the bike.

It has already been said that the price asked for a bike is just that—an asking price. Worn components, non-original parts, lack of maintenance and the general desirability of that model can all be used as haggling points. The presence or otherwise of an MoT certificate and tax disc can be haggling points too, and, of course, a valid up-to-date registration document (Form V5): the regulations concerning this piece of paper are covered fully in Chapter 4.

A little foresight will have alerted a potential purchaser to the fact that, if a deal is struck and cash exchanged, there follows the question of how to get the new machine home. Ride it? Well, if it's a runner, has current tax and MoT and you have valid insurance cover (ie, it covers you on that bike) and a suitable licence—and you have remembered your crash helmet—then by all means ride it. The chances of all these conditions being met is, however, not necessarily likely, particularly where your insurance is concerned. The different types of policy available are set out in Chapter 4, but unless you have one which covers you to ride any machine within a certain capacity limit, or you were so sure of your purchase that you arranged specific cover beforehand, you will have to consider another means of moving your machine or leave it and come back with a suitable cover note.

Most people transport old vehicles—when they're not running under their own power—by trailer or van. An owner of an old motor cycle may already have a trailer and a car fitted with a tow ball, or there may be a friend so equipped. Alternatively you may have to hire a trailer. In either case, you should be aware that cars towing are restricted to 40 mph unless properly 'plated', when 50 mph is permissible. Pick-up trucks are also limited to 50.

Hiring a van is a more expensive alternative, but it has the advantage of actually containing the bike in a safe place. Anyone who has strapped a bike to a trailer only to look in the mirror a few miles down the road and see it wobbling about will recognize and appreciate the peace of mind afforded by a van. In both cases, however, strong straps will be needed to hold the motor cycle upright (unless it's a sidecar combination) and these are available with more or less convenient fastening arrangements at most motor cycle shops. It's worth looking at them closely, too, for a good strap will never let you down, but a bad one will be a constant worry. Almost as great a worry as the motor cycle it supports!

Chapter 3

Ride or restore?

The decision as to whether you are going to ride your newly acquired motor cycle or restore it has—or should have—already been made, but, as is the way of these things, the purchase may not be quite what you envisaged. Perhaps it is in better condition than you had thought it would be, perhaps worse. Perhaps there is a current tax and MoT, in which case it would seem a pity to waste it; or perhaps you're simply itching to see how it goes. Many of the points of assessment will have already been covered while you were negotiating the purchase, but in your own time and space you will have more and better opportunity to learn about what you have just brought home.

Time to assess what you have just bought. Is it original? Is it complete? Is it a runner? Is it worth it?

Check the front forks for 'slop' in the head bearings, the stanchion bearings and the wheel bearings.

First of all, is it a runner? That does not just mean that it will cough and bang for a minute or so, but that it will start fairly easily and continue to run for as long as you want it to, preferably settling to an even tickover after a while, though this can be sorted out at a later stage.

If it runs, is it worn out or still serviceable? With the engine you'll soon be able to tell. Knocking bearings, clouds of blue (or indeed any colour) smoke, or generally rough-sounding mechanical noises indicate that you should not use the machine without further investigation into its health. However, if all is well with the motor, will the rest stand up to use? Check the cycle parts over really thoroughly—wheel and steering bearings, spokes, tyres, brakes, controls, chain and electrics. Don't pretend that something is all right if it's actually a bit dodgy.

Give the bike a thorough clean up, using paraffin or one of the proprietary cleaners to free oil and grease (though you should remember to relubricate the chain). This is not to demonstrate the pride of ownership, but to help you see it clearly! A number of things might be concealed by clinging muck—serious corrosion (perhaps unlikely under oil, but you never know), missing fasteners, badly worn or scored parts or even a cracked frame. Don't, however, start taking it to pieces yet, whatever the temptation. A strip-down begun in haste often ends in disaster; like everything else, it must be undertaken methodically and planned well.

Should your machine appear to be usable, you ought to use it, even if it is

At the back end, test the wheel bearings and the swinging arm (or plungers or chain stays, as the case may be).

not in the pristine state that you might prefer. A sound but scruffy bike is nothing to be ashamed of, and it is as capable of giving you as much pleasure if not more than a sparkling good-as-new mount. And there is another consideration: if the finish, scruffy or otherwise, is the original one, it gives the bike an authenticity which nothing can touch. A little delapidation here and there is more than compensated for by the knowledge that it left the factory in the same clothes, as it were, that it is wearing still. It might even win a 'Most Original' award at a concours or rally, and there is a growing number of people who believe in 'letting 'em be'. As long as all is safe, an original finish is something to be displayed rather than destroyed, for it is simply unrepeatable. The research you did earlier on will help to verify the authenticity of paintwork and details. The chances are, however, that far from being original, your old bike will have been treated to a coat or three of Valspar's best economy paint, brushed on in the days when it was simply an old motor cycle rather than a classic. It may be that you are perfectly happy with this state of affairs; should you want the thing for regular transport, what could be more sensible than a thick protective covering, whatever the colour? There are no rules in this game, and really, although purists may say that the model has been spoiled, it is entirely up to you what you do with it.

It is, in any case, a very good idea to ride the bike if at all possible, for by doing so you not only establish a bond with it (and stupid though that

Above *A scruffy but sound motor cycle is nothing to be ashamed of. Remember, too, the value of an original finish.*

Left *Acquire tools slowly but surely and you will end up with an invaluable collection. Multi-piece socket sets and cheap spanners are a waste of time.*

sounds it really is possible to become attached to this kind of mechanical artefact), but you will also gain a much clearer insight into what is right and what is wrong with it. The better you know the bike, the better you will understand what needs to be done, and in what order of importance.

It is sometimes possible to restore or refurbish a machine piecemeal. Provided you have a clear overall plan and you can find reliable services (for those parts which need it), it may be within your capabilities to have a season's worth of enjoyment out of the machine *and* end up with a better motor cycle at the end. Whatever path you choose to follow—restore, run or a combination of the two—the key to the whole thing is 'The Plan'.

Without exception, good and effective restorers keep a detailed record of progress. To this you can add a pre-restoration assessment and plan, especially if this is your first project. By writing down what you know needs doing and putting it into some rough order, you will save yourself the initial floundering around and doing unconnected jobs at random. It is very easy to fall into the trap of pulling lots of different bits to pieces with no clear idea of why you're doing it. You won't be able to assess the extent of wear or the necessity of replacement parts until you have examined the components in any case, but a general, external judgement—or the knowledge gained by using the bike—will be a starting point.

Before any of that, however, there are still more questions to be considered. In the first place, exactly what can you do? How good are you with mechanical things? And going on from that, how much of the work are you likely to have to farm out to experts? There are a number of factors which will determine what is within your reach and what beyond, not the least of which is finance. Restoring an old bike is not necessarily cheap, although getting an old bike on to the road in a sound state can be one of the cheapest means of acquiring personal transport. Note the difference.

Some of the processes will be out of the reach of the amateur anyway. Chrome plating, for instance, is extremely specialized (although nickel plating may be attempted at home with a kit), and heavy machining

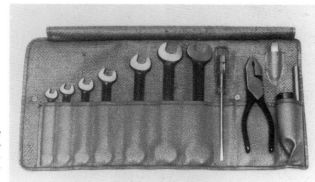

Useful for roadside repairs, tool rolls like this are hard to buy, but you can make, and stock, your own.

facilities are unlikely to be found in the average motor cyclist's garage. There is also, and let us not forget it, a social duty to keep skilled people gainfully employed, particularly at the moment—and how many of us are able to do as good a job as a time-served craftsman?

The trouble is finding one. The best recommendation is word of mouth, and that's another good reason to join the VMCC. There is bound to be a pool of knowledge in the local branch about where to get things done. It is also important to know just what you are asking the professional to do, and here again research will pay dividends. In this case it really isn't difficult, as the magazines *The Classic Motor Cycle*, *Classic Bike* and *Classic Mechanics* all deal with specific aspects of restoration in a very thorough way.

Once you have an idea of what you are going to do, *where* are you going to do it, and *when*? If you start in summer you will be wasting valuable riding time; if in winter—well, it gets jolly cold in a garage . . . However, it is generally possible to make a place warmish with heaters, and as long as it is dry and there's enough room to move around the bike, almost any kind of garage or shed will do. A source of electricity is, in these days of power tools, essential but it can be rigged up by sensible DIY types with the aid of a good book on home electrics. Others will have to call in an electrician—it need not cost much and it's far better to be safe than electrocuted. Or, if you want to use hand tools and paraffin heaters, don't bother.

Gathering together a good set of tools is another essential. Do not rush out and buy a 'Save £££' type giant socket set from the market or your local car accessory shop. These sets are usually poorly made, in inferior metal, and in any case most of them will be useless if you have a British bike. Modern socket sets generally come in AF (American Fine) or Metric sizes, and British

Some items require a surprisingly large spanner!

'Those who fail to plan, plan to fail.'

bikes were, on the whole, held together with Cycle, WC Whitworth and BSF (British Standard Fine) threads.

Don't discount the market or local bargain shops altogether though, for often there are second-hand tools to be found (also at autojumbles). Sizes and types should be clearly marked (if not, don't bother) and you can easily tell if the jaws have been butchered because the metal will be scarred. Markings to look for are W, BSF and, possibly, CEI. Common sense will tell you which sizes look most useful, although some bikes have one or two surprisingly large fastenings.

For these a decent adjustable spanner or Stilson wrench can be bought, though it is always preferable to have the exact size. Extra small fastenings such as those found on or in electrical equipment, are generally in BA thread, which will require its own spanners.

European and Japanese motor cycles are generally easier to cater for as they are almost certain to use Metric threads, and for these modern socket sets will suffice, although it's still a bad idea to buy a 999-piece special, and open or ring spanners will still be needed. If good sockets or spanners are bought one at a time, as you can afford them, or as your birthday or Christmas presents, they will last a lifetime. A well-made tool can be a joy to use, but a cheap one can cause a lot of grief.

Something which is almost always overlooked in a toolkit is the screw-driver—or, rather, screwdrivers. Both cheesehead (slot) and Phillips (crosshead) screws come in a variety of sizes and it really is a good idea to have a selection of screwdrivers to suit. Again, go for quality and don't buy Pozidriv types because they are different to Phillips although both are crossheads. An impact driver is another sound investment for shifting stubborn screws.

Pliers of the broad- and fine-nosed types are good buys (for holding things, not doing up nuts and bolts) and a pair of circlip pliers can be a god-send, though not all engines need them.

In the workshop, an engineer's vice is the single most useful fitting. These are expensive new, but can be found second-hand or in auctions and factory clearance sales. You will never regret buying one. An electric drill (hand, if you must) and a *good* set of twist drill bits come a close second.

Incidentally, a good modification for the workshop itself is to paint one wall white and lay in a supply of black felt-tip pens. You can then keep a running record of the restoration. A blackboard and chalk can be put to similar use, but you should still keep a notebook and pencil for recording details as you strip the machine.

First entries should be the parts you know to be needed from the pre-liminary examination. To identify these more clearly, a parts book or list will

A warm, dry and well-equipped workshop is a great bonus, and essential for top quality restoration work.

be needed, and the most likely source of these is BMS, whose catalogue of photocopied factory lists is extensive and invaluable. Autojumbles often have stalls selling literature and it's worth looking through the stock for your requirements. The same sources can be tried for workshop manuals, which are essential if a job is to be tackled in confidence—and sometimes safety. A lot of tasks are universal, but each model has its quirks and peculiarities, and a workshop manual can save much trial and error. They often include useful data for measuring wear and assessing serviceability too.

Also equip yourself with plenty of tie-on labels, cardboard boxes, plastic cartons, yoghurt pots or, if you are really serious, small parts storage bins. On the labels you will record the name and location of the parts *as you remove them*, and you can then keep them on their own or with their sub-assemblies in a suitably sized and labelled container. It is particularly important to keep nuts, bolts, screws, washers and spacers well tagged, and also to note, draw or photograph precisely how they fit together. For obvious reasons, it is best to do this before you start undoing them. In fact, the more sketches or photographs of details and assemblies you make before starting the job, the happier you'll be when you come to put it back together. If you don't have absolutely perfect recall, don't rely on your memory alone.

Before starting to strip the bike, make your rough plan. In a case where absolutely everything needs to be done, it is best to start with the engine and gearbox, for they are the biggest and most important sub-assemblies, and will keep you occupied for some time. Time spent waiting for a part to arrive or be found or be fabricated can be used to sort out another area or to make a start on the cycle parts.

The wheels, petrol and oil tanks, forks and the frame itself, plus all the fixtures and fittings, can be dealt with in turn, and although this is not the place to give detailed advice on particular jobs, there are a few broad hints which can be passed on. Now is the time to decide what kind of finish you want. Will it be chromium, nickel or cadmium (for fastenings) plating? Chrome was not in general use before 1930, but nickel will require constant cleaning as it tarnishes quickly, and some people sacrifice authenticity for ease of maintenance. Good plating of whatever kind does not come cheaply, and you should take pains to make it clear to the plater exactly what you want done. It is also an excellent idea to make a list (and sketches) of what you send for plating and go through it together.

Paintwork is an area open to much confusion. Many people now use modern 'plastic' paints, which are said to be very durable, but others claim that they do not take well to sharp corners and that in some cases they do not produce true blacks. Cellulose, the traditional type of paint, certainly produces strong and accurate colours, but it must be sprayed skilfully—or brush painted even more skilfully—if it is to look half decent. It is possible to lacquer over the top of cellulose, but an authentic finish would be just the paint, well polished.

Some patient souls get marvellous results from the cans of aerosol paint found in car accessory shops, but it must be said that it takes a lot of cans to get a good deep finish on a large surface, and there is an art to doing it well. Don't make the mistake of assuming that all aerosol paints are compatible. Different manufacturers use different types of paint, and if you get the wrong combination, the surface will blister and wrinkle.

There are so many variables in paintwork that it would take a whole chapter to cover all the kinds of paint, preparation techniques and methods of application (some perfectionists insist on hand-painting everything). However, as a rough guide, if you are after an authentic finish use cellulose on the painted areas and have the frame, and perhaps the mudguards, stove enamelled. Herein lies another morass, for some people call any process which involves heat curing 'stove enamelling', but this is not the case. Genuine stove enamel is applied wet and baked to a tough but brittle finish, which at its best has a deep gloss and true colouring. Many places now use epoxy powder coating, whereby a layer of powder is sprayed on to the parts and then baked to form a plastic skin. This is very tough, and done well it is almost as glossy as stove enamel. Done badly it looks very like plastic, and it is more difficult to get a true black. It is less prone to chipping than stove enamel, but it may tear and can then be quite difficult to touch in effectively.

Authentic lining or pinstriping should be done by hand (it can be sprayed on if masked effectively). Veteran machines with gold lining often used real gold leaf applied on to gold size (a kind of lacquer), but not many people can afford this treatment. A wide variety of stick-on lining is available now, and it's up to you to decide if it suits your restoration.

A respectable finish on a budget bike can be obtained by painting the frame and tinware with household oil-based paint. Providing that some care is taken with cleaning, rubbing down and brushing, such a job will look perfectly acceptable. The tank can then be sprayed with aerosol if your brushing technique is not up to scratch.

There are so many aids to preparing surfaces for painting now—primers, fillers, rust killers and so on—that it is impossible to give a full rundown here. However, for preparation it is hard to beat a lot of elbow grease, coarse, medium and fine silicon carbide paper (Wet or Dry) and red oxide primer. Allowing each coat of paint to dry properly is vital, too.

Serious restorers will want to have the metal parts thoroughly cleaned, and for this some form of blasting will have to be considered. This is generally referred to as shot blasting, but in fact a frame, for example, is best cleaned by grit blasting. Softer components can be brightened up by bead blasting, although controversy rages over whether a bead-blasted finish on a crankcase can be considered authentic and appropriate. There are probably more kinds of blasting medium than types of paint, and the best way of getting a good job done is to find a good person to do it and that brings up that problem again! As already indicated, the grapevine is the best recommendation. Wily old club members always seem to know where to go to get even the most obscure job done, so finding a good plater or blaster should be no problem at all.

Failing this, perusal of the classic magazines will reveal a host of establishments courting your trade. In the unlikely event of your finding a cowboy operator, the publication in which you found the advert should feel a moral obligation to help sort out the problem. The same advice applies when considering suppliers of parts. The well-known firms have become well-known by giving thousands of customers what they want over a number of years. Not even the most respected supplier can, however, be expected to have every single item you might want in stock. Often, spare parts are manufactured in batches, to ensure an economic price, and you may have to wait until there are enough orders to warrant a new production run. Or you may prefer to search the autojumble stalls and scan the small ads.

This is where a restoration can be seriously delayed, for not only do you not know what you may need, you can't tell how long it may take you to find it when you do know. It could be available off the shelf (quite likely with a popular model) or you might have to search a while, or you might have to have it made specially. All of the preparation, research and assessment undertaken previously should have left you with a pretty good idea of what needs doing.

Before starting, make a serious estimate of the time you think it will take—and then double it! The first rule of restoration is—'It always takes longer than you think'.

Chapter 4

Running an old bike

A classic motor cycle is free from many of the drawbacks of modern machines, but the need to display a road fund licence is not one of them. In order to get a tax disc three things are required; a valid registration document, a certificate of insurance, and an MoT certificate.

When you purchase a bike, you should receive from the owner a new-style registration document, issued by the Driver and Vehicle Licensing Centre (DVLC) at Swansea as a Form V5. *This is not the same as an old-style green- or buff-coloured logbook.* The DVLC has computerized all registrations, and unless the previous owner registered the machine before November 1983 (and that does not mean tax it—the DVLC was literally collecting all the numbers of all the vehicles in the country, whether they were being used or not), it will not appear on the database (as computer buffs say) and the registration number will be void—or, at least, it will not necessarily apply to that vehicle. If there is no new document, or the owner has not had the vehicle put on the computer, the DVLC's Vehicle Enquiry Unit (at Swansea again) will be able to say if the original registration is still valid.

Should it not be, and you still purchase the machine, you will have to apply for a registration, assuming that you want to use it on the road. If you can supply sufficient evidence that your bike is historically important you may be allowed to keep the old number. Perhaps it is the very model on which Ginger Hall crashed in the Isle of Man, leaving his name as a landmark; or perhaps you can prove that it is the only example of the model left in the country? There does have to be an exceptionally good reason though. It is more likely that if you can supply strong evidence of the date of manufacture, and the old log book, or a letter of authentication from a body such as the VMCC or one of the classic magazines should be good enough, then the DVLC will issue the motor cycle with an 'age-related' number.

This is something of a misnomer, since what it means is simply a number with no prefix or suffix. It will be left over from a series of registrations which was never completed, and will almost certainly be a 'spare' from somewhere like Caithness which, due to the low density of population, will have seen fewer new vehicles registered than, say, London. It will have no relation to either the age or place of registration of your vehicle, but it will look the part. It is, however, difficult to understand the DVLC's reluctance to leave a vehicle with a previously valid number, especially if it is only a matter of tapping a few keys on a computer keyboard—or perhaps that's the problem? But I dare say that it is very understanding of them to consider eccentrics like historic vehicle collectors at all.

If you cannot supply strong enough evidence of the date of manufacture of your bike but you still want to register it, you will have to apply for a 'Q' plate. As the name suggests, this is a registration mark prefixed with the letter Q, denoting a vehicle of unknown age or origin. Once your own vehicle has been registered, and if you are quite rich, you can purchase a 'cherished number' from one of the many dealers or a private seller, and have the mark transferred to your vehicle. Make certain that the cherished number has been put on the DVLC computer (the Enquiry Unit will tell you), or you will not be able to transfer it.

Of course, this whole number plate business makes absolutely no difference to the way your bike goes, and it is a peculiarly British thing since most other countries seem to attach little importance to their registration marks. In many countries they are issued annually, the motorist buying a number rather than a tax disc. It can be argued, however, that tracing a number can provide a great deal of history about a particular machine, and it has been known for someone who has restored a motor cycle to turn up on a previous owner's doorstep and delight them with their old friend made new.

The second item in the list of things required for tax purposes is insurance. In the past this may have been something of a problem for the classic motor cyclist, but with the boom in interest a number of firms have started to issue special policies catering for the needs of the collector and rider alike. Yet another good reason for joining the VMCC is the excellent insurance scheme it has worked out with its brokers. Under this, members can reap the benefits of agreed value, unlimited mileage cover and provision for one modern machine or for driving other motor cycles (ie, borrowing someone else's). Machines undergoing restoration or being displayed can also be covered, and there is a special fifteen-day, third party scheme, valid for VMCC events and road testing only.

This entire scheme is as near-perfect as one could want, which is not surprising considering that it was put together by what must be the biggest 'working' motor cycle club in the world. It is remarkably cheap, and contains all the items which should be looked for in schemes offered by other brokers. To wit: agreed value. This means, purely and simply, that a machine's value is agreed on by both insurer and customer. While the 'official' price of an old motor cycle may be written off as a few pounds, its market value may be several hundred (or thousand, in some instances), and it hardly seems worth paying a comprehensive policy premium to a company which will not reimburse you adequately in the event of a claim for the machine's worth.

The means of agreeing a bike's value vary. The VMCC scheme requires a senior VMCC official to confirm the customer's valuation, while others require a machine condition form to be completed or the receipts from the vehicle's purchase. All or any of the companies may request an independent engineer's or expert's report, the cost of which must be borne by the customer.

Most insurance schemes operate on the principle that the motor cycle will not be used as everyday transport and will, therefore, cover only a relatively small mileage in a year. One, two or three thousand miles per annum may be the limit of a basic policy, though there may be the option of increasing the distance for an additional premium. Companies operating this kind of scheme will probably ask for a milometer reading on the proposal form, and falsification of this would probably render the policy invalid. Much of the information is taken on trust, but it is not worth telling even a white lie, for the eventual consequence will be higher insurance premiums. There are enough schemes around to cover anyone's requirements and none of them are really costly, especially when compared with those for modern motor cycles.

A scheme which offers additional cover for your everyday car or bike would be worth considering, as would one which allows you to ride borrowed machines, but neither of these is essential to the running of your classic.

If your machine is not used on the road, or if you have one or more undergoing restoration, it is still a very sensible idea to arrange insurance against damage, fire, or theft. When enquiring about such policies, also ascertain whether or not they cover transport or trailering risks and the possibility of damage or theft while the machine is on public display. The number of machines to be covered—and this applies to road use too—is of great importance.

Something else to be kept in mind is the number of people who will be using the machine. It is not uncommon for a family to use one or more old motor cycles or three-wheelers for a vintage event, for example, and some policies allow for this.

A list of specialist insurance brokers appears at the back of this book. If you are considering taking out an insurance policy for an old bike, or a collection, make a complete list of your requirements and then spend some time discussing which scheme offers you the best deal. Current developments in the historic motor cycle movement could result in a VMCC-style insurance scheme being made available to any *bona fide* classic or historic club, through a federation or fellowship of such clubs.

As a final comment, if you are running an old bike on an ordinary policy, it could be worth your while making a couple of very specific enquiries. The

Opposite *No matter how old the motor cycle, it must pass an MoT test. Here a Zenith V-twin's brakes are being tested on a rolling road.*

Other testing stations may use a spring balance and pulley system to check brake efficiency.

first concerns the valuation of the bike; the second whether there is a date-of-manufacture limit on the policy, for some insurance companies write a clause into their policies which make them invalid if the machine is over a certain age.

The last requirement for a road fund licence is a valid MoT certificate. As most people undoubtedly know, every road vehicle over three years old must be tested annually by an authorized tester for roadworthiness. The test covers brakes, steering, lighting, exhaust and silencing systems, tyres and horn. Provided that a machine is in sound condition it is not a difficult examination to pass, and certain concessions are made for veteran and most vintage (pre-1927) machines as regards braking efficiency. However, even a modern machine has only to reach 30 per cent efficiency with one brake and 25 per cent with the other to satisfy current requirements. A veteran must be 30 per cent efficient on one brake, it being realized that many have only one brake.

Lighting regulations are fairly simple. If lights are fitted to any machine, they must *all* work, and show white at the front and red at the rear. If your

Lights will also be looked at. They must all work, be of the right wattage, and correctly aligned.

bike is post-vintage and has an electric sidelight it must have a headlamp with dip and main beams (15 watts each for up to 250 cc; 24/30 watt minimum over 250 cc). It must also have a stop lamp. However, no machine has to have any lights at all (as the law stands at present) and if you remove them all, together with their wiring, nothing and no one can prevent you using the bike during daylight hours. A simple reflector must be fitted in all cases. Acetylene lights are perfectly satisfactory, provided that they work when tested.

Most owners of historic machines will know of a friendly MoT tester. This is not to say that such a person will pass a machine if it is unroadworthy, but anyone familiar with older motor cycles will know what to look for, what is safe and what requires rectification. Rather than looking on the MoT as an annual hurdle to be struggled over, it will benefit both you and the tester to see it as an independent check-up—after all, your continuing good health may depend on it!

Steering includes checking the condition of the front forks and rear suspension (if any), the steering head bearings, and that the wheels are in line.

The tyres must have some tread all over, and though there is a specified minimum it makes no sense to try and squeeze through on a tyre that is obviously not going to last much longer. It is not always easy to find a tyre of the correct size, but a lot of digging around can turn up the most surprising things. If the worst comes to the worst, it is not unknown for riders to have different sized rims laced on to the hubs. Is it better to have a working machine with tyres of the wrong size or a laid-up one with original, but useless, wheels?

Exhaust and silencer requirements are fairly obvious—there must be no leaks and no excessive noise (this is somewhat objective, the ears of some testers being delighted at what others would wince at!). Likewise the horn—there must be one, even if only of the bicycle bulb type, and it must work.

Remember the value of appearances when presenting your machine for its MoT. There is no suggestion here that a bit of bull is any substitute for careful maintenance, but a little time taken to make things clean and tidy will reveal to you—and to the tester—that all is well, and that no faults are being concealed by clinging grime.

If anything nasty is discovered, one of the essential drawbacks of owning any kind of mechanical object will have been revealed: they go wrong, and it costs money to put them right. The amount it costs depends on the nature of

A selection of tyres suitable for vintage wear—specialist suppliers and auto jumbles are the main sources.

the fault and whether you are able to fix it yourself. When assessing the costs of running an old motor cycle this should be taken into account. There is no shame in not being able to work on your machine, though it can be useful sometimes if you can, but it will affect the running costs. Membership of one of the motoring organizations which operates a rescue system can alleviate the worst effect of a breakdown, being stranded with a useless lump of metal, but it is extremely doubtful that a patrol will be carrying a spare set of points for your 1912 Zenith Gradua—or even a relatively common Lucas K2F magneto!

Whilst thinking about such things, also consider the possibility of accident damage (which should be covered by comprehensive insurance, but not necessarily third party, fire and theft), bits wearing out and mechanical failure. The latter can range from an accessory falling off, to a con rod poking its way through the crankcase. Maintenance can prevent much, but accidents will happen and the largest costs always seem to come when the budget is stretched to its limit. If the bike is a hobby machine it can be set aside until the personal exchequer has built up reserves; a ride-to-worker will have to dig deep, or take the bus, if there is one.

If you are returning to the motor cycling fold after a layoff, it is probable that you will need to equip yourself with riding gear, and it is worth paying some attention to this. In the first place, waterproofs are essential, and if you buy cheap ones you will soon regret it. Traditional waxed cotton suits from Belstaff or Barbour are readily available, fairly cheap, and look very classic. They still have the disadvantage of getting grubby quickly (which rubs off on everything, including you), but against that they can last for years if reproofed.

A new development in waterproof material technology has seen the burgeoning of metallic-plasticized suits, by far the best of which is still the original Rukka, from Finland. These may not look classic, but they are a sight better than yellow plastic anoraks, and by golly they keep you dry. And, as with everything from Finland, they are washable.

Whilst good waterproofs are the basic clothing requirement for riding in this country, it is worth making an effort with the rest of the riding gear you will be wearing when it is not raining. The main point of owning an old bike is the bike itself, but the overall effect of bike and rider can be taken into account, and a smart and appropriately turned out ensemble is a very pleasing sight. Most of us harbour some desire somewhere within us to dress up, and choosing appropriate clothes can not only satisfy this, but can also ensure that a rider is warm (or cool), comfortable and even well protected. There is also the point to consider that while on a run— especially one which goes through highly populated areas—the riders are both representing the historic motor cycle movement and providing the casual spectator with an element of street theatre. In the first instance it is quite important to look a bit smart; in the second it is important to look interesting. This is not a frivolous point.

Right *Sensible classic cloth-ing is easy and cheap to acquire, and looks better than modern clobber.*

Left *Waterproof clothing is essential!*

There will always be people in power who want to put a stop to other people's enjoyment, and it could be argued that old motor cycles are a menace to other traffic on the open roads. It is therefore important to impress the casual or occasional spectator as strongly as possible: a colourful or amusing cavalcade of motor cycles will do so far more positively than a motley collection of flapping plastic and Hush Puppies. There are always a few characters at runs and rallies who dress to suit the spirit of the occasion, and ideas can be cribbed from them or from old issues of motor cycling papers. Jeans and a leather jacket will allow you to be the rocker you never were, while cloth or cord breeches and a Norfolk-style tweed jacket turn you into the pioneering squire.

Appropriate clothing can be bought new, even the breeches, but a little imagination and a few visits to the Oxfam shop can work wonders. Something which merits a little more expenditure is a crash helmet. Perhaps you've kept the old pudding-basin and you're happy wearing that—which is fine. If not, you can nowadays choose from a huge range of helmets, ranging from pseudo-pudding basins (with extra temple pro-tection), through the open-face jet-style, to full-face types. For casual, carefree riding an open-face helmet, with suitable goggles or eye protection,

Right *Failing all else, simple overalls can look very effective, and allow 'normal' dress beneath.*

Left *Or you can be the rocker you always wanted to be...*

is perfectly adequate, but regular main road mileage at speed is better accomplished in a full-face helmet. Oddities like the deer-stalker helmet are still available, as are pudding-basins, though they have to be bought from abroad. It is also possible to buy old helmets (often from autojumble stalls) which would not meet current standards; however, if you tell the vendor that you intend to use the helmet on the road, the transaction becomes illegal. When buying a new helmet, look for the British Standards marking (BS 2495.77 is the highest); also, if you want to use it for competition work, the ACU sticker.

Born again bikers might also like to consider the possibility of attending a motor cycle training school, just to get into the swing of things again. Naturally you will not have forgotten how to control the machine, but it is useful to brush up traffic riding skills, particularly since the volume of traffic on the roads has increased enormously over the past couple of decades, and motor cycles which were once immeasurably faster than the average saloon car may well now be left behind on the road. Your county road safety officer, contactable at the town hall or county headquarters, will be able to advise on training schemes in your area. Don't forget, either, that there are schools for racing, trials, motocross and speedway which will help you develop, or refine, the skills that you apply to your sporting classic.

Chapter 5

Veteran: Pioneering days

'You can't get people to sit over an explosion.' So said Colonel Albert Pope, one of America's leading cycle manufacturers in the 1890s. A damning pronouncement on the commercial prospects of the nascent motor cycle! Yet only a few years later, Pope's Columbia company was one of scores of manufacturers throughout the world, competing in a burgeoning new market. Most used proprietary engines, but Columbia chose to build their own, an inlet over exhaust (ioe) single-cylinder unit, which they slotted into their standard bicycle frame.

Industry, then, was forced to move with the times but the general mass of people must have viewed this turn of events rather differently; after all, most of us resist change, especially if we feel it is being thrust upon us. In the peaceful days of horse-drawn transport—when speeding fines were imposed on nothing more disruptive than an out-of-control penny-farthing or furiously-driven traction engine—the sound of a motor bike in full throttle must have been quite an intrusion.

Noise was one thing, but what about the practical applications of such an insane invention? In Europe, where the concept of a motorized two-wheeler is thought to have originated, the press as well as the public were not convinced of its necessity, or even desirability. The monthly magazine, *Engineering,* put it quite politely when they wrote, '. . .we think it doubtful whether the motor cycle will, when the novelty has worn off, take a firm hold of "public favour"'.

Out on the road, the pioneering motor cyclist could expect people to express their prejudice more strongly; catcalls, stone-throwing, even lead shot in the seat of the pants! It was a tough trail to blaze—and this is without taking into consideration the mechanical problems almost certain to be encountered on even the briefest of trips.

At the beginning of the century, £40 or £50 was the going rate for a machine and 'rich man's plaything' was a popular jibe amongst the many who didn't earn that much in a year. Few, in those far-off days, could have foreseen the enormous impact that motorized transport would have on the everyday lives of ordinary people. It would certainly rival, if not surpass, the railway as a utility vehicle for transporting raw materials and manufactured goods. It would perform a vital role in communications during the First and Second World Wars. Most significant of all, it would give individuals, whatever their class, the enormous mobility and independence that had only previously been enjoyed by the privileged few.

In the meantime it was the 'filthy rich' who provided the necessary financial backing to get the motor cycle beyond the complications of its embryonic state. During the 1870s and 1880s a feverish period of experimentation took place when every form of motive power, from coal gas to compressed air, clockwork to electricity, was considered, experimented with, and then abandoned. It was Gottlieb Daimler and Wilhelm Maybach who set the trend for running the internal combustion engine on benzine, although the fuel then used was very different from the specialized products of today and riders experienced enormous difficulties with ignition and carburation.

Engine configurations underwent a similar phase of wild permutation—there were flat, horizontal and vertical twins as well as more exotic formations, like Félix Théodore Millet's rotary five in 1894 and Colonel Holden's in-line four patented in 1896. Once mass-production was under way, all these fanciful ideas had to go on the back-boiler and make way for more practical designs with single cylinders, single speeds and belt drive.

Even with a relatively simple design, manufacturers could go to the wall simply because they lacked the foresight to test it adequately before going into production. Hildebrand and Wolfmüller, the first to build a motor cycle on commercial lines, are a good case in point. Their 2½ hp Motorrad flat-twin (the first two-wheeler to be called a motor cycle) achieved instant popularity when it appeared in 1894.

Their Munich-based factory expanded accordingly but before long complaints began pouring in from dissatisfied customers who had difficulty in starting up the large 1,488 cc engine. Ignition was by the unreliable hot-tube method which meant the H&W was liable to catch fire if the machine fell over—not an unlikely occurrence considering its propensity for skidding. By 1897, other makes, like the better-made Werner machine, were taking over the market. H&W found that the cost of producing their bikes exceeded the price at which they were sold and after four brief years production ceased completely.

Many other would-be manufacturers had their inventions strangled at birth simply through lack of adequate financial backing. It is universally accepted that Daimler, in 1885, was the first to build a motor cycle, although the four-stroke, single-cylinder Einspür was merely a test-bed for the motor cars that Daimler was later to produce with such success. But it was around the same time as this that a British inventor, Edward Butler, was perfecting his two-stroke, twin-cylinder Petrol Cycle, featuring a number of radically new ideas, including electric ignition, the first float-feed carburettor and rotary-type valves driven by chains from the driving wheel. A syndicate of investors was formed, but support was withdrawn before the Petrol Cycle got beyond the prototype stage and poor old Butler had to abandon his creation.

Lack of courage and foresight on the part of Butler's financiers can, however, be excused: the British motor cycle industry, unlike that of any other European country, was severely hampered by the Locomotive Acts of 1861 and 1865. These restricted motor vehicles to a maximum speed of 4 mph on open roads and 2 mph in towns. An added indignity was that each vehicle had to have a crew of three men, one of whom walked 60 yards ahead with a red flag, to warn other road-users of the vehicle's approach. (The famous London to Brighton Emancipation Run is an annual re-enactment of the celebratory run staged in 1896 when the speed limit was raised to 12 mph and the red flag dispensed with.)

Horses, dogs and local constabulary became something of an obsession with early motor cyclists, as reflected in the letters pages of the specialist journals *Motor Cycling*, founded in 1902, and *The Motor Cycle*, in 1903. From these it is evident that a class-based rivalry developed between motorists and users of horse-drawn vehicles, with each accusing the other of being a menace on the roads and a perpetrator of accidents.

If at times motorists felt persecuted by the general public, their paranoia was not entirely without grounds. For example, they were legally bound to stop on sight of a horse, to desist from making any sudden noise, and to avoid releasing smoke so as not to startle the animal. This could be quite tricky on a clutchless, single-speed machine, but offenders could expect little mercy if they were hauled up before the magistracy, composed as it was of horse-riding gentry! Fines were high, as were licensing fees. For

An early four—the Binks-engined Evart Hall of 1903.

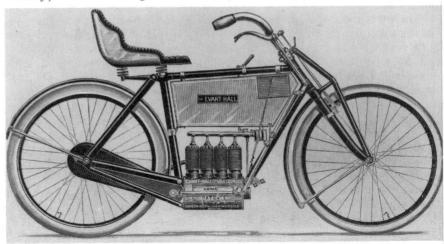

Right *The high-engine Werner sold well, despite its shortcomings.*

Below *By 1904 Werner had positioned the engine in what became the accepted place. The rider is Monsieur Derny, about to embark on the Paris-Bordeaux-Paris Reliability Trial, in which he won a First Class Award.*

example, in 1905 it cost 15 shillings to make a motor cycle street-legal, a considerable sum in those days.

The physical obstacles to motor cycling were also quite daunting. Most roads were unmetalled, deeply rutted with cartwheel tracks and full of potholes—not a comfortable prospect on a machine with little or no suspension and narrow, treadless tyres. In the summer, riders were enveloped in a thick cloud of dust stirred up by the wheels: in winter, the road became a quagmire to plug through as best one could.

Mud, wet and greasy cobblestones littered with horse manure, and roads where oolite (a kind of limestone composed of grains, like the roe of a fish) came to the surface, were conditions that the rider learned to dread. Side-slip, that is, the tendency for tyres to lose their grip with the surface of the road, was the bugbear of early motor cycling. Designers attempted to counteract this by lengthening the wheelbase and lowering the centre of gravity; a more immediate remedy was to have your high-frame cut down and substitute TT bars for the more standard swept-back handlebars.

Punctures were a common occurrence and the introduction of the quickly detachable rear wheel (first patented by Lea-Francis) was a godsend for those roadside repairs. Frequent culprits were nails from horseshoes and hobnail boots and one of the ways of preventing this was to stretch a piece of heavy-gauge wire between a pair of mudguard stays. The hope was that as the wheel revolved, the wire would trail against the tyre and whip out the nail before it could do any damage.

In addition to all the above were the purely mechanical problems of belts breaking, plugs getting oiled up, engines overheating, valves snapping and carburettors exploding. Ignition systems were unpredictable and early machines had no clutch to facilitate starting—you just had to run like hell and hop on. With no gears to help with hill-climbing, manuals suggested using a little 'light pedalling assistance'—a genteel euphemism for 'give yourself a coronary'. So it can be seen that as well as needing plenty of money, the pioneering motor cyclist was also likely to have stamina, determination and a well-developed sense of the ridiculous. In his popular column in *The Motor Cycle* magazine, Ixion painted an amusing portrait of just such a type:

'In his riding days an owner regarded a trip on his machine as something of an event. He spent odd bits of several days readying the machine for the perilous journey. He attired himself in very special garments. The whole family came out to see him off, and the eyes of the women folk were a thought anxious, if they were not actually moist. During the preliminaries every household in the street disgorged itself into the road, and stared. When he reached his destination similar scenes were enacted. The machine was petted, rubbed down with silk handkerchiefs and carefully locked up for the night, whilst the rider behaved like a subaltern who has come home to be invested with the Military Cross.'

By the beginning of the twentieth century the motor cycle was becoming less of a rarity. When registration of motor vehicles became compulsory in 1903 the increased reliability of the motor cycle, together with the lower cost of buying and running a machine, had brought the number up to 22,126. It was the sidecar in particular (a vast improvement on the forecar and trailercar which left the passenger exposed and vulnerable) which brought about the increase in popularity amongst the middle class sections of society. It meant that the whole family could now enjoy the benefits of a trip out into the country and manufacturers caught on to this new mood by promoting motor cycling as a pastime for improving one's health.

Muriel Hind, a competition rider and regular contributor to *Motor Cycling*, described a Mrs Gibb who benefited enormously from taking up the sport: 'for years this rider suffered from nerves, but since taking up motor cycling she has quite forgotten them. Some people may find this hard to believe, but it is quite true. Surely, if a motor-bicycle is going to act as such a splendid tonic, it will be an added inducement to take up the pastime.'

Women's lives especially benefited from this new period of change. With the coming of the telephone and typewriter more women went into employment as office clerks (although the vast majority who worked outside the home were still in domestic service) and yet another market was opened up. Motor cycle manufacturers were quick to take advantage of this and dozens of marques produced a Ladies' model as part of their range. Business was prospering but it wasn't until the First World War that motor cycling became a universal privilege and one which the working class people of Britain were to make a thing of their own.

The progress of the motor cycle through the pioneer years and the veteran period was, of necessity, one of fits and starts. Beginning from scratch, it was inevitable that basic principles would take some time to discover, and the essential components that go to make up a motor cycle were by no means established. Engines, wheels, transmissions and seating arrangements all went through a period of evolution, and it is worth examining these in greater detail, as they were applied to what might be called 'milestone' machines.

De Dion

In the 1890s and 1900s, the de Dion engine stood, according to *Motor Cycling* magazine, for 'all that is excellent in air-cooled engine construction'. Indeed, it could be said that the founding of the British motor cycle industry rested almost entirely on this French proprietary unit for the setting up of a workshop and finding the designers and skilled workers to produce an engine was beyond the financial limits of most of the pioneering marques. Fitting a proprietary engine into a standard bicycle frame was a popular way of entering the field and the de Dion motor was used by many well-known makes including, in this country, Royal Enfield (originally a branch of Eadie), Excelsior and Matchless.

During the 1880s the Marquis de Dion and engineer Charles Bouton began their successful collaboration with the manufacture of steam-driven four-wheeled carriages and tricycles. Before the century was out, they had turned their attention to the petrol engine and, under the influence of Daimler's Einspür, built a small single-cylinder ioe air-cooled unit with a bore of 50 mm and a stroke of 70 mm producing a cubic capacity of 138 cc. It had twin flywheels, one on either side of the crankshaft, enclosed in an aluminium crankcase. Both head and barrel had cooling fins and were held together with four long bolts screwed into the crankcase. Ignition was by battery and coil with an ingenious make-and-break mechanism which had its teething problems but eventually worked quite well.

Mounted in a pedal tricycle the de Dion drew a great deal of attention at the Place de l'Etoile in 1895 and in the following year, bored out to 58 mm and with output raised from ½ to ¾ hp, it competed in the 170-mile Bordeaux-Agen-Bordeaux race. Racing alongside the more highly developed steamers of the day, the de Dion not only beat a Hildebrand and Wolfmüller, but performed the remarkable feat of finishing fourth overall.

Over the next few years the little three-wheeler demonstrated its reliability again and again by virtually dominating long-distance racing in

An 1898 de Dion tricycle, splashing down Madeira Drive, in Brighton, at the end of a wet Pioneer Run.

France. It became a best-seller in Britain (H. J. Lawson acquired sole rights and built the engine at his Motor Manufacturing Company in Coventry) as well as on the continent and the engine's output was further increased to 2¾ hp. A light car was added to the range and later a two-wheeler with the engine mounted between the rear wheel and the saddle down tube. The latter never caught on in the same way that the inherently more stable tricycle did and the long-running question of where best to mount the engine was finally settled by the 'new Werner system', patented in 1901, which put it low down and centrally in the frame. By this time other manufacturers, like the Belgian Sarolea and British JAP companies, were rivalling de Dion with proprietary engines of their own.

Wall Autowheel

As motor cycle development galloped on ahead, there remained a core of manufacturers catering for the pedal cyclist who simply needed a little automotive assistance from time to time. Auxiliary units were designed which could be attached and detached from the standard 'safety' bicycle with the minimum of structural alteration to the machine.

Some of these cyclemotors were more ingenious than practical. For example, it was claimed of one machine, exhibited at the Stanley Show, that it could store energy. This was in the form of compressed air, pumped into the tubes of the frame when the rider descended a hill, which was then

Mrs Val Davies strides out with her 1914 Wall Autowheel. This machine often puts larger motor cycles to shame when climbing hills.

expended when assistance was required on upgrades. Another novel device was the Aerothrust which had an air propeller driven by a 2 hp two-stroke twin-cylinder engine and could be strapped on to the rear carrier of a bicycle. Also marketed as a power plant for rowing boats and canoes, it was claimed by the manufacturers that 'fitted to a four-wheeled truck known as a "motor bob" or "wind wagon" a speed of 30 miles-an-hour has been attained.' (They omitted to add that this was probably in gale force conditions and going down a steep hill.)

An attachment that actually did work, and sold in large numbers for several years, was the Wall Autowheel made by A.W. Wall Ltd of Birmingham. This comprised a small horizontally-opposed twin-cylinder engine mounted in a tubular frame which also held the single road wheel. One of the main points in its favour was that, apart from the ignition control lever mounted on the bicycle's handlebars, the Autowheel was entirely self-contained. When it appeared at the 1909 Stanley Show, *The Motor Cycle* thought it 'a most ingenious device' that could well 'revolutionize pedal cycling'.

The engine, a 1¾ hp two-stroke with automatic inlet valves (aiv), was fed by a floatless carburettor, had Bosch magneto ignition and lubrication by means of an automatic oiler. The flywheel and epicyclic gear were contained in the hub; there was no clutch but the engine was quite easy to start by paddling along a few yards with your feet. More unusual were the petrol and oil tanks which were cleverly formed out of the Autowheel's mudguard, in the same way that the rear mudguard of the Hildebrand and Wolfmüller housed the radiator for cooling the engine.

Overall design changed quite substantially over the years: in 1912 the two-stroke twin was replaced with a single-cylinder four-stroke engine with a capacity of 119 cc. A two-speed gear was added and drive was by means of a short chain instead of the former gear reduction. Most auto-cycles were driven by an engine clipped to the front or rear wheel of the bi-cycle, but the Wall Autowheel was of a more complex construction. It was pivoted in a flexible frame attached to the rear offside of the pedal cycle by means of clamps on the rear forks and the chainstay. This allowed the wheel to follow the cycle's direction at every movement—tilting over, if necessary, to take a corner, but always remaining parallel with the bicycle. In this way the Autowheel was able to propel the rider at an average speed of 10-12 mph!

Cyclemotors were not only used to augment the propulsion of bicycles, they were also applied to many other different pedal vehicles, like tricycles, tandems, tradesmen's carriers and even invalids' chairs. The constraints of social decorum and limited spending power made them especially attractive to women and in some districts they were even issued to nurses, particularly midwives, on which to make their daily rounds.

Fading away after the onset of World War I, 'Wilfreds', as they were popularly known, enjoyed a brief revival after 1945 when, once again, cheap and economical means of transport were needed.

Rover
During the period between the end of the Boer War in 1902 and the begin-ning of the Great War in 1914, Britain enjoyed a spell of relative economic stability. During this time the personal freedom offered by the motorized two-wheeler gripped the public's imagination in much the same way as the bicycle had before it, and an enormous number of motor cycle marques sprang up almost overnight. For example, in 1903 alone over eighty new makes in seven different countries came into existence; the most notable of these were Triumph in Britain, Harley-Davidson in America and Husqvarna in Sweden.

A temporary slump in sales between 1904 and 1907 put many out of business but did not deter the enthusiasm of those who survived. Nor did the fact that the motor cycle manufacturing industry was not the most lucrative of businesses. Few made their fortunes that way, but many grasped the opportunity to explore this exciting new territory.

Coventry, more than any other city, was where the motor cycle was developed to a high level of excellence. This was not mere chance: during the seventeenth century, clock-making was amongst the city's most important trades and later this was superseded by the sewing machine manufacturing industry. When trade began to slacken and unemployment became more prevalent, one of the leading factories, the Coventry Sewing Machine Company, sought to broaden its range by investigating new products. In 1868 a velocipede, one of the type made popular by Pierre Michaux, was brought back from Paris for examination. The velo, a 'bone shaker' as it was called in this country, was propelled by means of cranks and pedals fitted to the front wheel spindle. It was the forerunner of the safety bicycle, that pinnacle of light mechanical engineering and ergonomic design.

This was the start of the cycle industry in Britain. In 1869, the newly re-named Coventry Machinists Co Ltd went into bicycle production and its initiative was soon followed by many others. With the product vastly improved by the pneumatic tyre invented by John Boyd Dunlop in 1888, a craze for bicycling swept the country, with much of the impetus coming from the upper classes and the aristocracy. Famous names like Ariel, Excelsior, Hillman, Humber, Lea-Francis, Rover, Rudge, Singer and Swift—all have their roots in the enterprise of that one company, the Coventry Machinists. One name in particular, that of Rover, can be singled out for the major part it played in the development of the motor cycle.

Rover was the creation of an enterprising man, James Starley, who, feeling that he could improve on the design of the velocipede, left the mother company in 1869. He formed a partnership with William Hillman (the same Hillman who founded the motor car company in 1907) and within a year they had designed and patented the first tensioned wire-spoke wheel. This was used in the first all-metal, and relatively light, penny-farthing bicycle called the Ariel. It was a popular machine, both on the road and the racetrack, but it was Starley's nephew John who took the design a stage further by making the rear, rather than the front, wheel the driven one. By the simple addition of a chain and gearing the diameter of the rear wheel could be reduced and riding was made a great deal easier.

During the late 1890s the financier Harry Lawson was making his bid for the total domination of the nascent British motor industry with his licence-built Daimler cars. He approached, but failed to persuade, James Starley to join him in this project, but their meeting stimulated an interest in the combustion engine which was to result in the Rover 2¾ hp motor cycle. In fact Starley had already experimented with motive power as far back as 1888, when he built an electrically driven, battery-powered three-wheeler. Its performance was limited and the restrictions of the Road Act made it impracticable on the public highway.

In 1902 the Rover bicycle (so named because it gave the rider the freedom to 'rove' the countryside) was selling in enormous numbers—nearly 18,000 in that year alone. The time was ripe for expanding into the motor trade, and the first Rover motor cycle, a 2¾ hp model, appeared in November of the same year, quickly followed by a light car designed by Edmund Lewis. (Head hunting was as rife then as it is today, and Lewis had been poached from the prosperous Daimler concern.) Rover motor cycles rapidly

Note the exhaust cut out, the free engine device and the Bosch magneto of A.T.C. Lindsay's 1913 Rover.

developed a reputation for good design and workmanship. Their most popular pre-war model was a 3½ hp single which continued in production, with occasional modifications, for some time after 1918.

In 1911 a choice of two variants was offered. One was the single-gear type with direct belt drive, the other was equipped with a free engine clutch in the rear wheel, a Brown and Barlow carburettor with handlebar control, belt drive and Druid front forks. The exhaust was fitted with a 'cut out' to its silencer, a device which was eventually made illegal because of the noise it created. The cut out allowed gases to be released before reaching the expansion chamber, the idea being that you could reduce back pressure and also get an extra surge of power when you needed it.

Another interesting detail was the positioning of the Bosch magneto, which was carried immediately behind the cylinder instead of its more conventional 'tied around the tummy' point at the front of the motor. The magneto was chain-driven specially designed, it was said, to reduce the likelihood of backlash.

Triumph

If Rover can be said to have started the ball rolling with their diamond frame safety bicycles, Triumph is the name most commonly associated with the mass production of the motor cycle. When Siegfried Bettman started his cycle business in 1885, he chose a name which would be instantly understood in French and English as well as his native German. Joined by engineer and fellow countryman Mauritz Johan Schulte, the Triumph Cycle company became well established in Coventry.

It was the Hildebrand and Wolmüller which fired their interest in the motorized two-wheeler, and Schulte took delivery of one of these curious machines in 1896. After testing it on the Coventry Cycle track he found that he shared the misgivings that most people had about the unreliable ignition system. The Beeston tricycle was also considered but not taken up for production.

It wasn't until 1902 that Triumph built their first motor cycle, using the Belgian-made single-cylinder Minerva engine; proprietary engines by JAP and Fafnir were also used for a short while. It was around this time that the depression in sales set in; motor cycle sales dropped by a quarter and men and machines stood idle, just as they had done during the slump in bicycle sales in 1898. Although the 3 hp Fafnir was a good enough engine for its day,

Right *Unknown rider in an unknown event, but the year is 1910 and the bike is a 3½ hp Triumph.*

the directors at Triumph realized that their only chance of building up sales was to make a better engine of their own. This was the 3 hp single designed by Schulte and developed and used in many subsequent models. In it, Triumph invested all of their faith in the future of the motor cycle; many would claim that it was this persistence during some very difficult years which ensured the survival of the industry as a whole.

The Triumph was only a simple, clutchless side-valve with 78 mm bore by 76 mm stroke, but altogether it was a far more sophisticated affair than either the JAP or the Fafnir. The valves were mechanically operated and had adjustable spring tappets; carburation was by a Brown and Barlow spray type unit and ignition was by accumulator and trembler coil, although customers could have a magneto fitted if they preferred. Improvements in the manufacture of bearings allowed the Triumph to be fitted with all ball bearing mains instead of the usual plain components. It was found that because their rolling action reduced the surface contact area (compared to a large plain bearing surface) ball bearings minimized friction and were less prone to wear.

Although this power unit was of an advanced design it was mounted in what was basically only a bicycle frame with rigid front forks. This was rectified in 1906 when Triumph adopted a stronger frame fitted with a rocking fork with a horizontal spring. Consultations with a metallurgist resulted in better metal being used in the valves, piston rings and cylinders.

Excellent performance and reliability earned the machine its nickname of 'Trusty'. Respect for it throughout the trade was such that the Rev B. H. Davies (Ixion of *The Motor Cycle*) found it 'hard to guess where the Triumph people are going to find any more improvements; their machine is just about perfect'. Sales doubled with each new season until in 1907 the original Trusty was replaced with a 3½ hp model. This was also the first year of the Isle of Man Tourist Trophy race, when Jack Marshall took second place on the Triumph, and the factory was turning out more than a thousand machines a year.

Popularity was further increased when Marshall rode to victory in the following year's TT, at an average speed of 40.4 mph, and set a fastest lap of 42.48 mph. Triumphs were famous for their reliability rather than innovation, but one consequence of competition work was the development of their own design twin-barrel carburettor and a magneto ignition system which appeared on the 1908 models. A variable pulley, to facilitate hill climbing, was tried out but it proved rather inconvenient as, in order to change the ratio, the rider had to stop, screw the pulley in or out with a spanner and then adjust the belt length to take up the slack. A Sturmey-Archer three-speed hub gear was offered as an alternative, but it was simply a strengthened version of their pedal cycle component. With the increasing power of the engine, a stronger hub became necessary, and the increased weight of the rear wheel made riding over rough roads rather uncomfortable.

Triumph's contribution to the lightweight market was the 2¼ hp two-stroke 'Baby'.

A rear hub multi-plate clutch was also offered so that the machine could pull away from a standstill. Unfortunately a common failing was for the clutch to be let in too quickly, causing the belt fastener to rip out.

Another variation on the gearing theme came with Triumph's contribution to the lightweight market. This was the 225 cc, 2¼ hp two-stroke Baby, designed by Schulte for his young daughter. It had a two-speed gearbox operated by a handlebar lever; although clutchless, gear-changing was judder-free when taken gently, the starting-up required little exertion—you simply sat in the saddle and paddled along with your feet for a yard or two.

It was not only transmission systems that were under review. The growing interest in amateur trials and hill-climbing competitions also prompted manufacturers to raise the compression of their engines in the search for more power. This was not welcomed by all their customers, however, as high compression engines were not without their faults. These included difficult starting; pre-ignition (firing of the compressed mixture before the spark occurs); lack of flexibility when slowing down to take a corner; and a tendency to knock badly when going up hill (pre-ignition again). Triumph were able to appreciate that different customers had different requirements and met their needs by offering a range of machines, with different compression ratios. Each model range included a standard roadster as well as a TT machine for the sporting crowd.

In 1914 Triumph introduced a larger 4 hp version of their original single, with the same bore of 85 mm but with the stroke greatly lengthened to 97 mm. This was a dual-purpose machine to meet demands for a more powerful solo and a model better suited to sidecar work. By this time Triumph had undoubtedly done more than any other concern to popularize motor cycles, particularly amongst business and professional people, but they were now starting to feel the competition. As Schulte said in an interview with *The Motor Cycle*, 'I must go up hills fast and keep up with the rest of them.'

Lea-Francis

Local contemporaries Lea-Francis were one of those rare breeds who distinguish themselves not by volume, but by their never feeling constrained to run with the crowd. One of their earliest customers was the playwright George Bernard Shaw, who arrived in a chauffeur-driven Lanchester when he took possession of his first Lea-Francis motor cycle. Lea-Francis were certainly more expensive than other marques and one of their showrooms, in the best part of Piccadilly, was unashamedly aimed at the top end of the market. Yet there was a reason for this, and it was not purely a matter of snobbery.

Since 1895 when their partnership as cycle manufacturers was formed, Richard Henry Lea and Graham Inglesby Francis had built their machines with a keen eye for perfection. Never simply an assembly job, a high proportion of the components were designed and manufactured by the factory itself. Each and every bicycle was said to have been virtually hand built and rigorous quality control was exercised. Their policy was to build machines well and never to alter a good design simply for the sake of change: as Lea explained, 'The cycle should not be reduced to the level of a matinee hat—a mere cork on the ocean of fashion'. With equally florid language, the Lea-Francis catalogue described their patented inventions, of which there were many—42 before the Great War alone. Their brakes, considered to be the best in the world, were, 'like Caesar's wife—above suspicion' and their reflex rear lamp was, they said, 'a Moon in a Nutshell'.

Lea-Francis' first attempt at the motor cycle was a 3¼ hp JAP-powered side-valve V-twin which appeared in 1912. Some experimental work had already been done in 1902 with a Clement-Garrard 1½ hp unit (a Birmingham-made proprietary engine for fitting to pedal cycles) but nothing came of it, and some months after this the first (unsuccessful) car was built.

The 3¼ hp motor cycle, with two-speed gearbox, Amac carb and dummy rim front brake, was well received by the public and by 1913 production was well under way, despite a heavy price tag of £69 10s. It was instigated by Lea, with C. H. Ingall taking main responsibility for the final design, their purpose, from the outset, being to produce a machine of the highest engineering standards, with special emphasis on rider comfort and protection.

Large mudguards with deep valances shielded the rider from mud, rain and snow, as did the long curved running boards and splash shield mounted across the front of the frame. The all-chain transmission was fully enclosed in a rigid bicycle-type chaincase, which saved the rider's clothes from being spattered with oil and protected the chain from road grit and unnecessary wear on the chain rollers and sprockets.

That Lea-Francis should have chosen what was, at that time, a quite revolutionary mode of transmission was only what the public had come to expect of them. It was the culmination of years of attention to detail and extensive testing of pedal cycle components—right down to using round tubes for compression members of the frame and oval for tension members.

Needless to say, in using chain drive they were very much in a minority, for most British motor cycles of the veteran era were belt driven, although alternative systems were being experimented with on the continent and in the USA. Belt drive had much to recommend it: it was flexible, easy to replace and adjust, and initial costs were low although the frequency of breakage rather cancelled this out. Chain drive, on the other hand, was

It's not George Bernard Shaw, but would he give up his Lea-Francis? Not bloody likely!

much stronger and more positive in operation. It scored over the belt particularly when fitted to a motor cycle and sidecar combination or when used in wet and snowy weather. If fitted properly and regularly lubricated, the chain rarely needed attention on the road but, as we know, accurate adjustment is vital if misalignment is to be avoided.

It is easy for us, with an eagle's eye view of engineering history, to wonder why it took so long for belt drive to be abandoned in favour of chain, but initial problems of harshness and sensitivity to power impulses from the engine made the advantages of chain drive less obvious to riders used to the smoothness and simplicity of belt drive.

Even harder for us to imagine today is the fact that, despite widespread prejudice against noisy motorized vehicles, the single-speed belt-driven machine was comparatively quiet when running, with none of the grinding of gears and rattling of chains—just the steady thrum of the engine and the click of the belt fastener each time around. Full enclosure of the chains helped reduce noise, as it did on the Lea-Francis, and shock absorption was taken care of by a substantial four-spring cush drive incorporated into the multi-plate clutch.

The gearbox, one of Ingall's innovations, had dog engagement with gear teeth of a very fine pitch which ensured smooth and silent running. The circular casting of the 'box was eccentric in relation to the mainshaft, and mounted in a hollow bottom bracket of the frame. Adjustment was simply a matter of rotating the box in the frame.

Reliability trials, always a good means of promotion, provided the necessary exercise for Lea-Francis and their machines over the next few years. Factory riders including Norman Lea and Gordon Francis (sons of the founders) entered the Colmore Cup Trial in their first year of production, and although they came away without any awards, spectators were suitably impressed with the V-twin's handling and hill-climbing abilities, and their extraordinarily clean condition at the end of the trial.

Awards were not long in coming, however. In that same year (1913) D. W. Popplewell won a silver medal in the Land's End Trial and both Norman Lea and Gordon Francis gained medals in the ACU's Six Days Trial. Gordon also received a gold medal for his performance in the Scottish Six Days Trial, but the other two Lea-Francis entrants in the event were less fortunate, both machines suffering valve stem distortion as a result of overheating. This was a common problem with the side valve JAP if it was used hard over a long period, just one of the many aspects of motor cycle design which would benefit from the increasing knowledge of metallurgy.

Lea-Francis exhibited six new models, with 3½ hp engines, at the Olympia Show in 1914. These were similar in appearance to the 3¼ hp but had over-square dimensions of 70 mm bore by 64.5 mm stroke, giving 494 cc. A three-speed gearbox, built within the same circular housing as the two-speed unit, had also been designed but the outbreak of war interrupted production. Despite their attempts to secure a War Office contract with a specially made single-cylinder model, Lea-Francis were unable to compete with the well-established Douglas and Triumph concerns. Whilst the young men left for the trenches, the older generation continued producing the 3½ hp model, but on a greatly reduced scale. Many of these machines went to Italy for the use of despatch riders in the army there.

Zenith

Triumph and Lea-Francis were two of a growing number of manufacturers offering variable gears during the pre-war years. Discounting the lightweight models, of all the machines exhibited at the first Olympia Show in 1910, about 80 per cent had gearing of some kind or another. Riders needed greater flexibility in hilly country and for hauling sidecars, and the need for gearing was increasingly being felt on the enormously demanding Isle of Man TT course, particularly on the long climb up the eastern side of Snaefell, the 1,400 ft mountain incorporated into the circuit after 1910.

Triumph had already experimented with, and abandoned, the most basic means of altering the gear ratio—the adjustable engine pulley—in 1908. In the same year Freddie Barnes, chief designer and driving force at Zenith Motors Ltd, was able to take this curate's egg of a device and make its flaws, especially in the context of competition work, seem quite insignificant.

The Gradua gear which Barnes had developed worked by opening or closing the flanges of the pulley while the motor cycle was running. The gearing was thus altered, and belt tension was maintained by the rear wheel moving backwards or forwards in the rear fork slots, the movement being determined by the same mechanism that altered the pulley.

A 1911 6 hp Zenith. The rider is adjusting the 'coffee grinder' of the Gradua gearing system.

No, it's not stuck, just demonstrating the terrible state of Brooklands track in 1915!

Operation of the gear was originally by means of a wheel by the side of the tank but this was later replaced with a lever (the famous 'coffee grinder') which allowed a much quicker movement. In hill-climbing, the rider of a Zenith Gradua had a distinct advantage over other competitors as the ratio was altered while the bike was in motion. It was inevitable, then, that Zenith machines fitted with the system should be banned from entering competitions in the single-gear category, and the company exploited this fully by using the word 'Barred' in their trade mark. The subsequent publicity was all to their advantage!

To ensure commercial success, the Zenith Gradua was given a bit of a facelift in 1910 as its unconventional looks were thought to be off-putting to possible purchasers. The revamp was described by B. H. Davies as 'one of the prettiest mounts on the road, with a straight rectangular tank and the NSU type of change speed gear lever' whilst remaining 'as great a terror on hills with its 160-odd gear ratios'.

The new look came with a new engine, a single-cylinder 3½ hp unit, with 85 mm by 88 mm bore and stroke, a mainshaft supported on ball bearings and large mechanically operated valves. The unit was housed in a diamond frame with Druid front forks and handlebar control levers. The gear-driven magneto was positioned at the rear of the cylinder on a special platform cast integrally with the crankcase. The carburettor was situated behind this, so that if any flooding occurred (which was almost inevitable in those days) none of the petrol would drip on to the magneto and thereby cause a conflagration.

The oil pump was placed in an almost horizontal position so that the rider could see how much of the lubricant was being injected into the engine. Another novel idea was the petrol gauge fitted to the tank. A further refinement, adopted on the 1912 model, was a quickly detachable rear wheel, which Barnes claimed (and demonstrated at Olympia) could be removed in 30 seconds.

The Zenith Gradua enjoyed phenomenal success. Six and eight horse-power twins, with or without sidecar attachments, were added to the range and by 1914 all three models including the 3½ hp were powered by twin-cylinder JAP engines. The chief innovation in this range was, however, the introduction of a countershaft gear in front of the engine. Power from the crankshaft was transmitted to the 7 in diameter variable pulley by means of a chain, and from there to the rear wheel by belt. A chain-cum-belt system had already been employed by Douglas on their 2¾ hp single-speeder in 1911 with the idea of saving wear on the belt. On the Zenith it served the additional purpose of allowing a larger belt pulley to be employed, thus increasing the variety of ratios available; from 4:1 to 11:1 was now obtain-able. The countershaft also incorporated a metal-to-metal, pedal-controlled cone clutch which was fully enclosed and revolved in an oil bath. A kick starter was enclosed in the same case.

Based on a simple principle, the Gradua variable pulley could offer the rider a wide range of gear ratios. What it could not do was solve the problem of belt misalignment, and the Rudge Multi, which appeared in 1911, went some way towards correcting this fault. In fact, some decades later the pulley was to appear in a modified form on the Daf car.

Rudge
The Rudge concern started—and ended—life as so many other manufac-turers had done, with the production of pedal cycles. Its family tree is one of the more convoluted found in the industry, with branches shooting out and then being lopped off and frequent concomitant name changes. Its history begins not in Coventry but in Wolverhampton, when Dan Rudge, soon after his return from the Crimean War, spent free time from working in his pub, 'The Tiger's Head', to help out his friend Henry Clarke in his wagon-wheel building business nearby.

Dan started producing velocipedes, with Henry supplying the wheels, and built up a good reputation for high quality engineering. Never afraid to copy other people's ideas (he looked to well-established concerns like Ariel for inspiration) Dan would even resort to the odd dirty trick in his fervid quest for technical perfection. A good example of this was when a Frenchman came to pay a visit to Henry, riding a velocipede. Dan was so impressed with its smoothness that he took the man to his pub, got him rolling drunk and then stripped the machine down to find its hubs running on ball, rather than plain, bearings.

Nevertheless, Dan was himself an inventive man and his bicycles performed extremely well in the track races of the day. Sadly, his

Slight adjustment of the Multi gearing called for here. The bike is a 1913 3½ hp model.

connection with the firm was brought to a sudden end by his death, said to be caused by overwork, in 1879. The Rudge name was bought up, along with many others, by George Woodcock, a wealthy entrepreneur, who was himself to die early, but despite some ups and downs it was Dan's surname which survived.

Rudge's involvement with motor cycles did not come until some years after it merged with the Whitworth cycle company. Cheaper home-produced cycles had created a huge drop in exports to the USA, and Woodcock's death and the loss of several leading employees had caused the company to flounder. Charles Vernon Pugh, managing director of Rudge Whitworth, was the instigator of the initial dabblings with motor cycles and he made a deal with Werner of Paris to act as sole agent for the French machines in South Africa. When he found that other South African importers were in fact undercutting Rudge by £5 on every machine, Pugh retaliated by not paying Werner the balance, and unpleasant litigation ensued.

This was enough to put Rudge Whitworth off motor cycles for a while, until in 1909 it was decided that they could delay no longer and development work began. There was nothing terribly remarkable about the engine used in the first bike (it was a 3½ hp single) except the valve actuation. The problem of inferior materials and primitive metallurgy has already been touched upon, and this particularly affected the manufacture of valves, especially exhaust valves, which naturally run hotter than inlet valves. Under heavy loads, they tended to break, and while with a side valve design this would simply cause the engine to stop, in an overhead layout, the valve would drop into the engine and cause a considerable amount of damage. Most engines were side valves, but the overhead system was catching on as a means of getting more power out of a given capacity due to the better shape and efficiency of the combustion chamber.

Pugh decided on an inlet over exhaust layout, which combined the advantages of both. He also studied other motor cycles for their best features, and patents were taken out on several inventions. These included the hinged rear mudguard (which allowed easy wheel removal), a spring-up stand which was automatically released when the bike was wheeled forward, and front forks which had a large enclosed spring anchored at both ends and working in a piston and cylinder.

However, the most famous innovation was the Multi system of gearing. Rudge had offered a number of gear options, including the NSU two-speed 'box, the Philipson pulley (which adjusted the pulley automatically by means of a centrifugal governor) and the Mabon. The latter was an infinitely variable pulley system designed by a Rudge employee, and it can be regarded as the forerunner of the Multi.

Designed by John Pugh, a multiplicity of gears (hence the name) could be selected by opening and closing the engine pulley, whilst belt tension was maintained by the simultaneous opening or closing of the outer belt rim flange on the rear wheel. Both operations were controlled by a long gear

New Rudges for the 1914 season were shown in October 1913. Later in the year Cyril Pullin won the Senior TT on a Multi at a race average of 49.5 mph.

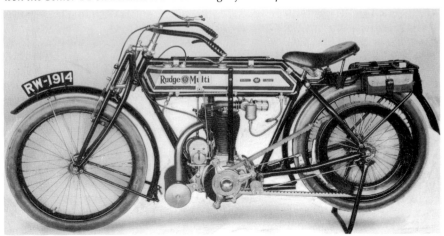

lever moving in a quadrant with notches, each of which represented a ratio.

The 3½ hp Multi was joined by a 5–6 hp twin-cylinder model (the Multwin) for sidecar use. Both engines had roller bearings on the mainshaft and on the big and small ends, and an important new kind of carburettor. Patented by Charles Pugh, the Senspray (named for the way it worked like a scent spray) had small subsidiary ducts over the jet, which enabled a much finer atomization of the fuel mixture.

The Multi gear system proved its worth in the 1914 TT when Cyril Pullin won the Senior race at an average speed of 49.5 mph. Sales were already at such a level that about eighty machines a week were leaving the factory and the Rudge Multi remained in production until 1923, a surprisingly long time considering that most had by then adopted the more efficient countershaft gearbox with all-chain transmission.

Matchless

The French were the first to appreciate the enormous value of motorized vehicles to the economic and industrial development of their country. Naturally enough, they were also the first to stage road races: these were chaotic inter-city affairs in which steam traction engines, cars and motor cycles competed side by side—with predictable consequences. As they attracted vast numbers of competitors, injuries—sometimes fatal—were not uncommon and accusations of cheating and rule-bending were all too frequent.

Following the French lead, other European countries began to stage more organized events of their own, and the motor cycle, as distinct from the motor-assisted bicycle, began to develop an identity of its own. Engine capacities and power output increased, frames and forks were strengthened and a seeming torrent of refinements made it more than an object for dilettantism. The most important of these advances were the sparking plug (1902), Robert Bosch's high tension magneto (1903) and Bowden control cables (1903).

In Britain the speed limit on public roads was raised to 20 mph, but this was still a heavy restriction on motors capable of 50 or 60 mph. Nevertheless, the authorities could not be persuaded to close public roads, not even for one day, so that road races could be held. Motor cyclists simply had to make do with using cycle tracks, like the ones at Herne Hill, Canning Town and Crystal Palace.

A dramatic change to this situation was effected in 1905. The Auto Cycle Club (formed in 1903 and later renamed the Auto Cycle Union) decided to enter a team of British riders in the French closed-circuit International Cup Race, in spite of the poor organization and cheating encountered in the first such event. Permission was given for the eliminating trials to be held on the Isle of Man, the only place the ACU could find, and more significantly, the Manx government also agreed to an annual Tourist Trophy competition, the first of which was held in 1907. Another important testing ground was opened up to motor cyclists the following year—Brooklands race track, for 28 years the only such venue on the British mainland. This lack of facilities makes the British industry's subsequent domination of the motor cycle market seem all the more remarkable.

The importance of trials and races to the improvement of the breed, as well as its value in advertising a product, was well appreciated by the Collier Brothers Harry and Charlie, co-directors, with their father, of the Matchless concern. The motor cycle was beginning to acquire a romantic, dare-devil image, and the Colliers provided a focus for such fantasies of speed and freedom, for they not only built fast bikes, they also raced them at all the major events. Harry, and even more so Charlie, became heroes of the race track—quite a coup for a company that started life as a humble laundry business.

As young boys with an interest in engineering, the Colliers were naturally enough inspired by the pioneering exploits of Michel and Eugene Werner with their 1¼ hp clip-on engine. After reading a do-it-yourself article in a journal called *The English Machinist*, the brothers set to work with a replica of the French unit. There followed many experiments with the positioning of the home-made engine and proprietary motors of continental origin. The problems they encountered were the usual ones of side-slip, unreliable ignition systems and dodgy carburation. Their first production machine was built in 1902 using a de Dion 2¾ hp engine manufactured by Harry Lawson's Motor Manufacturing Company. It had a Longuemare spray carburettor, battery and coil ignition and a much lower centre of gravity than their previous attempts, thanks to placing the engine beneath the steering head on the inside of the down tube.

Always ready to experiment, the Colliers built on the racing and commercial success of the 2¾ hp by adding an MCC-powered machine, this time a 3½ hp, to their range. Also included was a tricar with a wicker seat built on the same principles as their solo motor cycle. It was an unusual design as the seat was supported by two wheels in the front, with the driver sitting on a saddle in the rear. The solo machines sold well but the tricar suffered from overheating, and was dropped in 1906.

The first truly British proprietary engine was a single-cylinder 2½ hp unit built in 1903 by J. A. Prestwich. This was rapidly followed by singles and V-twins with side and overhead valves and different power outputs. Quick to appreciate the superiority of these JAP engines, Matchless adopted a V-twin for their 6 hp model in 1905. It had a single gear with flat belt final drive. Where the Colliers really excelled was in their early use of a suspension system when most still had rigid forks and frames. Their system featured swinging arm rear suspension with a spring unit under the saddle and leading link sprung front forks.

Harry gave a respectable performance on the V-twin in the 1905 International Cup Race in France, and in the following year Charlie came third. The first Matchless use of a JAP engine also coincided with Bert Colver

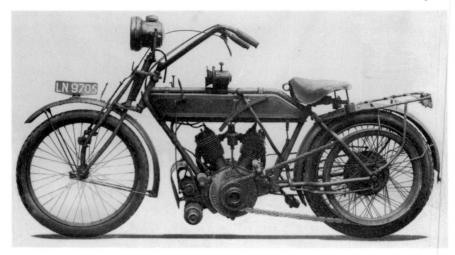

Side valve models were offered alongside the sporting overhead valvers. This is a 1911 touring model.

joining the company. He was a skilled tuner who played an integral role in the success of the Matchless marque. Colver was also a good racer, and together with the Colliers formed a works team, from which Charlie emerged as the star rider. On the 3½ hp he won the first TT at an average speed of 38.22 mph, in spite of broken front forks. Harry put in the fastest lap at 41.18 mph. Over the next few years, the Matchless team featured prominently amongst the winners at Brooklands as well as on the Isle of Man, in both Senior and Junior classes.

Having become somewhat accustomed to gaining first and second places at most events, 1911 was a disappointing year for Matchless. Charlie came in second in the Senior TT but was disqualified for stopping on the circuit to fill up with petrol, and as a result the Indian team walked away with the top three awards. But the outcome of the race was disappointing for another reason, for rising American star Jake de Rozier had also had problems, and the eagerly awaited US versus UK duel did not take place.

As compensation for this a three-race challenge was set up at Brooklands between Charlie Collier and de Rozier. The American on his Indian was the overall winner, but it was Collier who subsequently raised the world speed record to 91 mph on his famous red 7 hp machine. The Colliers were not bad losers, and they were quick to appreciate the good points of their opponents' machines. From Indian they learned that by dropping the top frame tubes and lowering the riding position you could improve the handling and appearance of the motor cycle.

Although they were still rather reserved about chain drive, of which

Indian were pioneers, Charlie started experimenting in 1911 with Renolds chains on his 91 mph racer. By September of that year an identical model, right down to the red enamel and gold-lined paintwork, was on sale to the public. The JAP V-twin was fitted with an Amac carb, Bosch magneto and handlebar controls. Transmission was by two chains via a countershaft mounted on an eccentric strap and running in ball bearings. The harshness of the chains was softened by a frictional slipping clutch fitted on the countershaft.

This machine was exhibited with ten other models for the 1912 season on the Matchless stand at the Olympia Show, with machines of between 2½ and 5 hp, with free engine and three-speed gears. The 5 hp model featured overhead valves and a six-speed gear with belt drive, and was based on the machine used by the Colliers in the TT. The gear was of the expanding pulley type, with belt slack being taken up by the back wheel. It was rather similar in principle to the Gradua system developed by Zenith, but Matchless were quick to assert that the design was entirely their own and nothing to do with the device patented by Zenith.

To get around the patent, the Colliers designed their system to be controlled by two levers (one for the pulley, the other for movement of the back wheel) working in a long quadrant on the side of the tank, whereas the Gradua patent covered only devices using a single hand control. Avoiding the patent rights was not done for purely parsimonious reasons though. One of the advantages of having two levers was that the belt could be tightened independently of any alteration to the gear ratio, thus eliminating any 'conking out' of the engine after taking a corner.

This point was taken up by *Motor Cycling* in their glowing test; 'The twin proved one of the most lively engines we have ever ridden,' it reported, 'whilst the six-speed gear provided an interesting experience. On this gear one can tighten or slacken the belt irrespective of the gear ratio employed, which is a very material advantage, especially in wet weather. The gear ranges from about 3½ to 1 down to 5½ to 1, which is an ample variation for solo work. One point worth noting in connection with the Matchless twins that we have ridden is that they start up so easily. Once bumped over compression the TT twin referred to above would be away like a shot from a gun; and yet with the use of the low gear it was possible to slow right down almost to a walking pace.'

By the end of the year, orders for 'Matchbox' machines, as they were affectionately known, were on such a scale that the Matchless works was forced to move to bigger premises in Burrage Grove, Plumstead. Customers sold on the fantasy of 'victories' of their own were not shortchanged, as throughout its seventy-year history the Matchless motor cycle was the epitome of good engineering standards at a reasonable price.

Douglas

The history of Douglas as a company begins with £10 borrowed in 1882 by

William and Edward Douglas to start a blacksmithing business. This turned
into a foundry, and the evidence is still to be seen in Bristol on cast iron street
lamps and manhole covers.

The history of the Douglas motor cycle starts with Joseph Barter, who
designed first a single and then, after witnessing the smoothness of a
horizontally opposed Lanchester car engine, a boxer twin. Unfortunately
his grasp of internal combustion theory would seem to have been
somewhat sketchy, for he arranged his timing so that both cylinders fired
simultaneously. Not unnaturally this destroyed the crankshaft assembly,
and his motor cycle, named the Fée, was not a great success.

Barter engaged a keen young engineer named Walter Moore (later to find
fame with Norton and NSU) to assist him. Moore explained the benefits of
altering the timing so that the cylinders fired alternately, which gave the
whole unit a much easier and smoother life. To market this new device,
Light Motors Ltd was formed and the cycle's name was put into English,
becoming the Fairy.

Douglas Bros supplied engine castings for the machine, which was little
more than a bicycle with the engine clamped into its frame, and William
Douglas Junior took an enthusiastic interest in the project. It was not a
surprise, then, that Douglas Bros should take over the design when Light
Motors Ltd went into voluntary liquidation in 1907, thanks to poor sales at
home. Barter, with Moore in tow, was taken on as works manager and
production was concentrated on an enlarged version of the twin. The Fairy
had been 2½ hp, but the first Douglas was 2¾ hp—a rating which was to be
associated with the firm for many years.

The Douglas motor cycle was displayed, with various other items, at the
1907 Stanley Show, but little business resulted. The following year,
however, *The Motor Cycle* called the machine 'well known', and went on to
describe the Model B, which carried its engine four inches lower in the
frame. There was a new carburettor, but the engine, with its automatic inlet
valve, remained essentially unchanged, having proved reliable in trials.

At the 1909 Stanley Show, Douglas displayed thirteen models (twelve
new and one of the previous season's to highlight the alterations). Once
again, the frame had been lowered, and the engine had undergone some
changes. Instead of being screwed on, as in the original design, the
cylinders were bolted to the crankcase, and the whole power unit could be
removed without first removing the petrol tank. Things were going well for
the Bristol company, for the following season they revealed three new
models. These were a touring lightweight, which was still equipped with
pedals; a two-speed model without pedals and therefore a much lower
frame; and an 'open frame machine, which can be ridden equally well by a
lady or a gentleman'. *The Motor Cycle* added that 'a professional man should
find this model particularly well suited to his wishes, as an ordinary coat can
be used with impunity, the transmission being encased'.

The pedalless models had a cone clutch, long footboards (pedals of any kind were *out*) and were started with a cranking handle. *Motor Cycling's* 'Lady Motor Cyclist', Muriel Hind, a well-known trials competitor, tested the open-frame model early in 1911, and found it smooth, comfortable and very pleasant to ride. Amongst other things she found the machine's hill-climbing ability—a real test in those days—exceptionally good. The two-speed gearbox, which had improved the Douglas' performance, was easy to understand and use. 'In all probability,' she concluded, 'we shall see a good many new lady riders on Douglas machines this season'.

It would appear that not only lady riders appreciated the Douglas, for *The Motor Cycle* reported that 'It is interesting to note the growth of the output of this firm. In their first year they turned out 50 machines, the next 350, and this year [1910] well over 1,000—a rate of progression they may well be proud of.'

The company did not rest on its laurels, however, for in 1911 there were more new models on show, with a redesigned engine and still lower frames. Four variants were offered, a basic single-speeder, a two-speed type, a two-speed and free engine (clutch) model, and finally the open frame two-speeder. The engine remained the same capacity, but now had both valves mechanically operated. Main bearings were ball type and the cylinders were easily detachable.

Not even the single-speed model had direct drive, for the company had found that a large indirect pulley improved the life of the belt no end, and there was a primary transmission by chain to a countershaft. The two-speed models now had kickstarts, with a heel-and-toe pedal to operate the clutch. The oil pump had also been improved, with an enclosed spring to remove the necessity for the rider to provide pressure manually. Once again Muriel Hind tested the model, finding the new kickstarter most convenient, and the engine smooth and powerful. Another lady trials rider, Rosa Hammett, commented that her Douglas had 'proved more suitable than anything I have previously owned'.

The year 1912 was an important one for Douglas, for they entered the Isle of Man TT races, then being run on the mountain circuit, for the first time. The 2¾s had already proved themselves in trials and hill climbs but this kind of racing was something new. Harry Bashall, one of the team of six amateurs, finished well, and was afterwards questioned closely by two officers from the War Department—which may have been significant, as we shall see.

Walter Moore was still busy in the design department, and in 1913 he created a three-speed gearbox, which played its part in gaining for the factory the Team Prize in the Six Days Trial. The following year Europe was plunged into the First World War, and Douglas at first had to reduce production, thus leaving the true veteran period on a slightly downbeat note.

However, it is worth following the story a little further, for the War Office soon began to appreciate the valuable role that despatch riders could play,

Douglases in Flanders in 1915: the 2¾ hp was pressed into despatch rider service in enormous numbers.

and Douglas (together with Triumph) were in a position to offer the right type of machine in the quantities demanded. Those two Army officers at the TT must have been impressed, for upwards of 25,000 Douglas 2¾s had been produced by the end of 1918. (This can pose something of a problem as far as dating goes, for all models were essentially similar.) Furthermore, the 3½ hp, introduced in 1913, was increased to 4 hp and put to work hauling sidecars. Initially, hill-climbing was a bit wheezy, but Walter Moore redesigned the cylinder heads to give what we now call a 'squish' effect. He should have patented the idea, but did not. A while later Harry Ricardo, a noted combustion specialist and a name to bear in mind, discovered the same principle. He did not fail to register his invention.

It is a measure of the success of Douglas motor cycles over the years that a good number of manufacturers adopted the horizontally opposed fore-and-aft engine layout, amongst them Bradbury, Montgomery (both these before the war), ABC, Coventry-Victor, Humber, Harley-Davidson and Indian. Granville Bradshaw, designer of the ABC, had another go with a fore-and-aft oil-cooled twin, which was eventually used by Zenith. What is it they say about imitation?

Bradbury

Bradbury, of Oldham, Lancs, began as a sewing machine factory in the Wellington Works, which is why there is a portrait of the Iron Duke to be

The Bradbury in action: it was renowned as a good hill climber.

found on the petrol tank. Motor cycle manufacture started in 1901 with singles of 2 and 2.5 hp built under a Birch Patent. J. J. Birch, of Coventry, built his own motor cycles, which had a triangular frame incorporating the crankcase—it was brazed on to the frame tubes—and bottom bracket casting. Birch also designed the rear-wheel-engined motor cycle that was built by Singer—another sewing machine manufacturer.

In 1904 Bradbury introduced 'at considerable expense, and after many experiments' a 4 hp forecar, but soon standardized production on a 3½ hp single-cylinder bicycle with an engine of their own manufacture. It seems that there was some hiatus in the business, for though *The Motor Cycle* of 18 November 1908 reported that the Bradbury had been noted for its 'special features in engine and frame construction' for five years, the issue dated 25 November states: 'a machine with a glorious past has been revived for 1909, and after a lapse is again to be seen at the Stanley Show. This is our old friend the Bradbury, which behaved so conspicuously in the early ACU and MCC Trials.'

The 1909 3½ hp model featured square bore and stroke measurements of 87 mm, mechanically operated valves and ball main bearings on the crankshaft. A Bosch magneto was driven by a chain enclosed in an aluminium case—sophistication indeed. The frame was said to be low, though cranked pedals were still provided and sprung girder forks gave a modicum of comfort.

Reviewing that show, Ixion was moved to comment, 'The Bradbury is an old friend I welcome again in a very up-to-date-form. I have not ridden a Bradbury for some years, but the early types possessed the steadiest engines on the market, capable of extraordinary plugging up long rises, thanks to an excellent flywheel system, and the 1909 type promises to reproduce this precious characteristic, besides being as completely equipped with refinements as any mount in its class.'

The 'precious characteristic' obviously helped Bradbury in their quest for success in trials, though more of it was deemed necessary the following year, when the 1910-season models were revealed. The 3½ hp was the factory's sole product, and it had been improved with better handlebars, stronger rear wheel spindle, larger diameter flywheels (for even more 'extraordinary plugging') and Druid spring forks. The Bosch magneto had been replaced by one of Simms' manufacture.

Riders in the colonies (where road conditions were far from ideal, hence 'Colonial' models) were thought to be interested in the greater ground clearance of the 1910 model, whilst home-based riders might well have appreciated the front rim brake, larger petrol tank and more conveniently placed oil pump. 'It is interesting to note,' *The Motor Cycle* commented, 'that Messrs Bradbury have profited well by the lessons they have learnt in this year's competitions.'

By 1913 the company had profited enough to expand its range. The 3½ hp single was still there, reliable as ever, but it was now fitted with a kick starter, two-speed countershaft gearbox of Bradbury's own design (with chain-cum-belt transmission) and a handlebar-operated clutch. There was also a 3½ hp horizontally-opposed twin (shades of Douglas here), with a three-speed countershaft gearbox and a choice of belt or chain secondary drive. Unusually for the time, an internally expanding rear brake was fitted. Completing the range was a 6 hp V-twin. With plated cylinders, detachable cylinder heads and light cast steel pistons, this model was quite sporty. It was also convenient, having the three-speed 'box and chain drive throughout which was totally enclosed in aluminium covers. It could be supplied complete with a coachbuilt sidecar (finished in dark green, the traditional Bradbury colour) which was as well built as the motor cycle.

Bradbury retained their reputation as manufacturers of quality machines which, though somewhat costly, could be relied on to give sterling service. Production continued after the war, up until 1925, but it is the models of the veteran era that will always spring to mind when the make is mentioned, for they incorporate all that was good of its time. Wellington would have been proud of them.

Bat

Most people, if they know anything at all about the company, imagine that the name Bat is an acronym derived from the advertising slogan 'Best After Tests'. True, the firm did use the slogan, but it so happened that the founder's name was Mr S. R. Batson, and he simply used the first syllable of his surname when registering the company in 1902. His first motor cycle, called the Model No 1, was fitted with a 2¾ hp de Dion engine, but initial sales were not as good as he hoped, and he sold the company to Theodore Tessier in 1903.

Tessier was something of a sporting rider, and he set about improving the Bat's image. A 3½ hp model was introduced in 1904 (along with an air- or water-cooled two-wheeler), and in the same year the company claimed to hold 217 world speed records, together with awards for hill-climbing. This was regarded as particularly important, as the Bat dispensed with bicycle pedalling arrangements very early on, a cone clutch offering further refinement and convenience.

The standards of acceptability in those pioneer days must have been rather different, for in a 1904 article entitled, '2,500 Miles on a Pedalless Motor Bicycle' Dr H. E. Denny recounts his experiences with a Bat. Far from sailing up hills effortlessly, the good doctor says, 'my engine has often stopped when going up a steep hill, due to poor compression, going too slowly, or carburettor needing adjustment, but in these cases, by either jumping off before it stops, or restarting on the hill (which is quite easy) and running alongside the machine, I always get up without delay or pushing.' So that was all right! Dr Denny had no complaints, indeed he felt, '. . .kindly towards the inventor, Mr Batson, for constructing what I consider a most comfortable, exceedingly safe, easy-riding, and as reliable a machine as one can find upon the market today.'

Exports played an important part in the firm's business, perhaps because continental riders appreciated the extra comfort of the Bat spring frame, which had been patented in 1904. Whatever the reason, it was one of the few British firms to establish a depot in Paris, and the Penge factory was kept busy.

According to *The Motor Cycle*, reporting in December 1908 on the Stanley Show, 'The Bat firm have a special reputation for tuning up machines thoroughly before delivery, and for meeting the requirements of individual customers.' Amongst their display models was a four-wheeled motor cycle and sidecar with a 7–9 hp motor, three-speed gear, chain drive and differential. The sidecar axle slotted into the cycle's driven axle making both rear wheels driven, but the whole thing was removable to allow for solo use. There was also an 8 hp side-valve twin, a 2½ hp lightweight, two twin-cylinder TT models (one of them with mechanically operated overhead valves, the other with an automatic inlet valve).

The TT models were important to the firm for T. H. Tessier had entered a Bat in the first TT held in 1907, and Harry Bashall (also famed for his exploits on the racing Douglas) brought a twin-cylinder model in second in the 1908 event. Bats were entered in nearly all of the pre-war TTs, and it is claimed that the speed put up by H. Bowen's model in 1910 (a lap record of 53.15 mph!) was partly responsible for the change of course. The first four TTs

It was 'V-twins only' for Bat after 1912: this side valve three-speeder has an 8 hp motor. Note the kickstart arrangement.

were held on the St John's circuit, but in 1911 the mountain circuit was used for the first time.

With Snaefell (the mountain) to climb, variable gearing became very important, and it is not unreasonable to say that the adoption of the new course greatly aided the development of the gearbox on motor cycles. Bat offered three models in 1911, a 3½ hp side valve, a 5–6 hp side valve twin and a similar 7–8 hp type. All were available with either simple belt drive or the P and M two-speed, chain drive gearbox. All of the engines were made by JAP, as they had been since 1908.

Despite their keen racing policy and the use of the ubiquitous JAP power unit, Bats were not noted for their reliability, and by 1913 there were signs of sails being trimmed. A new 4½ hp model was offered with a rigid frame and chain-cum-belt drive on a two-speed gearbox. A 6–7 hp model was also on show, with or without springing, the latter being seen as new models. This was a far cry from 1909, when *The Motor Cycle* was moved to comment that, 'other makers are slowly coming round to ideas of springing which Mr Batson first mooted in 1902 . . .' The last of the 1913 models was a 7–8 hp side valve twin (singles had been dropped completely the previous year) which came with a chain-cum-belt three-speed countershaft 'box.

It is not hard to perceive a decline in the fortunes of Bat by the end of the veteran period. One more nail was driven into the coffin when the post-revolutionary government of Russia refused to honour a contract for military motor cycles which had been drawn up under the Czar. Bat survived long enough, however, to incorporate the Martinsyde concern in 1923. That is a name we shall come across again, but for the record Bat-Martinsyde finally foundered in 1926.

Chapter 6

Vintage: The wartime influence

With the cessation of hostilities in 1918, it soon became clear that the old way of life had been lost forever. Many changes had been made, not least in the actual fighting techniques employed in this 'war to end all wars'. By 1916, as combat became centred on the battlefields of the Western Front, it was obvious that seapower had become outmoded and that Britain could no longer depend on its great naval force. The cavalry, too, had become obsolete, now that motor cycles and cars provided a mechanical substitute for the horse.

Speaking at a safe distance from the danger of the artillery, the squalor and misery of the trenches, H. G. Wells openly enthused about this latest stage in the mechanization of mass-murder. His article, 'New Arms for Old' drew up a very different line of battle from previous ones: 'An ideal modern pursuit would be an advance of guns, automobiles full of infantry, motor cyclists and cyclists, behind a high screen of observation aeroplanes. . . . It may be argued that horses can go over country that is impossible for automobiles. This is to ignore altogether what has been done in this war by recent devices. Mechanism can ride over places where any horse will flounder.'

One of the many ironies of this 'modern pursuit' was that the burden of fighting fell mainly on the troops of the regular Army—a body of men who until recently had been the object of hostility and prejudice. Nowhere was this more pronounced than amongst the working classes, the very people who made up its ranks. On hearing of her son's enlistment, one mother was fairly typical in writing '. . . there are plenty of things steady young men can do when they can write and read as you can. . .the Army is a refuge for all idle people. . .I shall name it to no one for I am ashamed to think of it. . .I would rather bury you. . .'

By 1918, with over 750,000 soldiers dead, the Great British Tommy had been elevated to a position of mythical proportions—a new kind of hero, obviously not of the officer calibre, but equally brave and always cheerful in his duty. Army despatch riders were used extensively throughout the war and, by association, the motor cycle drew up its own salvation in public opinion by becoming an indispensable tool in military strategy. Their duties included taking messages, acting as agents de liaison between various sections of a corps, and carrying out reconnaisance work. The busiest time for the 'Don R' or 'DR', as he was affectionately known, was when alterations were made in the troops' position while telegraph wires were temporarily disorganized. All communications devolved on the Don R until the wires had been smoothed out.

Sidecar outfits were as useful as solo machines—for carrying the wounded on stretchers, and for transporting top officials and military equipment. Royal Enfield, for example, supplied the army with their 6 hp JAP-powered combination as a mobile mount for the Vickers Maxim machine gun. A more ingenious adaptation was that made by Douglas who modified their 4 hp outfit to serve as the basis for a mobile wireless set; the generator, carried on a bracket mounted on the top tube, was driven by an outside flywheel via a Whittle leather belt and pulley.

In addition, stationary engines (often the salvaged remnants of a wrecked vehicle) were used to pump out water from the trenches and turn grindstones for sharpening bayonet blades. Statistics can only give a vague idea of the enormously important part played by motorized vehicles in the war. The petrol consumption of the British Expeditionary Force alone, rose from 250,000 gallons per month in 1914 to an astonishing figure of 10,500,000 gallons per month in 1918.

At the outbreak of war, more motor cyclists than were needed volunteered for enlistment as DRs (conscription was only introduced in 1916). Thanks to the increased sporting activities of motor cycling clubs during the pre-war years, most of the original Don Rs were quite experienced trials riders. Nevertheless, with the mud of Flanders, heat and dust of Egypt and rocky tracks of the Caucasus, they were hardly likely to have experienced anything quite as treacherous at home. And this is without taking shellholes and hostile fire into consideration.

The bashing taken by rider and machine alike is well illustrated in the following, a letter written by a DR based in Russia in 1917:

'We have been out here for the last fourteen months and have experienced every kind of road and climate during our 12,000 miles travelling from England, and have come to the conclusion that Russia wants a lot of beating for all-round test of a motor cycle. A most interesting and enjoyable run was to the Turkish front by the famous Caucasus Mountains. The road, or what there was of it, was hewn in the mountain side, but otherwise consisted mostly of cattle tracks and along these we had to ride at a height of some 10,000 feet. For a great distance one's attention is mostly centred on great rocks which stick up out of the road and sand-covered holes. Hairpin corners, as is easy to imagine, are very numerous, and the skid of a side-slip has soon to be corrected, otherwise a very unpleasant fall of several hundred feet to the depth below would be the result. . . The depth of the sand is a very great obstacle, footrests have been broken through landing and scraping in sand holes, and it is not uncommon to find the flywheel churning up clouds of sand and dust.'

The writer was using a 2¾ hp Douglas, a reliable model because even when kept in low gear for prolonged periods over rough terrain, the engine did not overheat or burn up its valves. Other machines used were the 3½ hp Sunbeam, 4 hp Triumph and 4¼ hp BSA, civilian models quickly snapped up by the War Office to meet immediate needs. DR recruits had their own motor cycles pressed into service, often to be ridden by someone else—much to their understandable disgust! As the need for more machines became apparent, manufacturers vied with one another for government contracts and a small selection of models, originally intended for the 1915 season, were chosen.

Best known of these was the Triumph Model H, with chain-cum-belt drive and three-speed Sturmey-Archer gearbox with clutch and kickstarter. A reliable machine, despite a tendency for the front fork spring to snap, 30,000 examples were supplied to the Army. The 3½ hp P&M two-speeder was the natural choice of the Royal Flying Corps (later renamed the RAF) who had thoroughly tested the machine during War Office manoeuvres before the war. Douglas, with their amazingly resilient horizontal twin, were also awarded a contract and by the end of 1918 they had supplied the military with over 25,000 motor cycles. Smaller contracts went to people like Royal Enfield, Norton, Clyno and AJS, some of which went towards satisfying the enormous Allied and colonial demand for motor cycles.

On the Home Front, motor cycles were increasingly being used by women in their capacity as nurses, Wrens and military chauffeurs. They worked as despatch riders for the Auxiliary Army Service and took wounded soldiers out on sidecar daytrips. Most were, however, involved in industry, both heavy and light, the most pressing requirements being the manufacture of munitions and vehicles.

In November 1916, the Ministry of Munitions imposed a ban on the manufacture of all civilian motor cycles. This caused serious problems for some businesses but for those under contract to the War Office, several prosperous years ensued. Indeed, war saved many companies from bankruptcy as an editorial in *Motor Cyling* predicted it would: 'When war broke out many men in the motor cycling trade held the most pessimistic views with regard to the future of the industry. All the young men would go to the war; none among the middle-aged men left at home would have any money to spend; trade would be utterly ruined. These were prophecies that might be heard everywhere.

'With these views we did not agree at the time, and we pointed out the enormous demand there would be for both solo and sidecar machines, not only for the British Government, but also for our Allies. Also, we foresaw that big engineering works all over the country, including those of motor cycle manufacturers, would be required to turn out vast quantities of all kinds of munitions of war.

'As everyone knows, these forecasts have proved correct. Today we are faced not by the ruin that the pessimists prophesied, but by a wave of industry and prosperity such as but few members of the trade dreamed of. Most of the well-known factories are working overtime, and even so are unable to keep pace with the demand. Others have only one complaint, and that is that there is a shortage of labour.'

Few modifications were made to these military vehicles although, for obvious reasons, substitutes had to be found for the German-made Bosch magneto. Because of the often difficult conditions under which WD machines were operating, some consolidation of technical developments was also achieved. All-chain drive, with clutch and countershaft gearbox became much more widely used, as did semi-automatic lubrication and high-tension magneto ignition systems. Some of the advances made in aero design were also to be of benefit to the motor cycle industry, not least in the development of suitable alloys for fabricating valves and pistons. It was this that would make possible the higher power outputs of overhead-valve and overhead-camshaft engines, as pioneered by JAP, Velocette and Norton in the 1920s.

Although the war ended in November 1918, it was not until January of the following year that motor cycle manufacturers were allowed to resume civilian production. Rationing of fuel, as well as food, was to continue for some time and private motoring was strongly discouraged. Those still running their own vehicles had by this time developed ways of eking out their meagre rations either by adding paraffin to the petrol or using paraffin, or other petrol substitutes, straight, in which case a special vaporizer was needed to aid combustion. Using acetylene gas was a rather more dangerous alternative and coal gas, though used by quite a surprising number of motorists, required a huge storage balloon to be carried around with the vehicle.

The first year of peace brought an overwhelming demand for civilian vehicles. Men returning from the Front, many of whom had had their first taste of motor cycling during the war years, wanted the freedom of personal transport. More women too, had discovered how enjoyable—and convenient—motor cycle ownership could be. Until factories were able to get production into full swing, demand was met by the second-hand market and factory reconditioned WD machines. Because there was little to distinguish one military vehicle from another, specialist firms sprang up offering components like exhaust pipes and aluminium pistons, with which owners could customize their bikes.

Prices were high, waiting-lists long and once production resumed, there were even some dealers unscrupulous enough to add a hefty surcharge if a customer wanted a quick delivery. Being a seller's market there were also the inevitable shoddy goods on sale, produced by manufacturers with no previous experience in building motor cycles.

At the 1919 Olympia Show, over 200 models were exhibited; those made by established firms differed little in basic design from pre-war machines.

All efforts were concentrated in producing sound, reliable motor cycles based on well-tried principles; experimentation with new ideas would just have to wait.

This isn't to say, of course, that no changes had been made. The rigours of military use in far-off countries had underlined the need for increased efficiency, resilience and ease of maintenance. Above all, soldiers returning from the trenches wanted a comfortable vehicle. A subaltern, writing in *Motor Cycling*, knew exactly what his colleagues wanted, 'And one and all they swear that "when once this blank war is over," mud and filthiness will have no part in their lives if they can possibly avoid it. They will not take to motor cycling if it remains the "dirty" hobby it has been considered in the past.

'. . . The motorcycle for *après* must be a cleaner machine. Mudguarding must be improved, oil leaks eliminated; cylinders must no longer require wire contrivances to prevent burning of the trousers; engines must start without injection or furious propulsion. For after the war it is the comfortable machine, the clean machine which will be the favourite of the new-type riders; tyres which do not puncture miles from home on a wet night, lamps which do not misbehave if unattended, saddles which give comfort instead of pain, spring forks which do not jar. These are the things which will be necessary to the new rider.'

The quest then was for what began to be referred to as an 'Everyman' machine— silent, flexible, comfortable and clean. Prudent manufacturers

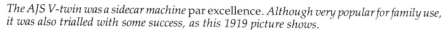

The AJS V-twin was a sidecar machine par excellence. Although very popular for family use, it was also trialled with some success, as this 1919 picture shows.

took heed and incorporated improvements in their civilian models: frames became heavier with more attention paid to suspension and steering, spring saddles and girder-type front forks being the norm. Quickly detachable wheels, 3-inch tyres, and weather protection in the form of legshields and larger, valanced mudguards; all-chain drive with three-speed gearbox, semi-automatic carburettors, high-tension magnetos and electric lighting (mainly Lucas dynamo) systems became standard. Riding was further improved by the (very) gradual adoption of small details like propstands, twist-grips and foot-gear pedals. Some of the earliest motorcycles with foot-control Sturmey-Archer gearboxes were specially designed models, like the one produced by Rover, for the war-wounded and disabled.

During the 1920s, the 'Golden Era', as many have since called it, the motor cycle industry settled into a fairly steady rhythm: price-cuts and the lower cost of petrol, oil and tyres made motor cycling even more attractive to those who could afford it. Motor cycling was more socially acceptable, cutting across class barriers, and used by both women and men, young and old, alike.

To meet their various needs a few basic trends emerged in the industry. One—a continuation from pre-war years—was for the simple single-cylinder 3½ hp, made popular by marques like Royal Enfield, Norton, and Triumph. With the growth in the market for lighter, cheaper machines, more attention was also paid to the versatile two-stroke, or 'baby'. The fact that a two-stroke required no valve gear and had a much lighter flywheel, as well as being cheaper to construct, played very much in its favour.

Machines like those built by Levis, Radco and New Hudson met the requirements of a large number of people who needed a cheap motor cycle for commuting an as a 'go-anywhere' mount. A basic aim in the design of the two-stroke lightweight was therefore to keep it within the 200 lb taxation limit for which the annual licencing fee was 30 shillings. This was quite a saving on the £3 it cost to tax a heavier machine.

The need for economy was also what made the sidecar outfit such a popular form of transport in post-war Britain. One only needs to look at the enormous range of sidecar attachments on the market in the 1920s to see that this is true. Made to cater for all types and needs, sidecars ranged from the simple lines of the single-seater torpedo attachment to the multi-seated family vehicle which came fully-equipped with hood, screen, luggage grid, rear locker and even curtains. The Acme, for example, was said to 'comfortably accommodate a family of six without recourse to the pillion' and with this type of vehicle more and more people were able to spend their free time in the country and at the seaside.

Sidecars were used by businesses as delivery vans and even as taxis; for example, the X motor cycle company in Torquay sold what they classed as a 'limousine' taxi outfit, luxuriously upholstered and with operable V-shaped windows.

Although light cars, like the Austin Seven and 8 hp Rover, started appearing on the market in the early 'twenties, initial outlay and running costs were too high for them seriously to compete with the sidecar combination and it wasn't until Morris' mass-produced and inexpensive Minor in 1928 that motor cycle manufacturers began to feel at all threatened. In its less elaborate form the three-wheeled cyclecar had strong appeal but over-development meant that many of these little runabouts were often as expensive as a moderately-priced car.

By 1929 there were 700,000 motor cyclists on the busy roads of Britain; by analysing the figures one can see that with economic depression setting in, customers were mainly concerned with reliability and comfort, rather than excessive speed. They expected their machines to function automatically without requiring too much attention, to be light, economical to run and easy to maintain; to coast uphill with ease and carry any amount of baggage without complaint. B. H. Davies could write vividly of this change in attitude:

'Before the war, motorcycling was sport. To-day it is transport. I don't say that the sporting type of rider is extinct; it is still every boy's dream that papa will remember his birthday with something which has short flat handlebars and an exhaust pipe like a stove funnel. But just as the pedal cycle began by being a society toy, and eventually economized the rural postman's shoe leather, so the motor cycle is now regarded, like the doormat, as an essential and unromantic part of many people's existence.'

This is not to say that sporting events had lost their attraction: reliability trials underlined the great technical improvements that had been made, as did the TT races where winning speeds rose from 52 mph in 1920 to over 74 mph in 1930. Captive markets in the colonies helped make Britain the biggest sellers of two-wheeled vehicles in the world but a challenge to this supremacy was developing on the continent where new and more progressive designs were being perfected.

Despite this, the British motorcyclist did not lack for choice. The variety of machines on offer is examined more closely in the following selection of collectable marques.

AJS

Albert John (Jack), Harry, George, Jack and Joe Stevens were brothers who started in business for themselves by making engines for motor cycle manufacturers like Wearwell. Then, in 1909 they started making complete bikes. Setting up in a factory in Retreat Street, Wolverhampton (where one of the family still runs an engineering business) they began with a range of 2½ hp, two-speed, chain drive models and a year later a 5–6 hp V-twin with mechanically operated side valves was added, with the sidecar market in mind.

The Stevens brothers were keen riders, and believed in entering sporting events in order to prove (and test) their products. In 1914 they entered a team of 2¾ hp (350 cc) machines in the Junior TT, and against all expectations they came in first and second. This was a surprise not because AJS motor cycles were unreliable or underpowered, but because no single-cylinder model had ever won either Senior or Junior TT. This victory (which coincided with a single-cylinder win in the Senior) set the seal on AJS's sporting image, particularly with their 350s.

After the war, during which the factory turned to munitions work, they brought out a new TT model which proved to be the fastest thing on two wheels. Much of the credit for its speed must go to Jack Stevens's study of combustion chambers. Taking a leaf out of various racing car designers' books (or should that be 'a trace off their drawing boards'?), he laid out a hemispherical chamber with the valves inclined, where most motor cycles had them upright. There was also a six-speed gearbox which was in fact a three-speed countershaft unit with a choice of two primary ratios. The new bike won the 1920 Junior TT, but in 1921 it went one better and won both Junior and Senior races, with Howard R. Davies (of HRD, later Vincent, renown) riding in the latter race, having come second in the former.

By the end of the vintage period, however, the V-twin had been refined rather more. Apart from the chromium plating, the valves had been enclosed and better brakes fitted. This 1930 model is one of the last genuine Ajays, before the takeover by Matchless in 1931.

The production model based on the TT machines passed into history as the 'Big Port' AJS. Its name is the subject of some discussion, with some authorities (and most enthusiasts) claiming that it derives from the huge exhaust pipe, while others claim that it was the size of the inlet tract which was referred to. Either way, the machine epitomized the sporting middleweight, and became the object of many a motor cyclist's desire.

Even *Motor Cycling* could not conceal its glee at getting a 1924 model to test; 'We have always been attracted', the report began, 'by the racy lines of the overhead valve 350 cc AJS.' They concluded that it was 'a mettlesome steed that will appeal chiefly to the enthusiastic class of rider, who considers that the little extra attention required in the garage is well repaid by the results obtained.'

Aimed at the other end of the market altogether was the 800 cc (7 hp) side valve V-twin which we first met in 1910 as a 5–6 hp model. By 1920 *The Motor Cycle* could say that the model was 'long famous as a machine embodying every luxury that care in design can provide', and then go on to prophesy that 'the new AJS will even improve its reputation.' It would do so by the enlargement of the engine, the fitting of roller big end bearings, three-ring pistons and better cooling arrangements. An internal expanding front brake was adopted, operated by a pedal, and the rear wheel was quickly detachable, a long-standing AJS feature.

Describing the 1922 models, the same paper began, 'One of the most popular sidecar outfits on the market—the 7 hp AJS—has been modified in one or two important points.' These turned out to be an engine shaft shock absorber (of the spring face cam type), better mudguarding and a Lucas Magdyno in place of a separate dynamo and magneto.

Hitched to innumerable sidecars, usually of AJS' own manufacture, for they liked to offer a complete package, the big Ajay hauled families around the countryside dependably and economically. It progressed in line with general developments during the vintage period; that is to say the brakes, lights and ancillary equipment were improved, for the basic construction had always been sturdy. In 1925 it was given a new frame and tank, while the engine was made even more reliable. A fourth piston ring was added, and oil was fed directly from the pump to the drive side main bearing and thence to the big end. In addition, the cylinder finning was changed, the new arrangement being described as 'pear shaped'.

In 1929 it grew a little—to 996 cc—and the design was brought more up to date with enclosed valve mechanisms and detachable cylinder heads. Thus it remained, still a favourite slogger, until the end of independent production by A. J. Stevens and Co (1914) Ltd. This occurred in 1931 when the name and most of the manufacturing capacity was bought by Matchless and shifted to Plumstead, where the two marques were combined under the Associated Motor Cycles (AMC) banner. AJS had, as a very successful company, diversified into the production of radiograms, cars and commercial vehicles, and when the Depression frightened the banks it found itself over-extended financially. The Stevens brothers sold up, paid their debts and started again under their family name.

AJS ended up as a badge-engineered variant of the Matchless, and although the big Matchless Model X V-twin was eventually passed off under an AJS badge, it was not the real thing. The sporting motor cycles, however, got their own back in a strange way. The 350 cc AJS overhead camshaft model designed in 1927 was developed into the immensely successful 7R 'Boy Racer', and after a couple of stabs at making an original 500 cc racer, Matchless found that they could do no better than to stretch the 350 7R to 500 cc and call it the G50. He who laughs last?

Scott

Following the boom in the railway industry, it must have been the most natural thing in the world for engineers, trained in steam-driven locomotion, to apply their skills to personal transport. Once it was realized that a nippy runabout could never evolve from all the cumbersome equipment that steam power entails, the logical step was to develop the two-stroke internal combustion engine. The principles of a compound steam engine, in which a charge of steam acts on both sides of the piston, and a simple two-stroke, in which both sides of the piston are also used, are surprisingly similar.

As early as 1859 Etienne Lenoir was working on a double-acting gas engine which, despite having no compression stroke, managed to produce ½ hp at 50 rpm. In 1880, Sir Dugald Clerk improved this considerably by adding a separate pump which compressed the mixture before introducing it into the working cylinder at bottom dead centre (BDC). Unfortunately for Clerk, the more immediate advantages of Dr Nicolaus Otto's four-stroke cycle, patented in 1876, were becoming well known. The rash of four-stroke building which broke out once Otto's patent had expired in 1890, almost killed the two-stroke stone-dead.

One of the few who kept the faith was Alfred Angas Scott from Bradford who explained his reasons in the technical press in 1914: 'My inclination towards the development of a practical two-stroke engine was no doubt due to early training in steam; attracted by the regular impulse, simplicity and sound mechanical motion of the steam engine which can thus be retained, in preference to the four-stroke's irregular torque, and complications of valves, gearing and cams. The crankcase compression two-stroke engine, in spite of its defects, is irresistible on account of its simplicity.'

Scott's earliest experiments, in 1898, were with a vertical twin of his own design, fixed to the steering head of a Premier bicycle frame with direct drive to the front wheel. In 1903, a more sensible position was chosen for the engine—this time behind the steering head with chain-cum-belt drive, via a countershaft, to the rear wheel. The engine had to double as a power source for Scott's small boat which he used on the Clyde, so by the time patent rights were acquired, in 1904, the vertical twin had been thoroughly tested!

Due to lack of finance, the first Scott production machines were built by local engineers, Ben and William Jowett; but after only six motor cycles had been made, they abandoned the project to concentrate on their own; the building of a light car. Scott managed to raise some money and in 1909 the Scott Engineering Company was formed in partnership with a friend, Eric Myers, and cousin, Frank Philipp.

Initially, the frame was built by the Royal Enfield Company, to a design and specification patented by Scott in 1908. Its construction was as unique and bizarre in appearance as that of the engine. Because of Scott's aversion to curved frame members, the whole of the design was composed of straight tubes. The rear of the frame was triangulated fully, and the steering head laterally, with the engine providing some of the overall stiffness.

The Scott was also unusual in having telescopic front forks, though without any damping, and probably the first kickstarter ever to be fitted to a motor bike. Engine capacity was 450 cc (increased from the previous 333 cc) and the cylinders were water-cooled while the barrels were air-cooled. A two-speed gearbox was fitted, with all-chain transmission.

Ridden in sporting events by Philipp and Myers, the Scott quickly gained a reputation for lightness, good handling and quick acceleration. This was in spite of a ridiculous handicap imposed by the ACU after Alfred Scott won several gold medals in hill climbs at Bradford and Coventry. In order to appease rival manufacturers, a formula was devised whereby the Scott's true capacity was multiplied by 1.32 (this was to compensate for the greater frequency of power pulses in the two-stroke) resulting in the little two-stroke being classified as a 640 cc machine!

In 1911, basic engine capacity was further increased, to 486 cc, and an

The late vintage Scott is often regarded as the peak of the company's development. This is a 1929 Flying Squirrel Tourer.

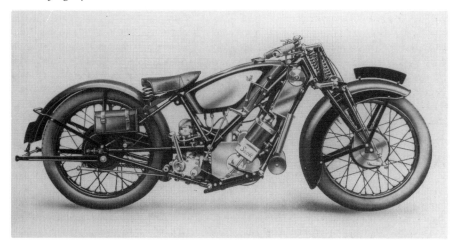

improved honeycomb radiator substituted for the old design. Although people like Jesse Baker were bringing home golds from trial events, Scott directed his energies to developing a machine for the new Isle of Man Senior TT course. Realizing the importance of improving the breathing system, he decided to employ a rotary valve to control the mixture. Philipp experienced some trouble with the timing during the TT that year, but managed to secure the fastest lap, at 50.11 mph, before being forced to retire.

The following year, Frank Applebee won the TT at an average speed of 48.69 mph, on a machine with a redesigned engine. This time the rotary valve was gear-driven to ensure the timing did not slip, the whole of each cylinder was water-cooled (and not just the heads, as on the road models) and each was equipped with two sparking plugs. With two TT wins, four lap records and innumerable trials victories, the Grosvenor Street works was flooded with orders. It was also at this time that their own annual event, the extremely difficult Scott Trial, was inaugurated, initially for Scott's factory employees only, but later extended to include all enthusiasts.

At the onset of war, Scott designed a gun-carrying sidecar outfit but this did not stand up well to military service and attention was instead diverted to one of the oddest-looking three-wheelers ever invented. (Scott himself referred to it as 'the crab'.) Intended originally as a guncar, it was powered by a 5 hp twin-cylinder, two-stroke engine of 578 cc capacity, with shaft-drive and a three-speed gearbox. The wheel configuration was that of a right-angled triangle, the single front wheel running in-line with the rear offside wheel. Viewed from the front, the crab looked rather like an ordinary four-wheeled car after a nasty accident with a low-standing bollard!

The War Office was evidently unimpressed and no orders were received. But Scott was undeterred and after the war he abandoned motor cycles completely, formed the Scott Autocar Company, and concentrated on producing a civilian version of his three-wheeled cyclecar, now christened the Scott Sociable. His aim was to offer the public the comfort, convenience and conviviality of the motor car at a little over the cost of a sidecar combination. Despite favourable write-ups in the press, and even with the price dropped from £273, in its first year, to £215, in 1921, the Sociable was never accepted as anything other than a curiosity and only 110 examples were ever sold. *The Motor Cycle* did not exaggerate when it wrote: 'Last year the Sociable was introduced to the somewhat staggered public as, perhaps, the most unconventional, yet sound, engineering job ever staged at Olympia. It was only known to a few favoured ones, and to be able to assert that one had driven it was to command wonder and respect.'

The first of the famous Squirrels was a 486 cc sports model on which the Scott team riders won third, fourth and ninth places in the 1922 TT race, as well as Team Prize for best manufacturer. Over the following three years the model evolved into the Super, and then Flying, Squirrel with further victories in national and international championships.

The 1926 production series of the Flying Squirrel marks the zenith of the Scott company's career. Improvements included a three-speed gearbox and mechanical oil pump which had an adjustable sight drip feed and was pre-set to provide lubrication at a rate proportionate to the speed of the engine. The TT full-frame tank was as an optional extra which greatly improved the appearance of the bike. The choice in standard machines was between a 498 cc at £66 and a 596 cc engine at £68; De Luxe editions, a Power-plus TT Replica, and grass and dirt-track specials, were also listed. The Scott Squirrel was classed as a 'thoroughbred' and an 'aristocrat' by press and public alike. It was a prestigious machine at a competitive price and sales were correspondingly high.

Scott suffered, as many other companies did during the 1930s, but seemed especially lacking in innovatory drive. This was more than likely a delayed reaction to losing the founder, Alfred Scott, who always had been the main driving force of the business. Although the company continued producing motor bikes with varying degrees of financial difficulty, until 1950, the design of the famous two-stroke never deviated far from Alfred Scott's original ideas.

Norton

Mention the name Norton to most enthusiasts and they will automatically think of its tremendous record of success in road racing and trials. The first of a long series of victories was in 1907 when Rem Fowler won the two-cylinder trophy at the inaugural Isle of Man TT. Fowler entered the race as a private owner but received active assistance from the factory where his machine was specially prepared. Its four-stroke, V-twin Peugeot engine was not exceptionally powerful but it had plenty of stamina and the single cradle, tubular frame was light and well balanced.

This early taste of glory could hardly be attributed to any great technical achievement. Nevertheless, it gave the company's founder, James Lansdowne Norton, sufficient encouragement to concentrate resources on producing racing machines and, more importantly, with engines of his own make. Thus committed, the Norton concern was probably unique in its attendance at every TT meeting until 1955 when it was the last British manufacturer to give up racing.

Though trained as a jeweller, 'Pa' Norton, as he was popularly known, was intensely interested in precision engineering. He followed a well-trodden path, from the manufacture of cycle components (founding the Norton Manufacturing Company in 1898 in Birmingham), through to his first motorized two-wheeler which he built in 1902 using his own bicycle frame with a 1½ hp Clément engine attached to the front down tube. Other proprietary engines used at the small Bradford Street works included single-gear, Moto-Rêve with belt drive, and Peugeot singles and twins with automatic inlet valves and the option of a two-speed countershaft gear and all-chain drive. But, following the TT success, Norton hurriedly designed

An early Norton 16H, a model which, with some modification, was to be in production from 1921 until 1954.

and built his 'Big Four' single of 633 cc (with 82 mm × 120 mm bore and stroke), in time for it to be exhibited at the 1907 Stanley Motor Show. The 4 hp engine was a simple side-valver, with aluminium crankcase and cast-iron head and barrel, although the breathing system was quite sophisticated for its day.

The 4 hp was followed in 1911 by a 3.5 hp model (79 mm × 100 mm bore and stroke, producing 490 cc), a forerunner of the hugely popular 16 and 16H models which appeared after the war. Norton himself competed on the 4 hp and 3½ hp models but without success and as a result of his poor health, coupled with a lack of business acumen, the Norton Manufacturing Company was forced to liquidate. Norton Motors Ltd was formed by amalgamating with R.T. Shelley and Co and, under their joint management, the 3½ hp and the Big Four continued, with the 4 hp offered as a sidecar as well as a solo mount.

Sales picked up enormously when Dan Bradbury, on the 500, made the record books with a fastest speed of 70 mph while Jack Emerson won the 1912 Brooklands TT, well ahead of the other competitors and simultaneously gained three long distance world records. 'Unapproachable Norton' was a slogan that had caught on in the early days of Fowler's hill-climbing successes and, indeed, speed was to become an increasingly dominant factor in Norton designs—in 1914, for example, the 3½ single established many world speed records, with a maximum of 81 mph.

Apart from the standard models, customers were given the option of a Brooklands Special (BS) and a Brooklands Racing Special (BRS), tuned by the well-known record-breaker, D. R. O'Donovan. Before being fitted into the standard chassis, the engines were tested and a certificate was supplied with every unit, guaranteeing, in the case of the BS, that it had attained a speed of at least 75 mph, and the BRS, 70 mph.

Like most motor cycle manufacturers, Norton satisfied the enormous post-war demand for transport by updating their pre-1914 models and reconditioning their military machines. (They had not been awarded any WD contracts in this country but did supply the Russian Army, and later the Allies, with Big Fours.) Three-speed Sturmey-Archer gearboxes were fitted to the 4 hp and 3½ hp models (the latter now designated No 16, under Norton's new cataloguing system), with all-chain transmission; customers who preferred the more peaceful belt-drive transmission were also catered for.

In 1921, the 16H appeared—the H affixed to identify it as the Home model, as distinct from the Colonial one—with a new low frame, as used in the 1920 TT. The 16H became one of Norton's biggest sellers and continued in production until 1954. In the meantime, new designs were drawn up and considered. James Norton had a fertile imagination and at one time had toyed with the idea of using steam power and even radium energy to drive his machines. So it wasn't a particularly wild flight of fantasy on his part that led to the introduction of overhead valves on the 1923 range of Norton models, a feature that the founder had been contemplating for some time.

On the competition track, the 1922 prototype, ridden by Rex Judd at Brooklands, created a new mile record speed of 88 mph. The 1923 Maudes Manufacturer's prize, together with second, fourth and fifth places in the Senior Isle of Man TT were followed in 1924 by a first in the solo race with Alec Bennett in the saddle and another victory in the sidecar event, with George Tucker at the helm. (Tucker's passenger was none other than Walter Moore, who joined Norton in 1923 and designed their first overhead camshaft engine in 1927.)

The overhead valve, or Model 18, as it was called, was easily identified by its head valves which were set at a 100-degree angle, with long pushrods and hefty rocker gear exposed. It had three gears, with ratios of 7½ to 1, 5½ to 1 and 4½ to 1; fuel consumption was an economical 80 mpg. A *Motor Cycling* road test in 1924 was surprised that such a powerful machine, with its quick acceleration and torque, could be so smooth and flexible: 'One might imagine, with a machine possessing such a formidable list of Brooklands records, that the ohv model would be a fierce and uncomfortable thing to ride—a machine for a young blood on a billiard-table type of road. But this is not the case, for the machine, although capable of very high speed, is perfectly simple and safe to handle.'

A justifiably popular machine, the Model 18 continued in production for many years, but by 1927 its racing days were practically over and Walter Moore's Camshaft One (CS1), with overhead camshaft, was beginning to take centre-stage.

Martinsyde

Towards the end of the First World War, Martinsyde developed a fighting aeroplane which turned out to be more advanced and faster than anything else in the world. Many orders were taken, but before they could be fulfilled, the Armistice was signed and the demand for fighters, indeed for aircraft of any sort, ceased.

Just like Tommy Sopwith, who commissioned a motor cycle design from Granville Bradshaw, Martinsyde decided to keep the large factory in Woking occupied with the production of two- and three-wheelers. By the time the 1920 Motor Cycle Show opened, the company could display two sidecar taxis and a light delivery outfit, each powered by a 6 hp motor of Martinsyde's own design, which was said to have made a distinct hit. A novel feature of the motor was the valve layout—exhaust over inlet—which gave better gas flow and more cooling for the exhaust valve.

The 3½ hp model was also announced, very similar in general specification to the larger machines, but 'built with one eye on efficiency and the other on speed'. The frame was lighter and shorter than the 6 hp's, though like that model's the chains were totally enclosed and the AJS-pattern three-speed gearbox was fitted.

In 1921 *The Motor Cycle* looked at the 3½ hp more closely, and found it to have been considerably changed in the year. The main difference lay in the frame, the original of which tended to break. It now had parallel top stays, with the rear of the upper one sloping sharply at the saddle end, at the same angle as the upper rear frame tubes. The petrol tank was rounded at the

The light delivery outfit was one of Martinsyde's first production machines: seen here at the motor cycle show in 1920.

front and of cylindrical section where the original had been far more angular. Two sets of footrests were fitted (in place of footboards), with the rear brake pedal placed midway between the offside rests.

The primary chain was totally enclosed, with an inspection cap to allow adjustment of the clutch spring, while the secondary chain was just well guarded. Despite the clutch, no kickstart was fitted to the first run of models. The 496 cc engine was identical to the larger 678 cc model, apart from a bore of 60 mm instead of 70 mm; the stroke was common at 88 mm. Crank and cams ran in ball bearings, while the big end had rollers.

An idea of the problems facing Martinsyde can be gained from *Motor Cycling*'s road test of a 1921 3½ hp model; 'very few production models have been completed, so that, with detail alterations only, the description which follows may be taken as applying to the 1922 model'. The reasons for the delay were the problems with frame breakage, and a strike by component suppliers. However, the 3½ hp was found to have good acceleration and flexibility (it could be ridden down to 12 mph in top gear), excellent cooling and good brakes. One point of criticism concerned the noise generated by the exposed valve gear, and also the likelihood of grit-generated wear at that point. This is lent some irony by an article carried in the same paper some eighteen years later. Reporting on a highly-modified Martinsyde owned by Mr P. J. Tait, Peter Barrett said, 'there was less mechanical noise than I have heard from many 1939 engines'.

The 1921 tester also noted the sturdy construction of the frame, which added considerably to the bike's all-up weight. His conclusion was that, 'the sports model is undoubtedly a machine of great promise, and we think it will fill the requirements of a large number of motor cyclists. It is built on sound lines, and, with the experience of such old hands as H. H. Bowen and the brothers Bashall at the command of the manufacturers, it is only to be expected that the Martinsyde will be a make much to the fore during the 1922 season'. Bowen had taken the 50 miles and one hour records at Brooklands with a Martinsyde and, together with the Bashalls, the team prize.

The reference to experienced old hands was not without point for, as has been mentioned, the founders Helmuth Paul Martin and George Harris Handasyde were not motor cycle manufacturers by choice. If Sopwith found Bradshaw, Martin and Handasyde were joined by Howard Newman, whose family was associated with Ivy machines. Newman had a design (which may or may not have been fairly acquired) for the unique exhaust over inlet engine. The first few machines were known as Martinsyde-Newmans, but the latter name soon disappeared from the scene—as did its owner.

Sadly, the former name disappeared within a fairly short time, too. Neither of the founders was a businessman, and despite the launch of a supersports 'flagship' in 1922—the Quicksix—a fire in the factory caused enough damage to leave the firm unable to pay for repairs, but insufficient to allow an insurance claim. Caught in this dilemma, an Official Receiver was brought in, and the firm tried its luck with a 2¾ hp single-cylinder economy model. It was not a success (only six were made, of which one is known to survive) and Martinsyde closed its doors in 1923.

It was not the end though, for Bat, itself not in the best of health, bought both the name and whatever engines and components were left. In its short life the Martinsyde factory had established a reputation for engineering excellence second to none. Today a band of committed enthusiasts, members of the Martinsyde Register, ensure that the marque is remembered as it deserves to be, and that those machines which have survived can continue to be run.

Triumph Ricardo

Sir Henry Ricardo, 'Harry' to his many motor cyclist friends, was a busy man in the 1920s. His name has been mentioned previously, in connection with a cylinder head design which Walter Moore failed to patent for Douglas. But Ricardo was obviously an originator of ideas or he would not have acquired his reputation for being able to make a faster engine than the next tuner.

It was natural, then, for Triumph to turn to him when they needed a machine with which to contest the TT. His brief was to use as many existing components as possible, and when the new overhead valve 3½ hp model, intended 'exclusively for solo use' was unveiled in June 1921, the only truly new items were a barrel machined from steel, a new cylinder head and a special piston.

The production version shown that year was slightly different, but in essence it was the same design, with four inclined valves opening into a

A 1924 example of the four-valve Ricardo.

Bottom half of the motor was standard Triumph, but the barrel and cylinder head were special indeed, although the model never really fulfilled its potential.

hemispherical head. The finning was extensive, to ensure adequate cooling and, rather unusually, one of the lower cylinder fins doubled as an anchorage for the head bolts. The valve gear was exposed, one-piece nickel steel rockers running in ball bearings located in cast-in lugs or 'ears'. Cylinder and head were now both cast in iron, but the piston was still an aluminium slipper job, and the bottom half of the engine was basically standard Triumph, apart from a flat base to the crankcase. Reciprocating parts were suitably lightened and balanced.

Pointers to the fact that the Ricardo, or Model R, was a super-sports machine rather than an out-and-out racer can be found in the mudguarding, the comfy saddle and the oil-bath primary transmission. A Triumph three-speed 'box drove the rear wheel through a chain. TT-type handlebars, and Druid forks, rather than the usual Triumph 'fore-and-aft' jobs, rounded off the specification.

A road test in *The Motor Cycle* found that the new 3½ was as different from the standard 4 hp, Model SD 550 cc side-valve, as 'an anti-aircraft gun is from a trench mortar' (a strange choice of simile, even in 1921). The aluminium slipper piston was found to have the advantage of not gumming up as readily as the cast-iron type, though that was perhaps due to the smaller surface area presented to the cylinder. Conversely, there was found to be more piston slap with the aluminium job.

Acceleration and steering were well up to expectations, though the tester could only claim to have estimated that, 'we appreciably exceeded the elusive "sixty", since no speedometer was fitted. However,' he continued, 'a fairer criterion of the machine's all-out capabilities is afforded by the well-authenticated fact that one of the production models to standard specification has lapped at Brooklands at 68 mph, which, in effect, means that it has exceeded 70 mph. It should also be remembered that the racing four-valve Triumph holds the 500 cc hour record at 76.74 mph.'

Indeed it did, for Major Frank Halford had undertaken a record-breaking session just before the 1921 Olympia Show. As well as the hour record, he had taken the Flying Mile at 83.91 mph and the 50-mile at 77.27 mph. The racing Ricardo returned to the Isle of Man in 1922, substantially altered. The bore and stroke, previously 80.94 mm × 97 mm, had been changed to 85 mm × 88 mm, the valve area was considerably greater, and lubrication was now of the dry sump variety. In this trim, a Ricardo came second in the Senior TT, Walter Brandish finishing just seven seconds behind Alec Bennett on the Sunbeam, despite having only two of the three gears operational.

A series of competition successes followed, with gold medals in the ISDT among them; but the Riccy never did win the Senior, for in 1923 Brandish, who was heavily tipped to win, crashed in practice at what subsequently became known as Brandish Corner, breaking a leg.

The Triumph factory apparently lost faith in the four-valve design, for it then bought another racing engine, a two-valver, from Brooklands racer Vic Horsman, and marketed it as the TT model.

The Ricardo was dropped from the range in 1928, but in its relatively short life it had established a good and lasting reputation as a sporting machine. And the four-valve layout did not go unnoticed or unappreciated, for shortly after the Ricardo had demonstrated the layout's potential, in those early record-breaking and racing successes, it was adopted by Rudge, who used it to great advantage in both racers and roadsters.

Chater-Lea

Chater-Lea was founded around 1900 to make components for the bicycle industry. This led naturally into the making of parts for motor cycles, particularly frame lugs (each one stamped with the firm's name), spring forks and brake components.

Experiments were made with clip-on-engined bicycles and, by 1909, *The Motor Cycle* could declare, 'A machine that has caused a good deal of interest recently in the motor cycle world is the Chater-Lea No 7 motor bicycle. . .' This was the first full motor cycle, a 7–8 hp side-valve vee-twin, produced by the firm, and it made its appearance at the Stanley Show held in November

The AA used a great many Chater-Lea outfits for their mobile patrols. The AA has recently restored one such model, which was in production from the early '20s until 1936.

1908. Initial reaction was rather muted, for the specification was very advanced for its day—a three-speed countershaft gearbox, all-chain transmission and an effective cone clutch. Suspicions about its practicability were soon allayed, for it proved itself reliable in long-distance trials and hill-climbs, and formed the mainstay of Chater-Lea production for the next five years.

The reliability of the machine was no accident for, as *The Motor Cycle* was moved to comment: 'Mr Chater-Lea is himself a practical motor cyclist, and designs his machines after much experience on the road. This fact, coupled with mechanical abilities of the highest order, and the best material, naturally results in the production of a really first-class mount'.

By 1911 Chater-Lea had started to make their own 8 hp motors (a variety of proprietary units had been used previously), which were said to be designed along the lines of the JAP engine, though with very different timing gear arrangements, and they also featured a metal-to-metal disc clutch with no fewer than 29 plates. Never slow to adopt new ideas, the company redesigned its frames for 1914 to give a much lower saddle position. The same year saw the adoption of internal expanding, cam-operated hub brakes, running in large ball bearings. The engine, too, was altered to give quieter running, the side-valve tappets now being driven directly off the cam instead of through rockers.

After the Great War, Chater-Lea expanded its range. The enduring Model No 7 was still there, but to catch the market for cheap, or in this case cheaper, transport, a 2½ hp lightweight, fitted with a Villiers engine, was introduced. In 1919 both machines were shown with the new, quickly-detachable rear wheel, which allowed it to be removed without disturbing the brake and chain sprocket assembly. Most other manufacturers had not caught up with this simple, but extraordinarily convenient, system twenty years later.

Chater-Lea were never exactly a volume manufacturer, but one of their most numerous machines was introduced in the early 'twenties—a 550 cc Blackburne-engined side-valve single. This was used extensively by the AA for its sidecar patrols, and proved a well-made, dependable and enduring mount, for it survived until 1936. Rarer, but infinitely more exciting, was the 350 cc 'face cam' sports model, on which Dougal Marchant and Ben Bickell did so well at Brooklands; the family was still heavily involved in practical motor cycling too, for J. Chater-Lea used one of the 350s for a record-breaking session at Brooklands on 31 August 1928. The factory took home the 9, 10, 11, 12 and 1,000 kilometre records that day.

At the end of the '20s Chater-Lea had consolidated their reputation for well-designed motor cycles (they had been in the forefront of styling changes by introducing saddletanks in 1924), for *Motor Cycling*, previewing the 1929 models, could say that, 'certain modifications have been made which add still further to that general cleanliness of design which has long been an enviable distinction of this particular make'. A sign of the times, however, was that Sturmey-Archer gearboxes were fitted instead of Chater-Lea's own, which was presumably more expensive to make than the proprietary item was to buy in.

Eventually, economic circumstances forced more drastic cuts on the company. The sporting face cam 350 was dropped, and in 1936 the company ceased to make motor cycles of any sort. By concentrating on more profitable areas of engineering, Chater-Lea ensured its survival, and the factory can still be found in Letchworth today, turning out precision engineering sub-contracts.

Morgan

Built as a light and economical substitute for the car, and a more comfortable alternative to the motor cycle and sidecar combination, the cyclecar enjoyed a small degree of popularity in Britain, especially during the 1910s and '20s. It was constructed on the same basic principles as the two-wheeled vehicle and, according to ACU definition, could have three or four wheels as long as its weight did not exceed 7 cwt and engine capacity 1,100 cc. The essence of the cyclecar was simplicity and inexpensiveness but many of the fifty or so makes at one time in existence became over-elaborate and for this reason few survived beyond the First World War. Of course, the advent of the Austin Seven and other cheap cars did not help matters.

Morgans were widely used in trials, and this 1922 photograph shows a competitor approaching Duffton in Westmorland.

By far the most popular and successful of these manufacturers was the Morgan Motor Co Ltd which, pre-1914, offered well-built machines for less than £90. Regarded with almost cult-like veneration, the Worcestershire-based firm is still going strong and still producing surprisingly inexpensive sports cars; all machines are hand-built, just as they have always been ever since the business first started in 1909. With no commercial interests in mind, H. F. S. Morgan built his first three-wheeled single-seater for his own personal use. He used it as a runabout in the beautiful Malvern hills, a good testing ground for reliability trials in which the Morgan was later to excel.

Like many of the more popular cyclecars of the day, the Morgan had chain-drive transmission to a single rear wheel, with two wheels and the engine at the front. The power unit was a single cylinder air-cooled JAP giving the vehicle a top speed of 50 mph. The driver had a choice of two gears, selected by means of a lever on the left side and steering was controlled by a tiller, later replaced by a wheel.

In many ways, the Morgan handled like a conventional motor cycle whilst offering the driver far greater weather protection, with its car-like body and optional hood and screen. It was eminently suited to trials work and won numerous competitions, notably the 1911 London to Exeter trial and the 1913 Cyclecar Grand Prix in France. Enthusiastic write-ups and test reports appeared regularly in *Light Car and Cyclecar*, a magazine catering exclusively for this new breed of motorist.

For many years JAP units, especially their ohv racing engines, gave the Morgan its distinctive front-end appearance; post-war models utilized other proprietary power plants, like those made by Blackburne, MAG and French Anzani. Morgans were not developed for racing purposes only and the 1921 range is fairly representative of the variety of models on offer to the public. There was a Grand Prix and an Aero model, a De Luxe machine and a family car with adequate seating for two adults and two children. Specifications for all models were broadly similar with either JAP or MAG engines, AMAC or B&B carburettors and a two-speed Morgan gear with ratios of 4½ to 1 and 8 to 1. A four-speed gear was an optional extra at £20. Drive was transmitted from the engine to a cone clutch and from there by shaft to a bevel box on the countershaft. Final drive was via a pair of chains, made interchangeable in order to equalize wear.

One of the most important modifications of 1921 was the introduction of a quickly detachable rear wheel: after slackening off the axle-nuts and disconnecting the two band brakes, the axle could be slid forward and would then drop out of the rear fork ends.

Under the new directorship of George Goodall, the sporting, and consequently commercial, success of the Morgan cyclecar continued well into the 1930s. This was at a time when most other cyclecar manufacturers had been killed off by the cheap car, or opted to join 'the enemy' by producing four-wheelers of their own. Morgan built their first *bona fide* car before the Second World War but it wasn't until 1950, and several models later, that the last of the famous three-wheelers was to leave the factory in Malvern.

Levis

William and Arthur Butterfield were engineers who became drawn by the spirit of the times into motor cycle manufacturing. William developed an efficient two-stroke engine, and a year later the brothers had made the move into manufacturing a complete machine. The name they chose was Levis, meaning 'light' in Latin, and the product set a standard for other two-strokes—indeed, other motor cycles—to aim at. The prototype was of 198 cc, but the first production model was 269 cc, with a smaller 211 cc version soon made available.

By 1913 the firm was doing well enough to become a limited company, with the Butterfields as directors and Howard Newey, their brother-in-law, as works manager, engine tuner and leader of the design department. They kept going through the war years, and afterwards the great demand for cheap lightweight motor cycles helped the company to grow. In 1920 Levis were showing 2¼ hp (211 cc) models and a longer 2½ hp (247 cc) variant. The smaller machine had been subjected to a petrol consumption test, wherein it achieved 320 mpg at an average speed of 20 mph—figures verified by the ACU—and the production model was *guaranteed* to do 120 mpg; 150 mpg was said to be possible, with careful riding.

If economy was the watchword of the 2¼ hp, the 2½ hp had proved its turn of speed in the Isle of Man TT. Competing in the Junior race, against a field of (mainly) 350s, R. O. Clarke had brought a Levis home in fourth place overall and first in the 250 cc class. Levis also gained second and third in the class.

Reliability was a prerequisite for the TT, and Levis ensured that their engines were well lubricated. Oil was fed by drip through a pipe to the cylinder, which covered the gudgeon pin and one main bearing, and another to the other main bearing, which also took care of the big end.

A TT model was, naturally, made available to capitalize on Clarke's success, and it was thought that it would appeal to sporting riders. Other types of motor cyclist were catered for, the low frame of the standard machine being thought particularly suitable for 'feminine use'.

An interesting sidelight on the factory's concern with weight was shed by *The Motor Cycle*: 'More than interesting evidence that the standard Levis, as applied to the public, is a genuine lightweight, is forthcoming in the fact that, when the railways refused to carry machines that were over 112 lb by passenger train, Messrs Butterfields continually despatched their products

A young businesswoman (The Motor Cycle *informs us) attends to a minor problem on her 1915 Levis, a machine which 'fulfilled to perfection' her transport requirements.*

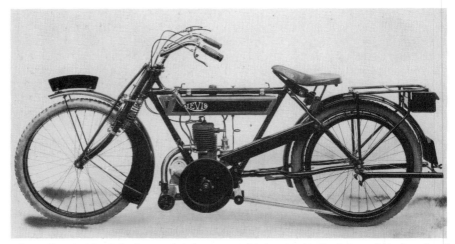

Above *By 1920 Levis had expanded the range. This is a 2¼ hp 'Lady's model', though, of course, it was suitable for either sex. This type of engine was guaranteed to do 120 mpg.*

Below *At a motor cycle meet at Richmond, Yorkshire in 1921, a Levis is prominent. They were popular competition machines, and found great success on the race circuits. The car in the foreground, incidentally, is a Jowett.*

so, and only rarely found it necessary to send on the tool-kit under separate cover'. In this case, light did not mean flimsy, for Butterfields always made their products up to a certain standard rather than down to a price.

The following year, all models were available with or without a two-speed gearbox, clutch and kickstart. The 2½ hp engine ('the TT power unit modified for touring purposes') was fitted into a new frame, which had a sloping top tube and correspondingly different petrol tank. This alteration was adjudged a great success, both motor cycle papers praising the attractive appearance of the new machine. The new Levis did more than look good, however, as rider Geoff Davison proved. In 1922 he won the Belgian and French Grands Prix, as well as the Lightweight TT, the first ever held. He also won a gold medal in the ISDT.

By 1923 other two-stroke manufacturers were catching up with the Levis and the company's racing career was virtually at an end. Instead of putting effort into competition success, Butterfields expanded the range of models, but of all the machines they produced, the Popular, the basic, single-speed version of the 2¼ hp, was, as the name says, the most popular. Despite that, its production was brought to an end in 1924, the 250 cc chain-drive model M (later known as the Levisette) taking its place.

In the late 1920s, Levis took a somewhat unexpected step in introducing a range of four-strokes of 250 and 350 cc capacity. By 1929 the complete range consisted of the Popular Model Z, a basic 250 cc two-stroke; the 'Six-Port' sports two-stroke (first seen in 1928); a 350 cc ohv single-port four-stroke; and a new twin-port version with enclosed valve gear. When it came to the 1929 Motor Cycle Show, a couple of 250 cc four-strokes had been added, one with overhead valves, the other with side valves. The A2 (the twin-port 350 ohv) was a very successful machine, as was the 250 variant, providing riders like Percy Hunt with a lot of racing victories; sales boomed, and the two-strokes took a back seat.

Although its last years were notable for competitive four-strokes (including a 600 cc model which Bob Foster rode to great effect in trials and scrambles) it is the two-strokes which characterize Levis in the vintage period. The Second World War brought to an end all motor cycle production but the firm turned to other things, and Levis industrial pumps can now be found all over the world. Good engineering is well appreciated, whatever the product.

Sunbeam

How did the Sunbeam get its name? Legend has it that Ellen Marston, wife of the firm's founder John, suggested it after seeing his prototype bicycle leaning against a sunlit wall. John Marston and Co were primarily involved in tinsmithing—the manufacture of saucepans and the like—and japanning, or lacquering as we would now say.

Bicycling was a favourite family pastime with the Marstons, and as it boomed in general popularity it is not surprising that Marston, with his

Sunbeam's most successful early model was the 3½ hp introduced in 1913. Tommy De La Hay and Alec Bennett both won TTs using such machines.

business partner William Newill, started manufacturing high-quality cycles. One of the make's distinguishing features was the 'Little Oil Bath Chaincase', which totally enclosed the chain, thus protecting it and the rider's clothes. One of the firm's most famous customers was the composer, Sir Edward Elgar, who had two machines, both of which were nicknamed 'Mr Phoebus'.

Towards the end of the century, the firm was doing so well that another factory was purchased, in Villiers Street, Wolverhampton. Called the Villiers Cycle Component Company and placed under the direction of son, Charles Marston, it made cycle parts, supplying a great number of manufacturers and assemblers. Later on, of course, the famous Villiers two-stroke engine was developed, although John Marston refused to have anything to do with it. In fact, he refused to have anything to do with any motor cycles for a long time. Cars were, however, considered acceptable, and various prototypes and limited production four-wheelers (like the Sunbeam-Mabberley, which had a wheel at each corner of a *diamond*-shaped chassis!) were made. Eventually, a conventional but very high-quality car was designed and developed, and this part of the business prospered too.

By 1911 there was potentially a lot of money to be made from building and selling motor cycles, and John Marston's reservations about their safety and nuisance value were overcome. Work began on a bike, under the able direction of John Greenwood, who had already worked for Rover and JAP. Greenwood, who became inseparable from Sunbeam, had to produce a machine for the top end of the market, as convenient and mechanically advanced as the car had become. Harry Stevens (one of the Stevens brothers who formed AJS, another Wolverhampton company) was brought in as the engine consultant, while Greenwood laid down the general specification and determined the final appearance. The result was the Sunbeam 2¾ hp, a 350 cc side-valve (85 mm × 85 mm bore and stroke) with clutch, two-speed gear, magneto ignition and all-chain drive. The Little Oil Bath name was carried over from the bicycles for the chain enclosures. At 60 guineas the price was rather high, as might have been expected from the full specification and high level of engineering. Despite some success in ACU trials, such as the London to Exeter, sales were a little disappointing, although not discouraging.

In 1913 the range was augmented with a 6 hp JAP-engined V-twin for sidecar work and a new 3½ hp machine, which was to be one of Sunbeam's most successful models. All three types were finished in black paint with gold lining, a scheme invariably associated with Sunbeam.

The following year the 2¾ hp was dropped, with development work continuing on the initially troublesome 3½ hp. Once the engine had been redesigned, it proved very reliable, and both the French and Russian Armies used Sunbeams in the Great War. These bodies insisted, however, on belt drive, and military Sunbeams are instantly recognizable by this transmission: all civilian models were fitted with chains.

Demand for motor cycles after the war was keenly met by Sunbeam, but at their quality and price, of course. The car factory was hived off as a separate company in 1919, which doubtless aided the firm's concentration on two-wheelers. The 3½ hp was entered for trials and TTs, and did well at both, with Tommy de la Hay winning the 1920 Senior TT and Alec Bennett following suit in 1922.

A *Motor Cycle* road test of the 1920 model was fulsome in its praise of the machine: 'By reason of its good name,' the writer says, 'one, of course, expects a great deal from a modern mount with the now familiar black and gold tank, but those expectations are fulfilled in their entirety—nay, more—on acquaintance with the machine'. This tone is maintained throughout the report: 'the engine is smooth but powerful'; the gearbox, 'a pleasure to use'; the brakes, 'most effective'. It concludes thus: 'In brief, our experience of the machine, extending over several weeks, has been entirely devoid of untoward incident, it has failed at nothing, started easily with wonderful consistency, not even a puncture has marred our enjoyment, and consequently one may justly dub the Sunbeam as a machine of unfailing reliability'. This sums up the essence of the Sunbeam for many people.

Sporting success continued, with George Dance in charge of development and tuning, but the side-valve engines were no longer up to the task. Overhead valve models were experimented with (as was an overhead cam type) and in 1923, a new ohv 3½ hp (80 mm × 98 mm bore and stroke,

A 1936 Model 8, made the year before Sunbeam's takeover by AMC, and therefore one of the last of the original line.

producing 493 cc) was announced. The old models continued, eventually redesigned into the Longstroke (and at 77 mm × 105.5 mm, it certainly was) and Light Tourist machines, which continued in production until the outbreak of the Second World War.

The new ohv 3½ hp was soon renamed the 500 cc Model 9 and, with a 350 cc Model 8, it proved a natural successor to the side-valve 3½ hp as the backbone for the company's range. Competition development was entrusted to Harry Weslake, who perfected his scientific application of gas-flowing techniques during the operation, and under his guidance the firm began to prosper at Brooklands.

Gordon Cobbold won a gold star for lapping at over 100 mph, and the factory broke the world records for seven, eight and twelve hours, plus the 1,000 kilometre category. In 1927 Sunbeam catalogued a model based on the racing machines, named the Model 90. It had dry sump lubrication, necessitating a separate oil tank, hairpin valve springs and a close-ratio gearbox without kickstart.

The works 90s proved to be fast and reliable; riders like Charlie Dodson, Graham Walker and Italian, Achille Varzi, winning many TTs and GPs including the Isle of Man Senior race of 1928. This was particularly important as the motor cycle factory had been bought by ICI (or the Nobel Industries part of it), who did not have much of a tradition or interest in motor cycle manufacture.

In 1929—just before the end of the traditionally defined vintage era—all the models were redesigned with new frames and saddletanks. These machines are not now considered to be as good-looking as their flat-tank predecessors, though contemporary reports described them as 'delightfully clean and satisfactory' in design.

The racing success continued with victories in France, Belgium, Germany, Austria, Italy and the Isle of Man, where Dodson won the Senior TT with Alec Bennett second. But the Sunbeam was reaching the limits of its rather conventional design. Rivals were beginning to get results with overhead camshafts (Norton) and four-valve heads (Rudge) and in 1933 there were no major victories to keep ICI sweet. Economies were made: the works team was disbanded, and production models were made cheaper—welded petrol tanks, for example, replacing soldered ones.

The Model 90 was retained in the Sunbeam catalogue until 1933, although after 1932 it could no longer be considered a special racing model, as it utilized many components in common with the Model 9 and other, less exalted, models. The end came in 1934, when a Model 95 was listed in two versions—L for touring and R for racing. Although it was a highly developed roadster, it was not the 90, but it had an image of which many other manufacturers could be jealous.

The name was taken over, together with most of the range, by Associated Motor Cycles in 1937. AMC consisted of the Matchless and AJS marques, and would later include James, Francis-Barnett and Norton (who, in turn, would amalgamate with Villiers), but the Sunbeam name was not with them for long. The Second World War brought motor cycle production to an end, and afterwards the name was sold to the BSA group, who applied it to a new twin and a disastrous scooter. *Sic transit gloria mundi.*

Royal Enfield

Royal Enfield's experience as motor cycle manufacturers began in the 1880s and spanned more than seventy years. Throughout that period they produced machines of varying capacity, configuration and quality, with perhaps none more successful (particularly in competition) than the single-cylinder middleweights.

Like so many others, Enfield started as a small pedal cycle company; run by George and Foster Townsend they built their own brand of two-wheeler, the Ecossais. When financial difficulties necessitated reorganization, the Townsend company was made a branch of the Eadie Manufacturing Co, with Albert Eadie as managing director and Robert Walker Smith as works manager. The Eadie Co was, in turn, made a part of the BSA empire in 1907, but a steady management was maintained by Smith, who was succeeded at Enfield by his son Frank. Frank Smith continued in the post until his death in 1962.

Based in Redditch, the Enfield Cycle Co acquired its name and field gun trademark as a result of contracts with the Royal Small Arms factory in Enfield, Middlesex. The 'Royal' prefix was added in 1893, together with the slogan 'Made like a gun'. The first motorized vehicles were built in about 1899; these were quadricycles, shortly followed by tricycles using de Dion engines. Experiments with two-wheelers soon followed, one with a Minerva engine clamped to the front down tube of a heavy bicycle frame,

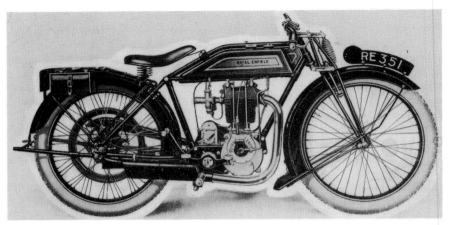

One of the first 350 cc overhead valve singles, this is a 1924 JAP-engined sports model. The two-speed Enfield gear is fitted, but this was dropped the following year, and at the same time the braking (somewhat sketchy here) was improved.

the other with a 1½ hp engine clipped on to the front of the steering head. Both were fitted with belt drive to the rear wheel, with the 1½ hp's rawhide belt being twisted in order to get a better grip on the engine pulley.

By using the Werner formula of 1901, the stability and handling qualities of early Enfields were greatly improved. This involved positioning the engine in the frame under the petrol tank, in what became accepted as the normal place. Other improvements that Enfield included on their machines were the carrying of oil in an extension of the sump (an enduring habit) and the early use of mechanically operated valves.

An abortive attempt was made at building motor cars, and this meant the postponement of any further development in the motor cycle department until 1910, although the company was still producing cycle and motor cycle components for the trade. This time a small 2¼ hp V-twin Motosacoche was used, and soon afterwards a 2¾ hp unit based on the Swiss design, with the option of an expanding clutch, two-speed gear or a single gear with countershaft.

This two-speed gear, similar in design to that adopted by Phelon and Moore in 1906 and Scott in 1908, was one of the simplest and most reliable of the early gear systems used on motor cycles. It incorporated two separate primary driving chains which ran on sprockets of different ratios. The appropriate gear was selected by connecting either of the primary chains with the single secondary chain via separate expanding clutches. Enfield used this system up until 1924, when customers were given the option of a Sturmey-Archer three-speed countershaft 'box; it was dropped altogether in 1925.

Enfield's close connection with Motosacoche in those early days was witnessed by the number of components that both firms had in common. For example, the all-chain transmission with Enfield's patent rubber cush-drive rear hub, which did much to soften power impulses from the engine, was fitted to all Royal Enfields right through to their last models in the mid-'60s.

The company expanded and prospered, building their own engines, but also occasionally making use of proprietary units, as in the 1912 sidecar combination. This model marked the beginning of a long line of Enfield V-twin sloggers. These outfits were so popular that, for a time, the Enfield name was chiefly associated with 6 and 7 hp machines. Later versions were powered by their own make of side valve units, but the initial model had a 6 hp (770 cc) JAP engine with the two-speed gear.

A solo machine, designed by W. H. Guillon, was introduced in the following year. Powered by a 3 hp inlet-over-exhaust V-twin engine, the most novel feature of this machine was the fully automatic dry sump lubrication system, which was in stark contrast with the standard hand-operated pump used by most other manufacturers. The double-acting oil pump design was yet another long-lived Enfield fitting.

Although regular competitors in trials and track events, Royal Enfield made a less than dramatic impact on the racing world until the 1914 season, when scaled-down versions (from 425 to 350 cc) of the solo model gave some creditable performances at Brooklands and in the Isle of Man. The TT was, however, marred by F. J. Walker's fatal accident only seconds after he finished in third place.

In 1914 Royal Enfield made the unusual move of adding a single cylinder two-speed two-stroke to their range (active development of the lightweight unit was only just beginning to take off at this time) and its production continued, with modifications, in 2¼ hp (275 cc) form for several years after the war. Post-war production also included an 8 hp sidecar outfit which had been used to great effect as (amongst other things) a mount for the Vickers machine gun. Appropriately enough, some engines were supplied by Vickers.

It was quite some time before any new models emerged from the Redditch works, but the growing trend for middleweight singles could not be ignored for long. In 1923 Enfield made the decision to return to their original market but, their experience being limited to big twins and two-strokes, they made the wise decision to use proprietary JAP engines, at least initially.

The first of the line was a 349 cc four-stroke with an aluminium piston and a bore and stroke of 70 mm by 90 mm. It was a side valve, the valves being fitted with aluminium cooling domes in place of the ordinary caps, and the mainshaft ran on roller bearings. Lubrication was forced through oilways to all the principal internal parts of the engine by means of a mechanical oil pump. Transmission was all chain drive, and the well-tried Enfield gearbox provided ratios of 5.7 to 1 and 10 to 1, with operation by a heel-and-toe pedal; this was an advance on the previous hand change. Other details, common to all Enfields, were the well-sprung Terry's saddle and detachable carriers and rear mudguard for quick tyre repairs. The rear dummy rim and front stirrup brakes were not very effective, but these and other features were the subject of improvements in subsequent years.

The two-speed gear could cope well enough with general riding and gentle hills, but for freak hills encountered in trials events a more suitable system was required. A change was made, in 1925, to the close-ratio, three-speed Sturmey-Archer countershaft gearbox. This coincided with the introduction of two new 350 cc singles to the range: a single port ohv model, and a specially tuned ohv engine with twin exhaust ports for those with racing pretensions. Additional improvements included internal expanding brakes both front and rear, and heavier tyres.

In the meantime, Enfield had been working on a 350 cc engine of their own design and manufacture. It had a Dural light-alloy con rod and an aluminium piston, and the rocker gear and pushrods were totally enclosed. Introduced as part of the 1927 range, the new engine was as successful in trials as its JAP-powered predecessors, and for the first time in the history of the company Royal Enfield won the manufacturer's team prize in the Junior TT. Despite the impending slump, sales were on the whole good and it was necessary for a large extension to be built at the Redditch works. A famous name was added to motor cycling's hall of fame with the continuation of the single cylinder sporting model—the Bullet.

Raleigh

Raleigh is one of the few names to survive the heyday of British motor cycle production—if only on the side of a bicycle frame. History, it seems, has come full circle as the Nottingham-based firm was a leading bicycle concern before branching out into motor cycle manufacture in 1899. One of their earliest designs was based on the Werner and in this, the simple single-cylinder engine was attached to the steering head of their own bicycle frames, with belt drive to the front wheel. The high centre of gravity resulting from this configuration made the bike especially prone to sideslip, and subsequent models had the power unit lower down the frame.

In 1919, after a gap of some years in motor cycle production, Raleigh began to set their sights on the luxury end of the market with a 5–6 hp (698 cc) flat twin for either solo or sidecar use. Comfort and convenience were given precedence, and the twin featured a shock absorber on the engine shaft, fully enclosed all-chain transmission and quickly detachable wheels. Most outstanding for its time was the Raleigh's spring frame with quarter elliptic springs which insulated the rear of the machine from road shocks. At 155 guineas it was certainly a pricey machine but, to many, the quality of design and finish no doubt justified the expense.

Raleigh's 2¾ hp (348 cc) single-cylinder model, introduced in 1922, was a more standard machine at the relatively modest price of £66. In their bid for lightweight trade, both touring and sports versions, each with the

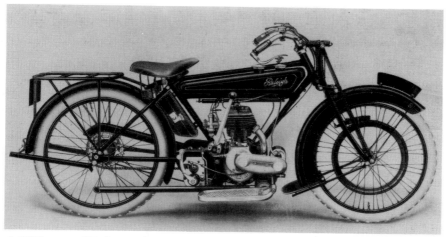

A 1923 season 2¾ hp touring model, with all-chain drive. The sports version featured different handlebars and footrests instead of the boards.

appropriate type of handlebars and footrests or boards, were offered. The side valve engine had drip-feed lubrication, a two-speed gearbox and chain-cum-belt drive, though an all-chain version was introduced soon after. A three-speed Sturmey-Archer gearbox could be substituted at an extra cost of £5. The frame was rigid, made in steel with brazed-on lugs and having a low riding position. Front forks were the popular Brampton Biflex type, made under licence by Raleigh, and the brakes were of the dummy belt rim pattern.

For sidecar use, Raleigh marketed a 3 hp version, made by boring the single out to 76 mm (from 71 mm, with a stroke of 88 mm), producing a capacity of 399 cc. Priced at £78, the light sidecar could be added for an extra £25. The company had learned to keep down manufacturing costs by simplifying the design without skimping on the quality of the materials they used.

Both the 2¾ hp and the 3 hp were enormously popular during the 1920s and were exported to, amongst other places, Japan. They possessed, as *Motor Cycling* put it, 'that indefinable air of "class" which distinguishes most high-grade productions'. Competition successes confirmed this widely held opinion and daring deeds by trials riders like Hugh Gibson and Marjorie Cottle gave the name even greater charisma.

Marjorie Cottle's association with Raleigh was completely fortuitous. On the eve of a 24 hours trial from Aberystwyth to Birkenhead and back, a jealous rival 'cooked' her Powell machine and nothing could persuade it to go. Raleigh dealer Victor Horsman came to the rescue, having previously offered the loan of a machine should she ever need one. Competitors rode in

the worst weather imaginable, and over half of them retired, but having got
her Raleigh Marjorie felt compelled to go on and as a result was one of the
few to win a gold medal.

One of the best publicity stunts of all occurred when Marjorie on her 348 cc
side-valver and Hugh Gibson on a V-twin sidecar outfit did a round-the-
coast run of Britain. With Marjorie heading south whilst Gibson rode north,
they completed the 3,404 miles in 11½ days. Their crossing point was the
subject of a popular competition run by the manufacturers—over 60,000
entries were received—and the prize was a model similar to the one used by
Miss Cottle.

In 1929 the side valve 348 cc model was dropped from the range, but the
MT30 twin-port overhead valve machine continued to excel in trials events.
As with all but the smallest of Raleigh's machines for 1930, the MT30 was
converted to the popular semi-dry sump lubrication system but only after
prolonged experiments. This pursuit of perfection was the hallmark of the
Raleigh concern, and a great asset as long as the economic climate was
stable. A slump in demand brought the motor cycle side of the business to
an end in 1933, and Raleigh's three-wheelers lasted only a few years longer.

BSA

BSA, at one time the biggest manufacturer of motor cycles in the world, was
built on solid foundations going back to the sixteenth century and beyond.
As its full name— the Birmingham Small Arms Company Ltd—suggests,
this long tradition in engineering evolved from the formation of a pool of
smiths and craftsmen in an area rich in materials vital to their trade. Their
consolidation became necessary during the Napoleonic Wars when the
government of the day set up an ordnance factory in Enfield. It then
proceeded to import machinery from America which the local craftsmen
knew would, in time, put them out of work. To counteract the threat, the
men formed the Birmingham Small Arms Trade Association and set up a
factory of their own at Small Heath, equipped with machine tools. This was,
of course, in direct competition with that of the government but BSA soon
found that as long as there was a war going on there was more than enough
work for the private sector. The sad truth of the munitions industry is that
peace is never desirable and during lulls in trade, when all routine orders
(the few that there were) were directed to the ordnance works, BSA found it
necessary to diversify.

First dabblings with cycle-making came in 1880 when the intrepid E.C.F.
Otto demonstrated his Dicycle by riding it up and down the company's
boardroom table. Inherently more stable than its contemporary, the
penny-farthing, both wheels were of an equal, if huge, size and set side by
side with the rider sitting between them. Work on the Dicycle was,
however, abandoned when another order for guns came from the War
Office: with the subsequent and inevitable slump BSA gradually converted
their shell-making plant to manufacturing cycle parts for the trade.

BSA waited some years before attempting a motorized vehicle. It was 1905 before they experimented by fitting a proprietary engine to one of their own bicycle frames. Enthusiasm gathered momentum when an amalgamation was formed with the Eadie Manufacturing Company (the first of many firms to become a part of the BSA empire) and Albert Eadie was given the task of developing the idea further. Eadie formed a team with two other distinguished engineers: Frank Baker, TT racer and designer of Precision engines, and Charles Hyde, ex-works manager of the James Cycle Company. They examined machines on the market to decide what they did and didn't want and, even at this early stage, they determined that all mass-produced parts should be made to the highest precision standards and that as many components as possible should be interchangeable.

During the five or six years leading up to the First World War, the 3½ hp belt-drive single emerged as the most popular engine design so it was natural enough for BSA's motor cycle division to adopt the layout for their debut machine. Though similar to the Triumph single which appeared in 1907, the BSA was notable for its superior front forks, said to be the first ever example of cantilever springing. Also of their own design was the two-speed hub gear using a clutch of the concentric-cone type, which customers could buy as an optional extra for £6 10s. The basic model, priced at £50, sold well, and quickly developed a reputation for hard work and unfailing reliability, combined with simplicity. A 4¼ hp model, primarily for sidecar use, was added to the range and this was adapted for military use during the 1914–18 War.

Reverting to its traditional craft, the Small Heath concern supplied, amongst other things, several million Lee-Enfield rifles and Lewis automatic machine guns to the Russian and Belgian Armies, as well as to British troops throughout the world. To cope with this enormous output it was necessary for new factory buildings to be added and for the number of employees to be raised from 3,500 to 13,000. This stood BSA in good stead once the production of civilian motor cycles could be resumed in 1919. As ever, the emphasis was on silence, serviceability and reliability and, apart from the usual round of competitions, BSA motor cycles were used to pull off a number of attention-grabbing stunts.

One of these, in 1924, involved trials rider H. S. Perrey who led a team of four on a climb up Snowdon. The machines used were a 3 hp ohv sportster, designed by Harold Briggs, and a 2¼ hp lightweight which was to become a familiar sight on Britain's roads during the 1920s. The feat took less than thirty minutes to achieve and was subsequently emulated by other marques. In another popular stunt the manufacturers built a machine from spare parts gleaned from a number of dealers throughout the country—the resultant motor cycle started first kick, demonstrating the remarkable precision with which BSA fabricated their components.

Commercial production recommenced with both singles on offer: the 4¼ hp with chain and belt or all-chain drive, and the 3½ hp, in TT form only. To

Seen outside the offices of W.W. Greener Guns Ltd, manufacturers of rifles, pistols and ammunition, Major Burne Glen sits astride his 'Round Tank', doubtless on his way back to the Small Heath factory.

these were added a sidecar machine with a 6–7 hp V-twin, four-stroke engine with side-by-side valves, AMAC carburettor and EIC magneto. It was fitted with fully-enclosed all-chain drive, a seven-plate clutch and three-speed gearbox with kickstarter, a redesign of an earlier BSA unit. Rider comfort was catered for by the sprung saddle pillar and a modified version of the spring fork, a single long compression spring being used in place of the previous short compression spring and recoil spring.

These three machines continued for some years, providing a solid foundation for the difficult times ahead, but the real money-spinner was the 2¼ hp Model B introduced in 1924. This was a simple side-valver, easy to maintain and, at £39 10s, a popular machine with the less well-to-do; it also became the official mount of post office telegram boys, and of gas and water board inspectors.

The 249 cc engine had a bore of 63 mm and stroke of 80 mm; it was equipped with a flat-top aluminium-alloy piston, fully floating gudgeon pin and a piston skirt specially grooved to prevent binding. It had a roller bearing big end and the main shaft was fitted with a plain bearing on the gear side and ball bearing on the drive side. Transmission was all-chain with a cam-faced cush drive on the engine shaft to ensure a smooth ride. The two-speed gearbox provided standard ratios of 6.25 and 11.66 to 1 and the dry plate clutch was contained in the large chain wheel and controlled from the left side handlebar grip.

The Model B's distinctive, cylindrically-shaped petrol tank gave the machine its better-known title of Round Tank, although this was later replaced with the more usual wedge-shaped receptacle. The tank was secured to the front down tube by studs and tied to the top tube by a pair of metal bands; it contained 1½ gallons of fuel and 2¼ pints of oil and lubrication was drawn by a hand-operated pump housed in the magneto gear cover and driven off an intermediate gear wheel.

The wheels were shod with 24 × 2¼ inch tyres and the rear wheel was fitted with not just one but two brakes operating on a dummy rim and controlled independently—one by a hand lever and the other by a foot pedal. This was in order to comply with the Motor Vehicles (Construction and Use) Act which stated that all motor cycles should be equipped with two independent brakes—the Act omitted to specify, however, that they should be fitted to two independent wheels!

The Round Tank's frame was built with a sloping top tube to give a low riding position; it had an adjustable saddle, for more capacious riders, and a toolbox containing a comprehensive set of tools, in addition to the 'inflator' held by clips on to the top tube. Weighing only 170 lb, the little bike was capable of a top speed of 45 mph and of taking a 1 in 6 gradient, like that of a favourite testing ground—Sunrising Hill, at 20 mph. In *Motor Cycling*, a road test of the 2¼ stated that BSA had good grounds for confidence, and a rosy future was predicted. The company's quality-control technique was also much admired: 'With a view to testing in the most violent manner the strength of such parts as the forks and frame a special bumping machine has been perfected, and on this a machine laden with a weight equivalent to that of a rider has been battered for hours on end, with the result that the possibility of any failure from forks or frame has been quite eliminated'.

Over the four years of its production, the Round Tank underwent a number of changes, notably the more sensible arrangement of one brake on each wheel and a three-speed gearbox. Over 35,000 were sold and in its practicality and lightness, as well as its enormous popularity, the Model B was the clear ancestor of the post-World War Two Bantam which was to be BSA's most successful motor cycle of all time.

Ariel

Ariel was the name James Starley used in 1870 when he and William Hillman patented their tensioned wire-spoke wheel; 'the Spirit of the Air' imagery was evoked again in 1871, when they patented an improved version of the penny-farthing bicycle. Starley it was who went on to even greater things with the Rover car and motor cycle company, and both Rover and Ariel amalgamated in 1877 with Cycle Components Ltd, a large and growing firm in Selly Oak, Birmingham.

When Charles Sangster took over the management of the company, Ariel had already produced a number of tricycles and quadricycles using de Dion engines. Unlike the French manufacturers, Ariel placed the engine in front of, instead of behind, the rear axle, thus giving the machine much greater longitudinal stability. The tricycle was extremely well-made, with carefully thought out details, like the enclosed driving gears ensuring protection from road grit, and efficient lubrication of the gear teeth. It performed well in the 'Thousand Miles Trial' of 1900 and sold in large numbers.

The two-wheeler that followed in 1902 was equally advanced: it was powered by a Kerry engine, and featured magneto ignition and a float carburettor. Sangster's contribution was to encourage Ariel's participation in trials competitions to stimulate sales, and in 1905 J. S. Campbell won the ACU race on the Isle of Man riding a 6 hp model.

1910 saw the introduction of a robust little Ariel with a 4 hp White and Poppe side valve engine (later built by Cycle Components, who bought the design rights in 1911) which carried on in production right up to 1925. Bikes with V-twin engines made by Abingdon King Dick and MAG were built for sidecar use but sales were not tremendous in spite of the generous part exchange deals offered by Ariel.

Sangster himself designed a lightweight two-stroke, coyly named the Arielette, but the war put paid to its production and, in any case, much more attention was now being paid to the car side of the industry. Sangster's son, Jack, was the driving force here, with his flat-twin engined Ariel Nine. In 1922 the Ariel Ten with an in-line four-cylinder engine was added, but neither motor could compete with the mass-produced Austin and Morris machines.

Although not on the same scale as Triumph or Douglas, Ariel played their part in supplying military vehicles and munitions, and when restrictions were lifted in 1919, they reaped the benefits of a seller's market. The 1920 range featured no essential changes, and the single and V-twin continued in solo and sidecar form for several years with only a few modifications.

In 1925 a couple of new employees, Val Page and Victor Mole, proceeded to give Ariel a much needed shake-up. Page and Mole scrapped all the old models and came up with a couple of new, though fairly safe, designs for single cylinder 557 cc side valve and 496 cc overhead valve machines. The engines had roller bearing big ends, mechanical oil pumps, aluminium pistons, a Burman three-speed gearbox and all-chain transmission. The frame was the conventional diamond pattern, with Druid front forks, but in 1927 the riding position was lowered with a new cradle frame. A combined petrol and oil saddletank and an exhaust system fitted with a Brooklands

The 1928 5 hp overhead valve de luxe Model D, designed by Val Page and Ariel's most sporting single.

can added to the general improvement in styling.

A new slogan—'Ariel, The Modern Motor Cycle'—and the horse logo completed the rejuvenation. Ariel became well established in people's minds as makers of tough and sporty machines, and the new singles sold in vast numbers. Some of the credit for this must go to the imaginative salesmanship of Vic Mole and Harry Perrey, the latter an Ariel employee who was well known for his expertise in trials events.

In one of their more bizarre stunts, Perrey took a sidecar outfit up to the summit of Snowdon. On another occasion, he crossed the English Channel on a solo machine mounted on floats. The press, it seems, were happy to go along with this light-hearted bid for attention. One of those who tested the Ariel 'Sea-Horse' was Torrens, the well-known technical journalist who found it 'very like driving a belt-driven sidecar outfit up a Welsh mountain in a heavy storm'. He added, 'A point which will appeal to all motor cyclists is that punctures are impossible; also, there is no need to "test your tyres every Friday" '. The highly camouflaged Ariels used in George Formby's film *No Limits* (they made up the Rainbow team) was another bit of publicity that the sales department was quick to exploit.

Successful performances at Brooklands and in long-distance endurance races led to design improvements in production models, such as fully enclosed valves, dry sump lubrication and straight tube frame construction. Two ohv machines, the 497 cc and a prototype 248 cc, won the Maudes Trophy in 1929—the second time that Ariel had received this prestigious award. For the 1930 season these two 'Specials', as they were called, were hotted up with high-compression pistons and polished ports. Their appearance, notably the chromium-plated petrol tanks, set them apart from the rest of the range, although all models featured some interesting changes.

The new shaped tank, remodelled to fit flush with the peak of the saddle, incorporated a speedometer and oil pressure gauge. No major changes were made to the engines of the standard range, except for slight modifications to the cylinder heads to improve performance. In the case of the 497 cc ohv single, this was to be developed further, as young Edward Turner, brought into the company to design and develop a four-cylinder engine of 'square' disposition, revamped it into the sporting Red Hunter, first of a line bearing that name.

The 1930s were a difficult time for everyone, and Page's singles and Turner's Square Four became the mainstays of a slimmed down range and were offered with few changes throughout the pre-war years.

Chapter 7

The build-up to war: Depression or expansion

During 'the hungry years' of the 1920s and '30s the burden of economic depression— with its unemployment, poor health and malnutrition—fell predominantly on the communities centred round Britain's heavy industries. Civil strife amongst these declining sections of the economy—principally in mining, shipbuilding and the railways—was not infrequent, and the divisions between the haves and the have-nots continued to widen.

Following the collapse of the New York stock exchange in 1929, the value of Britain's exports plummeted and by the mid '30s unemployment had risen to over two million, with many people living in desperate poverty. One of the most potent expressions of their plight was the Hunger March of 1936 when a quarter of a million people, travelling on foot from Glasgow, Jarrow and South Wales, gathered in London's Hyde Park.

As the old industries languished, so a new order emerged centred around the light industries. There was still great deprivation but those in employment were increasingly able to spend their money on more than just the basics in life and therein lay the means of escape from the problems of social reality.

New materials, new technology and the development of mass-production techniques, together with the increase in 'easy' hire-purchase terms, gave industries the means of satisfying consumer demands. Plastics, electronics and the service industries all prospered; private transport, private housing, leisure activities and entertainment were all catered for by trades that were expanding and, in turn, encouraging a new consumer culture that was making Britain look more and more like America.

Throughout these years the motor cycle industry remained in a position of great commercial value to the country. In 1935, the Manufacturers' Union was able to report that the motor cycle was maintaining its popularity as a sporting and utility machine all over the globe. Britain was still far and away the biggest exporter of motor cycles: of the nearly three million machines in use throughout the world, British manufacturers could claim 548,461 and their nearest rivals, the US marques, only 3,566. Retrenchment in the economic and industrial structure of the country was reflected in the policies of the motor cycle manufacturers. The entrepreneurial spirit of the golden era in the '20s was over and the job in hand, as it was then perceived, was to provide the public with simple, dependable workhorses based on tried and tested designs. For this reason the single-cylinder machine became almost synonymous with British motor cycle design. Ranging in

Above *The side valve single remained very popular, with models like this AJS 3.5 hp Sports selling at £40.*

Below *Progress was often confined to technical refinements: this 1932 Panther has open valve gear—but also note the front brake, linked to the rear.*

capacity from 150 cc to 600 cc and with a moderate compression level, one of the side-valve single's most enduring attractions was its great flexibility—slot it into top and it would still run at just a few miles per hour, without any risk of snatching.

Although its basic design remained the same, a large number of technical refinements raised the single to a high level of excellence. Power outputs were increased and engines became tidier and more compact, some with unit-construction gearboxes. Valve gear, tappets and springs were made fully-enclosed, thus keeping them well protected from the elements as well as constantly lubricated by oil-spray from the crankcase. Detachable cylinder heads made maintenance work much easier and extensive use of aluminium-alloy and extra finning improved cooling efficiency.

Sophisticated new valve steels and aluminium alloy pistons with scraper rings reduced the frequency with which routine jobs like valve-grinding and decarbonizing had to be done. Lubrication systems, previously of the total-loss variety, were now dry or semi-dry sump which made starting easier and reduced the tendency for gummed-up pistons.

Despite Britain's dominance of the world market, there were many critics, at home as well as abroad, who felt that the motor cycle industry was lagging behind in not adopting more innovative designs for their production machines. Strictly speaking, the single was obsolescent and considered by many to have been around for far too long.

What was needed was for the British industry to develop the smoother multi before the Germans and Italians snatched the opportunity, and the market, clean out of their hands. Dedicated singles riders might refer to them derisively as 'pussy-purring fours' but the multi-cylindered continental bikes were becoming increasingly advanced in design and standards of reliability, and it was only a matter of time before they would take over the market.

Four-cylinder machines, like the popular Motobécane in-line ohc 500, were smooth, quiet and easy to start. They could be tuned to rev much higher than a single, as all parts were light and better balanced. Less fatiguing to ride, the multis achieved a more even torque and consequently enjoyed better road adhesion.

The manufacturers' defence was that keeping costs down and prices to a minimum was an absolute priority in order to keep business ticking over. Bright, original ideas would have to wait until the economic climate would allow them to be put into practice; even then, manufacturers were dubious about the response they were likely to get, accusing the public of being too conservative for unorthodox designs.

Of course, there were two sides to this argument. There might have been those of the old school, like the correspondent to *Motor Cycling* who sighed 'for the days when motor cycles were motor cycles, the vital adjustments accessible to other than specially trained snakes and with nothing but the most necessary fittings to embellish them.'

But what most British manufacturers failed to realize was that a new type of motor cyclist was emerging: a rider who would be attracted to the greater comfort of the spring framed, multi-cylindered foreigners and learn to reject the British motor cycle for its noisiness, difficulty in starting, frequent electrical problems and numerous other headaches.

Overhead camshaft and unit-construction engines were innovations (and not very recent ones, either) which the Brits were surprisingly reluctant to adopt in their production motor cycles. Production models of the overhead valve single were almost all of the pushrod-operated variety, in spite of the tremendous racing success of overhead camshaft machines, like Norton's CS1 350 and 500 cc models, and the many years of the overhead camshaft's use in the motor car industry.

The advantages of unit-construction, its compactness, lightness and reliability, were well appreciated by the continentals. Nevertheless few British manufacturers felt compelled to adopt unit-construction of the engine and gearbox until the 1960s, and then only in a rather half-hearted form. Instead of redesigning the engine as a unit, marques like Triumph and BSA simply incorporated a separate engine and gearbox in one set of cases while retaining primary chain-drive, the very thing that most needed to be eliminated, being noisy, quick wearing and in need of regular adjustment.

Two of the more notable exceptions to this ingrained conservatism in the British industry were both designed by that whizz-kid of motor cycle engineering, Edward Turner. The Ariel Square Four (1930) and Triumph Speed Twin (1937), are examples of Turner's genius for creating machines which caught the imagination of the public and sold in vast numbers.

The Square Four, a highly unusual design, with four cylinders arranged equidistantly in a square formation, overhead camshafts and twin crankshafts, was probably too complex for others to imitate. But the vertical twin was simplicity itself and inspired a long line of post-war imitations.

In the meantime the British public continued to exalt motor cycling as a national sport. 'The Blue 'Un' and 'the Green 'Un', as the motor cycle papers were called, kept enthusiasts up-to-date on national and international competitions; touring articles and tips on camping emphasized the health-giving nature of the pastime, while Sir Malcolm Campbell, a keen motor cyclist himself, wrote that motor cycling represented the best form of training for driving any motorized vehicle—being more vulnerable made one fully aware of the potential hazards on the road. It is interesting to note that the driving test was introduced in 1934 and motor cyclists of 17 years and over who passed were then entitled to drive a car without having to take a further test.

For motor cyclists in those days, tinkering with the works was an essential part of the enjoyment. The small ads for parts and accessories testify to this—forty-odd pages at the back of each motor cycle paper was not at all unusual. Perhaps people were more sporting and individualistic at that time, although economic considerations undoubtedly played an important

By 1938 the valve gear has been enclosed, and since the footbrake (still linked) has changed sides, hand gear change has given way to foot-operated change.

part in this as the cheapest form of transport was still the motor cycle and sidecar outfit.

Tax and insurance were major expenses which most people would have been happy to avoid. During the 1930s, Ixion observed, with envy, that in Germany Hitler had abolished tax on all motor cycles, irrespective of size; there was no compulsory insurance either, although vehicle owners had to pay tax on fuel.

By catering for the needs of the commuter, the Hitler regime was able to treble the number of people employed in the motor cycle industry and thereby dramatically reduce unemployment. State subsidies were procured and the beneficial effect on the development of the German motor cycle soon became apparent. British competitors could do no more than watch helplessly as supercharged BMWs, NSUs and DKWs began to overtake them—this was brought painfully home when Jock West, on a BMW, won the Ulster Grand Prix in 1937.

There were many who argued, unsuccessfully, for a reduction, if not outright abolition, of tax and insurance in this country too. They were aware of the important role of the motor cycle as the wage earner's means of transport and there were those too, like Lord Sandhurst of the BMCA, who remembered a time when motor cyclists had saved the country's bacon.

Presenting his case in the House of Lords, Sandhurst reminded his audience, 'that the cyclists, and particularly the motor cyclists, provided in the last war practically the whole of our Flying Corps. Today they are still a great source, but a dwindling source, for the supply of pilots. Italy and Germany have realized the value of the motor cyclists to the full, and do everything they can to encourage them.'

It was only a short time before the government would have to call on the services of the motor cycle industry again. 'The Phoney War' of 1939-40 was a belated response to the warning signals that had for some years been emanating from the continent. Two Emergency Powers Acts were passed, giving the government almost unlimited authority. Food and petrol rationing, evacuations and black-outs became a part of everyday life; conscription was introduced with a list of 'reserved occupations' precluding skilled workers who were needed at home for the production of munitions.

Up until the eleventh hour it was still hoped that war might be averted. 'Peace in our time' was Prime Minister Neville Chamberlain's promise to the people of Britain on his return from talks with Hitler and Mussolini. It was in this spirit of optimism that over sixty British competitors entered the 1939 International Six Days' Trial in Germany, only to receive strong advice from the British embassy, halfway through, to pack their bags and head for home.

With regret, *Motor Cycling* reported: 'History will record that Germany won the event, but the Germans will be the first to admit that their victory is both inconclusive and unsatisfactory. The excellent performance put up by our Trophy and Vase ''B'' teams, and the quiet efficiency of the BSA-

Most British manufacturers ignored unit construction, but New Imperial were an exception—this hard-used 1938 250 was competing in the Talmag Trial.

BSA's M20 500 cc side valve provided transport for many a military despatch rider. The rider here is only dressing up, but his bike and the one next to it are ex-WD relics.

mounted Army men, gave every promise of British successes in the concluding scramble test, and we are certain that our regret in withdrawing was shared by the organizers who proved themselves to be thorough sportsmen.' Peter Chamberlain sums up the whole unhappy affair when he says, '. . .a miserable and wretched end to what might have been a memorable International!'

During the Second World War, the motor cycle again proved invaluable, this time almost solely as a vehicle of reconnaissance and communications. Yet again, the DR was praised to the skies, sometimes in the most unlikely places. In a series of articles from the fighting fronts, a writer in Blackwood's literary magazine described his experience of travelling in convoy: 'But it was not till a group of RASC (Royal Army Service Corps) motor cyclists arrived that I knew we would soon be moving. These motor cyclists acted as mechanized sheep-dogs during our voyage; competent, attentive, allowing no lorry driver to go too fast, smoothing out congestion at crossroads with the efficiency of London policemen, rendering aid and making arrangements should one of those over-worked, hard-used lorries happen to break down. Admirable, courteous, sun-tanned young men they were, to whom we owe no mean debt of gratitude for a comparatively comfortable, well-regulated journey.'

Another military favourite, the Norton 16H.

Most of the machines produced for the British forces were middleweight 350 cc singles with side or overhead valves. A popular example was the Matchless WD G3L, based on the civilian Clubman G3. This had a 347 cc single-port, single-cylinder engine with overhead valves controlled by hairpin valve springs and enclosed pushrods. Mounted in a strong duplex cradle frame, drive was by chain which was fully enclosed in a quickly detachable primary oil bath.

For military use, the engine was detuned to provide a more flexible performance, and in 1941 a new set of forks was fitted. These were the 'Teledraulics', a pair of hydraulically-damped, telescopic front forks based on the famous BMW components introduced in 1935. The Matchless Teledraulics were the first forks of their kind to be made by a British manufacturer.

Over a quarter of the bikes used by the British forces were provided by Norton, who supplied over 100,000 examples of the well-tried side-valve 16H fitted in a high trials frame and with crankcase shield and 'snubber' springs in the front forks. They were well suited to their task, being simple, dependable and easy to maintain. On a much smaller scale, Norton built Big Four sidecar outfits for the War Department, and these were used mainly for reconnaissance work in North Africa.

At Triumph, a light, 350 cc twin was specially designed for the British Army and the first fifty units were actually on the assembly line when the factory, along with most of the centre of Coventry, was destroyed by German bombers. The 350 twin had to be abandoned but in a remarkably short period of time, work was resumed at new premises, this time concentrating on the 350 Model 3HW single.

Ariel and BSA contributed to the war effort, the former with the 350 Model W/NG and the latter with the 500 cc M20, although both were more occupied with other military projects. One of the more unusual two-wheelers produced at this time was the 98 cc two-stroke Corgi, a folding scooter, originally made for Air Force paratroopers but continuing in production, on a small scale, until 1948.

During the latter half of the year, the improved reliability and range of military radio systems reduced the motor cycle's usefulness. Fortunately, a good few years were to pass before the popularity of the two-wheeler was to decline in the civilian sector and, once restrictions had been lifted, a large variety of models was made available in increasing numbers to all types of people.

The watchword, then, in the post-vintage period was, by and large, conservatism. Many vintage models were simply continued, with cosmetic changes. This is not to say, however, that there was nothing new or that everything was dull, as scrutiny of some of the more interesting or outstanding machines will show.

Brough

William Brough built some pretty good machines, starting with his de Dion-powered motor car and tricycle built in the late 1890s and followed by his first motor cycle in 1902. Concentrating, for the most part, on engines of flat-twin design, Brough's machines earned a reputation for being solid and reliable; this was amply demonstrated in the 1920 London to Edinburgh trial, when seven Brough entries brought home seven medals—six gold and one silver.

It was in one such long-distance trial, the Auto Cycle Club's 'End to End' which went from John o' Groats to Land's End, that Brough's sons, William and George, competed on two of their father's machines. Only sixteen years old at the time, George put on a good show but nevertheless finished three days behind all the other competitors. Fortunately, he did not allow this less-than-encouraging experience to stifle his interest and enthusiasm in motor cycles and motor cycling. On the contrary, he became more determined than ever to pursue his ambition to build a really superior machine of his own. Over the next few years, the dream machine took form in his mind while the necessary technical knowledge was gained working in partnership with his father at the Vernon Road factory in Nottingham.

The partners were unable to see eye to eye on the matter of basic engine design— the son preferring V-twins and the father, flat-twins. So in 1919,

George decided that, rather than compromise any further, he would start up his own business at new premises in Haydn Road. In order to avoid any ambiguity, he decided, at the suggestion of a friend, that he would call his marque Brough Superior. This was hardly a compliment to his father, who interpreted it as meaning that, by implication, his own product must be considered inferior!

Although Brough Superior's first machine, the Mark I, was not completed in time for exhibition at the 1920 Show, *The Motor Cycle* built up expectations by giving the big V-twin a lengthy and highly complimentary write-up: 'Mr George Brough informed us that it was his intention to produce a fast, light and well-equipped motor cycle, which should include all necessary fittings, but no fancy attachments, and, after inspecting his latest production, we may safely say that we have never examined a more sensibly equipped big twin solo mount.' George Brough's reputation, as a successful competition rider as well as an engineer, was such that even without seeing the machine for themselves, let alone the benefit of a road test in one of the technical journals, eager customers sent in orders and deposit money long before the machine was officially launched.

As a solo mount, the V-twin was well established in the United States, with makes like Indian and Harley-Davidson producing their first monsters as far back as 1908. In Britain, the JAP-engined Mark I, or '90 Bore' as it became known, was quite a departure from the norm. Additional details, like the oval saddletank and unusual silencer and exhaust system—all heavily nickel-plated—have since become characteristics automatically associated with the Brough Superior name.

Quiet, luxurious and expensive, it was indeed the 'Rolls-Royce of motor cycles', as one appreciative customer called it. The Mark I was also remarkably fast, and George Brough himself demonstrated this characteristic with great skill in trials and roadracing events. In 1922 and 1923, he won 51 out of 52 consecutive races, on his own personal sprinter, 'Old Bill'—quite a kick in the teeth for those who, prior to its first race, had scathingly dismissed it as 'Spit and Polish'!

Brough's first SS100 model was based on a competition machine developed by Bert Le Vack at Brooklands; he it was who recorded an astounding 113 mph in 1924. Appearing in the same year at the Olympia Show, the SS was powered by a new ohv JAP engine housed in a duplex cradle frame and fitted with Castle forks—a parallel ruler design patented by George Brough and Harold Karslake in 1925. So confident were Brough of the model's performance, that they issued each machine, as it left the factory, with a guarantee that it had been timed over a quarter of a mile at over 100 mph.

At £175, the SS100 was probably the most expensive motor cycle in the world and certainly beyond the price range of the average enthusiast. But George Brough had no interest in mass-producing cheap motor cycles; his concern was with building high-quality machines and, with customers like

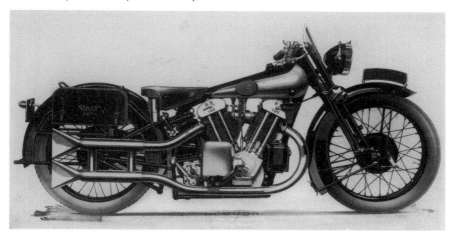

The 1931 version of the Brough Superior SS100. A refined and tireless tourer, it became a legend in its own production lifetime, and that legend has persisted.

T. E. Lawrence, there was no shortage of people with the necessary cash to make the marque a success.

George knew he had gauged his customers well when he wrote: 'I knew the public did not want a machine which was virtually a sidecar model, adapted for solo use merely by the fitting of a higher gear. I knew they wanted a type of machine designed from the experienced solo rider's point of view'.

Redesigned in 1933, the 996 cc JAP engine (80 mm × 99 mm bore and stroke) was capable of producing 74 bhp at 6,200 rpm with a compression ratio of 8 to 1. Both cylinder walls were deeply spigoted to ensure greater rigidity and reduce vibration. Specifications included twin carburettors and twin magnetos, dry sump lubrication, with no less than four oil pumps, and a Sturmey-Archer four-speed gearbox. An alternative engine, made by AMC Ltd, was introduced in 1935. This had hairpin valve springs, bore and stroke of 85.5 mm × 85.5 mm, and the crankshaft and mainshaft running in phosphor-bronze bearings. With its compression ratio of 6.5 to 1, a top speed of 102 mph was quite easily attained, although for racing purposes compression could be further raised to 8 to 1.

In 1934 William Brough Senior died and George decided to move back to the family concern in Vernon Street. Here he worked on what was to be his ideal machine—a 997 cc flat-four which he called the Golden Dream. Unfortunately it never went into production, remaining a dream forever and also marking the beginning of the end for Brough as a motor cycle business. War intervened and, from 1940 onwards, the factory continued to function as manufacturers of precision components for aircraft; no more motor cycles were ever made.

BSA Blue Star

Shock waves, resulting from the Wall Street Crash in 1929, were felt throughout the business world for some years and BSA, like any other manufacturer, had to make adjustments to allow for a drop in demand. The Small Heath concern was so robust, though, and still offered such a wide and varied range, that sink or swim was never an issue. Losses were made, of course, especially during 1931 and 1932, but by the following year profits were up by £245,000 and a new range of solo machines, the Blue Stars, played a major part in this upturn in events.

The Blue Star was not the first of the Star models: in 1928, Harold Briggs designed the 493 cc ohv Sloper, with an inclined single cylinder and the oil carried in a forward extension of the crankcase. This, and a 350 cc model, were produced in overhead valve and side-valve form and despite poor handling characteristics, both machines became best-sellers, carrying on well into the 1930s. A tuned-up version of the Sloper, with special cams and a high-compression piston, was also offered; a red star decal, fixed to the petrol tank, distinguished it from the standard models of the range.

Cashing in on this renewed interest in speed, the Blue Star models were a sportier variant on the Sloper theme, this time with a two-port vertical engine, although the oil sump was still cast integral with the crankcase. Two overhead valve sports models were available, in 348 cc and 499 cc, soon followed by a 249 cc Junior which was well within the lowest tax class of 30 shillings. Standard versions of the sports models were also offered, with overhead-valve and side-valve engines, while the old Slopers were redesigned and increased in capacity, to act primarily as sidecar haulers.

In 1932 a 499 cc ohv Special, derived from a competition machine which had been raced with some success by Bert Perrigo, was added to the Blue Star range. 'A Blue Star only more so' as *The Motor Cycle* described it, the Special differed little in outward appearance from the rest of the Star line, except that it had straight-through pipes with tubular silencers, instead of its counterpart's upswept exhaust system, and the addition of a crankcase shield. Internally, the specially-tuned engine was kitted out with a slipper-type piston, giving a compression ratio of 7.5 to 1, and quick cams and valve springs. Every part was highly polished, including flywheels and con rod.

With financial recovery well under way, BSA introduced a second generation of Stars, called Empire Stars in commemoration of George V's Silver Jubilee in 1935. With a design originating on Val Page's drawing-board, the Empire Star featured such innovations as dry sump lubrication, a saddle-mounted oil tank, telescopic forks and rear end suspension. To coincide with the new range, the Blue Stars were relaunched with a number of improvements; nevertheless, from this time on they lived in the Empire's shadow. Of an enduring nature, the basic design of both ranges enjoyed a long life and they were eventually turned into the B31 (350 cc) and B33 (500 cc) models, continuing until 1959 and 1960 respectively. And let us not forget, of course, the famous Gold Star.

The Blue Star eventually evolved into the Empire Star, for which the engine was largely redesigned. This is a 500 cc model of 1937.

Norton CS1

Norton's intention in 1927 was to enter the TT with their successful ohv machines, but designer Walter Moore persuaded the company to take a change of course with a new design of his for an overhead camshaft, single-cylinder engine.

The merits and demerits of the overhead camshaft layout had been hotly debated for some years and when Moore designed and built the Camshaft One (or CS1, to give it its snappier title), he was following a precedent first set by JAP in 1922. J. A. Prestwich's 350 cc and 500 cc prototypes had achieved some degree of success in the TT races, but it wasn't until Velocette's 350 cc four-stroke single that the overhead camshaft was given the opportunity to demonstrate what it was really capable of. Ridden by Alec Bennett, the Model K achieved a stunning victory in the 1926 Junior TT, coming in more than ten minutes ahead of all the other competitors.

Most of the early ohc designs employed a chain-drive to the camshaft but Moore, in common with Percy Goodman of Veloce Ltd, chose shaft and bevel gear to drive the single camshaft running in a separate cambox on the cylinder head. Lubrication was by means of a reciprocating oil pump—another Moore design—placed below the gears; when adjusted to a high setting, the oil level could be raised to produce a semi-wet sump effect.

In 1927 Bennett gained another victory in the TT—this time in the Senior event and riding a Norton CS1; Stanley Woods, also on a Norton, scored the fastest lap at over 70 mph. Presented in its production form at the Show that year, the CS1 was, in outward appearance, rather similar to the ohv Model 18. It had the same capacity engine, 490 cc, the same bore and stroke, 79 mm × 100 mm, and was therefore equally tall in the saddle but with appropriate alterations made to accommodate the camshaft drive. Other points in common were magneto ignition, Webb front forks and three-speed Sturmey-Archer gearbox. The CS1, like Norton's ES2 ohv model, was mounted in a new cradle frame which had excellent steering and handling abilities. This sturdy frame continued to be used by Norton for another twenty years or so.

Two 348 cc versions, with lighter cradle frames and cycle parts, were added to the works team. The ohv model proved rather under-powered, but all five machines entered in the Junior TT—the ohc included—were forced to retire, and Norton's Senior team fared little better. The following year, 1929, two 350 cc production models were added to the range—the JE (Junior Enclosed pushrods) and CJ (Camshaft Junior): on all ohv models the rockers and pushrods were enclosed, the cams slightly modified and new silencers fitted, in order to reduce noise. In 1929 Moore left Norton for a more lucrative post with NSU, taking his camshaft design with him. The German machine which resulted from this switch in allegiance was basically the same as the Norton model, except that it had a four-speed gearbox.

Brought in to replace Moore, Arthur Carroll set to work, together with Edgar Franks and additional assistance from the new development engineer, Joe Craig, to redesign the ohc models. Sticking to the vertical drive-shaft layout that Moore had used, Carroll made several improvements which completely transformed the machine. Chief of these was the vernier adjustment for the bevel drive which made the engine much easier to tune. The new engine was also fitted with a more efficient oil pump and a three-speed gearbox with footchange. After further minor modifications, a string of victories, spanning the period 1931 to 1938, ensued with star performances from riders like Jimmy Simpson, Stanley Woods, Jimmy Guthrie and Harold Daniell.

During this remarkable period, Norton won every Senior and Junior TT race bar two, and development of the racing machines continued apace. The four-speed gearbox, with positive stop mechanism, became standard; so too did the famous 'garden gate' spring frame with plunger rear suspension. Other exceptional models were added to the range: the International, the Manx GP and the twin ohc engine, introduced in 1937.

In the 1938 Senior TT, Harold Daniell achieved a fastest lap of 91 mph, but Norton withdrew their support for the following season to concentrate on fulfilling their military contracts to supply 16H and Big Four machines. In any case, there was much stiffer competition gathering steam on the continent. With BMW, DKW and NSU all developing superchargers, the single-cylinder engine was rapidly going out of fashion.

After much reworking and development, the ohc unit reached its zenith in the Manx Norton racers which, against all the odds, continued winning right into the 1960s.

Rudge

The Rudge four-valve engine first saw the light of day in 1924. Disposed in a parallel arrangement, the design had as much to do with metallurgy as improved gas flow, for opening out the cylinder head to take two enormous valves would have weakened the overall structure too much. The answer, doubtless after due study of Ricardo's four-valve Triumph, was to make four smaller holes. The disposition was changed in 1930 to a fully radial one and then, after that proved less than entirely successful, a semi-radial one, which is how it stayed until the end of production.

Another feature for which the Rudge is renowned is the linked braking. Operating the foot lever brings a spring compensator into play, from which a second cable runs to the front brake operating cam. Thus, by using one control balanced braking is achieved, although the compensator must be set up correctly.

In 1926 Graham Walker, a racer and later the editor of *Motor Cycling*, was appointed sales manager of the company. Shortly after his arrival, the model range was diversified, to extend the appeal of Rudge motor cycles. Three models were marketed: the Roadster, with a 'cooking' motor and utilitarian trim; the Special, with brighter paintwork but the same engine; and the Sports, with a tuned motor and the Special's cosmetic finish. Walker won the Ulster Grand Prix in 1928, after an epic race against Charlie

The first year of full valve enclosure for Rudge was 1937. Note the centre stand lifting handle, designed to be operated from the sitting position.

Dodson on a Sunbeam 90, and gave the factory a new name—the Sports was rechristened the Ulster.

Apart from altering the disposition of the valves, the engine was developed to accept a double- or triple-row roller bearing big end (triple-row for the Ulster only). The lubrication system was changed to a centre-fed crankshaft and in 1937 the valve gear was, at last, enclosed. In the same year the gearchange pedal was shifted. Originally it had been on the left (which is now the accepted side) but after the rear wheel hub had been redesigned, the brake and gear pedals could be swapped over, to fall into line with the practice of the day.

Rudge went into receivership in 1935, and was bought by the EMI conglomerate. The new bosses moved the factory from its home in Coventry to the parent plant in Hayes, Middlesex, but in September 1939 motor cycle production was shut down to make way for radar needed for the war effort. EMI sold the Rudge name to Raleigh, and thence Tube Investments, who continued to use it on push bikes.

Rudge motor cycles today benefit from a devoted and active enthusiasts' club, who operate a very good spares scheme. An Ulster or a Special would be an excellent proposition for someone who required a motor cycle which could be ridden regularly, for they are reliable, will cope with modern traffic and have the back-up to keep them on the road.

Triumph Tiger 80 and 5T Speed Twin

Despite its war success with the Model H, Triumph was hit badly by the economic recession of the 1930s and the motor cycle side of the business was forced to keep prices to an absolute minimum. When plans were then drawn up for, of all things, a luxury car—the Gloria Dolomite—new finance was desperately needed and the decision was made to sacrifice motor cycle production completely. In 1936 Jack Sangster, who had previously salvaged the Ariel motor cycle business, bought the nominal share capital of the Triumph Engineering Company and reinstated its founder, Siegfried Bettman, as chairman. The next 25 years were to be the most eventful of Triumph's life.

In 1932, top engineer Val Page had left Ariel to join the Triumph concern where he established a tradition for simple, reliable and inexpensive machines that amateur mechanics could easily maintain themselves. His range of single cylinder machines included 250, 350 and 500 cc side-valve and overhead-valve models in touring and racing guise, the latter being equipped with high-compression pistons, polished ports and racing cams.

At a time when harsh practicalities had to take priority, the stolid, reliable touring models were, quite naturally, the biggest sellers of the range. It was natural enough too that when Triumph hit trouble, yet again, in 1935, it was the popular single that was selected for review. As Val Page had, by now, left for BSA, the task of redesigning the range fell to his former apprentice, Edward Turner.

Turner, who had already demonstrated his engineering genius with his design for the Ariel Square Four, was installed at Triumph in 1936. Acting as

Val Page's worthy and solid Model 3/5 of 1935. When he left Triumph for BSA, his former apprentice took over the designer's reins. His name? Edward Turner.

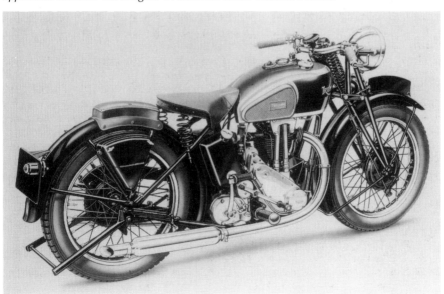

managing director, as well as chief designer, he gave the company the organizational shake-up it needed. His genius also lay in offering the public what they wanted and, more to the point, offering them what they could afford.

The redesigned singles, finished in chrome and blue, were as stylish, fast and glamorous as their names—Tiger 70 (250 cc), Tiger 80 (350 cc) and Tiger 90 (500 cc)—suggested. They were also enormously popular. Each model number was an indication of the top speed the machine could attain but, with a little persuasion, this could be raised quite a bit. Ace tuner Freddie Clarke demonstrated this when he fed his Tiger 80 on dope to win the 350 cc Brooklands lap record at 105.97 mph.

The Tiger 80 was a reasonably priced (£57 when it first appeared in 1936), sporty, ohv machine of 349 cc with 70 mm × 89 mm bore and stroke. It had enclosed valve gear and a special alloy piston with the choice of high or low compression ratios. The duralumin pushrods were encased in telescopic tubes which allowed easy access for adjusting the tappets. Lubrication was by dry sump and an oil pressure gauge was fitted in the petrol tank panel, together with the ammeter and the switchgear.

The Tiger family was cosmetically similar to the Ariel Red Hunter which Turner had also prettied up. The 1937 Tiger 90 500 seen here sports all the trade marks—upswept exhaust, a chrome tank with contrasting panel and a 'leaner' look overall.

In spite of the almost obligatory oil leak, the verdict of the road test in *Motor Cycling* was that the Tiger 80 '. . .was "gentlemanly" in every respect but nevertheless, a veritable tiger, living up to its name, when it was a matter of sheer performance.' In 1937 the petrol tank was restyled, in common with the rest of the Triumph range, and the exhaust pipes were upswept.

During the Second World War, Triumph concentrated on building military machines: the 350 cc ohv single, based on the Tiger 80, and its more prosaic counterpart, the 3H, redesignated 3HW. The main difference between the military 350 and its civilian counterpart was the use of a one-piece cast-iron cylinder head. With the destruction of the Coventry factory during the Blitz of 1940, production of the Tiger series was brought to a halt.

After the war Triumph led the field again, this time with the first of a long line of twins with evocative names like Bonneville, Daytona and Thunderbird. The foundation of this new generation of solo machines was laid by Turner in 1937 when his 498 cc ohv Speed Twin was introduced. Lighter and narrower across the crankcase than the Tiger 90, the parallel twin was, to all intents and purposes, a single, save for the fact that it had two vertical cylinders: its pistons rose and fell simultaneously, thus allowing even firing periods. The beauty of its simplicity in operation was immediately discerned by keen motor cyclists and many a single-cylinder die-hard was converted by Triumph to the multi faith.

It is often assumed that Turner invented the parallel twin with this model, but the design had been experimented with from the earliest days of internal combustion engineering. A remarkably advanced prototype parallel twin was already in existence at Triumph in 1913. It had a cast-iron cylinder block with integral head, two exhaust valves at the front and two inlet valves at the rear. The 180 degree crankshaft was a one-piece forging, turning on two ball-races. However, it was not until Val Page's 649 cc ohv Model 6/1, introduced in 1934, that a vertical twin was put into production. This was a sturdy, dependable machine built primarily for sidecar use, but the oil being carried in the sump made the 6/1 rather tall in the saddle and this gave it an ungainly appearance. A hand-controlled gear lever, at a time when foot-change was coming into fashion, meant that it was never very popular and production lasted only three years.

It was the Speed Twin, incorporating some of the 6/1's design features, that was really responsible for what *Motor Cycling* called the 'bloodless revolution' in public taste. It was an instant success and, costing only a few pounds more than the equivalent single, it soon killed off the 500 cc singles that remained in the Triumph range. Other manufacturers followed the new trend but production was interrupted by the war, and it wasn't until after 1945 that the vertical twin really came into its own and became the most popular type of engine on the market.

The only weak point on the first season's model was the method of fixing the cast-iron cylinder block to the high-tensile alloy crankcase: this was by

The Speed Twin in 1938, by which date it was already on the road to immortality.

means of six short studs, increased to eight in the following year and
thereby curing the problem. The high camshafts were driven by gear-
wheels fore and aft of the crankcase mouth, and the fully-enclosed valves
were operated by pushrods between the cylinders. Lubrication was by
double plunger pump, and the Triumph four-speed foot-change gearbox
gave ratios of 5.0, 6.0, 8.65 and 12.7 to 1. The unit was housed in a cradle
frame and finished in chromium and Amaranth red with gold lining. The
Magdyno electrics system was replaced after the war with an automatic
advance magneto and separate Lucas six-volt dynamo. Post-war models
also featured new telescopic front forks with hydraulic damping and the
option of rear springing which greatly improved the Speed Twin's roadholding and shock absorption capabilities.

In 1939 a hotted-up sports edition of the Speed Twin was introduced.
Called the Tiger 100, it was fitted with a high-performance engine with alloy
pistons and had a compression ratio of 7.75 to 1. Equipped with a large-bore
Amal carburettor, the Tiger 100 was, as its name suggests, good for 100 mph
and petrol consumption was near enough the same figure. Cosmetically,
the 100 was similar to the single-cylinder Tigers—finish was in black enamel
and chromium, with silver-sheen tank panels and rim centres lined in blue.
To maintain a high level of quality, each unit was tested on a Heenan and
Froude brake, then stripped, examined and reassembled before being sold
with a certified test card.

The Speed Twin received a different form of certification. Given the
official seal of approval by the Metropolitan Police, the Speed Twin was
chosen as their standard machine, thus initiating a decades-long
association between Triumph and the forces of law and order.

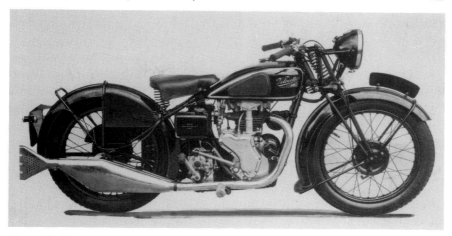

First of the high cam Velocettes was the 250 cc MOV introduced in 1933—it looked this way in 1935, though this is actually the 1936-season model.

Velocette MOV/MAC

For a long time Velocette's reputation rested on two-stroke models, but in 1923 it was decided to design and manufacture a high performance four-stroke. This idea became reality as the overhead cam K models, the most famous of which are the KSS (super sports) and KTT (racing) variants. Their success, both on the track and as sporting road machines, led Veloce to believe that a simpler four-stroke would sell well. The result of this was the 250 cc MOV, first of the M-series of ohv singles, designed by Charles Udall to the specifications of Eugene Goodman (one of the family which owned the factory). The MOV was introduced in 1933.

With almost square cylinder dimensions of 68 mm bore by 68.25 mm stroke, the most distinctive part of the design was the high position of the camshaft in the crankcase. This kept the pushrods short, thus reducing the reciprocating weight and lessening the likelihood of whip. The cam was driven by a train of gears, with an intermediate pinion mounted on an adjustable spindle, to allow accurate meshing of the teeth and thus silent operation. The pushrod Velocette engine owes its distinctive appearance to the high-cam design.

The new engine was mounted in a new cradle frame with a new, hand change, four-speed gearbox (the internals of which were based on the K-models). Velocette's Harold Willis patented the positive-stop foot change mechanism in 1929, as a racing modification, and it was soon applied to the roadsters. The company also developed a quick-action, push-pull throttle twist grip, which may or may not have enhanced the MOV's acceleration, but in any event it soon proved itself a fast machine, capable of 60 mph, which was excellent by the standards of the day.

A sales success, the MOV was shortly joined (1934) by a 350 cc model, created by increasing the stroke to 96 mm. The new machine was dubbed the MAC, and it offered performance almost on a par with the more expensive and heavier ohc models. The 250 and 350 M-series shared many components, were easier to make than the rather specialized cammy models, and brought considerable financial advantage to the Veloce concern.

Initial production runs encountered some teething troubles with the lubrication system, including a few bad leakage points, and poor material specification for the crankcases. A continuing trouble spot was the clutch, which was a single plate, cork-lined device, very similar on both 250 and 350 models. During the war (for which the MAC was converted to the MAF for military use) the larger pushrod model was fitted with the multiplate clutch as used on the K-series.

The next step for the factory, in the light of the MAC's success, was the obvious one of making an M-series 500. In 1935 the MSS appeared, having a stroke of 96 mm (common with the MAC) and a bore of 81 mm, giving a capacity of 495 cc. A more robust frame was used, together with heavy duty Webb girder forks, and K-type pinions filled the gearbox. The new machine was apparently intended more for the sidecar market despite the SS tag previously reserved for super sports models like the KSS and USS. Road tests found it to be exceptionally flexible, running from 16 mph to over 80 mph in top gear.

All three M models were kept in production until the outbreak of war, when the MOV and MSS were dropped. The MAC was adapted for military use, as already mentioned, but was never used in any great numbers. After the war the 250 cc and 500 cc models were reintroduced, but in 1948 they were dropped again. The new models which replaced them were, respectively, radically different and recognizably similar—reflecting, perhaps, the mixed social attitudes in post-war Britain.

Chapter 8

Post-war: Boom before the collapse

The austerity of the war years, with the rationing of food and petrol in particular, continued for some time after hostilities had ceased. In some respects this austerity was intensified but this served only to emphasize the need for 'fair shares for all', and a new mood of consensus, even at government level, began to develop. Official reports were made of the health, social welfare and education of the people, drawing a sharp contrast between the world before the war, and the world as it might be.

It was a time for ideals, for dreams of social equality, as evidenced by the measures proposed by Beveridge in his National Insurance Bill, introduced in 1946. It was also a time of great material change. Living under the shadow of the Bomb, social life in the Britain of the 1950s became increasingly dominated by the growth of the mass media, particularly television. The little box in the corner of the room was a powerful means of promoting the 'candy-floss culture' of consumer goods with attractive images of a new utopia where everyone would have their own house, their own car and a multitude of accessories to add glitter to their lives.

With the newly-formed welfare system and full employment, it looked as though Macmillan's vision of a new world might actually come true. In what is probably his most famous speech, during a long prime ministership, Super Mac was confident that 'most of our people have never had it so good. Go round the country, go to the industrial towns, go to the farms, and you will see a state of prosperity such as we have never had in my life-time—nor indeed ever in the history of this country'.

Of course there were still those who lived in poor conditions without any decent sanitation; nor did the new era obliterate class differences, although with more money in their pockets the working classes could now afford to replace the family's sidecar outfit with the more practical Ford Popular or Morris Minor. It is strange, then, to think that in 1953 motor cycle sales were enjoying a post-war boom—there were over one million British machines on the roads of this country alone—and yet within a few years the British industry would be all but extinct.

Before the collapse, production of the single-cylinder touring machine continued, although the vertical twin, ranging in capacity from 350 to 700 cc, was churned out in larger numbers than any other type of two-wheeler. In this, Triumph, who pioneered the vertical twin with its built-up 360-degree crankshaft, led the field; similar models made by manufacturers like AJS, Matchless, Norton and Ariel were also big sellers.

Machines at the luxury end of the market, for example the Vincent 1000, had a few more years to run but, on the whole, the manufacture of more exotic multi-cylinder camshaft engines was left to the continentals. There were huge war debts to be paid so the government's first priority was to export as many goods as possible in order to strengthen the economy. It was a frustrating time for customers at home who were fobbed off with reconditioned WD machines and the more mundane pre-war models. The long-term effects were, of course, far more serious as, without the necessary finance for research and experimentation with new ideas, the motor cycle industry was failing to lay down the necessary foundations for future growth and prosperity.

A notable exception to the general lack of progression was the development of the small capacity lightweight which answered the need for cheap personal transport and appealed to a wide range of people. Post-war designs had more efficient combustion chambers and higher compression ratios which meant that power outputs were raised and the units were more economical to run; performance was further improved when higher grades of petrol were again made available. Popular British lightweights included the Triumph Terrier and the BSA Bantam, as well as numerous models made by James and Francis-Barnett.

Although British sales figures of the 1950s still looked good, the motor cycling press was not oblivious (even if the industry seemed to be) to the competition being posed by the foreign marques. *Motor Cycling* warned 'that motor cycle manufacturers on the Continent, and notably in Italy, are pushing forward vigorously with the development of ultra-lightweight machines. Already they are marketing new models that are real post-war types and that show definite advances upon 1939 practice. It will be unfortunate, to say the least, if our country's foreign rivals should gain a predominance, both in design and production, in the lightweight field in the immediate future'.

These fears were well founded. In 1946 the Piaggio Vespa (meaning wasp) motor scooter was exhibited at the Turin Motor Show where it received much adverse criticism. In spite of this the Vespa was a huge commercial success which inspired a considerable number of imitators (notably the Lambretta) and launched a craze for scooters which swept through Europe.

The Vespa design was a unique combination of totally-enclosed, two-stroke, air-cooled engine with an open, stressed-skin spot-welded spine framework and small wheels carried on stub axles. It owed much to its inventor Corradino d'Ascanio's experience as an aircraft engine and frame designer, and little to anything that had ever been done before in the motor cycle industry. As a consequence of its unusual pedigree, the motor scooter inspired some extreme reactions. Ixion, in *The Motor Cycle*, wondered how such 'squat, funny little frog-like machines' could exercise such a powerful spell on those who had previously resisted 'half a century of wooing by normal designs', while the *Financial Times* called the scooter boom 'an outstanding economic event in post-war Europe. . .a political and social phenomenon affecting the outlook on life of hundreds of thousands of people'.

The British motor cycle industry was caught napping by this dramatic upsurge in the popularity of the scooter; worse, it stood aloof, thinking the manufacture of scooters to be rather beneath its dignity and only a belated, half-hearted attempt was made to enter this lucrative market. Unbelievably clumsy examples, which inevitably failed with the public, were grudgingly produced by the big names—the Velocette Viceroy, BSA Beezer and Triumph Tina were all monumental flops and quite deservedly so.

For a time Vespa scooters were made under licence by Douglas in Bristol, and together with the Lambretta they became the favourite machines of the Mods during the late '50s and '60s. The Mods were part of a social phenomenon that was quite unique to the post-war years. As wages steadily improved, personal powered transport became one of the many consumer goods which ascribed social status to its owner. This was especially evident amongst the young people of Britain who, with greater independence from the demands of their parents' generation, were free to create a style and culture of their own.

The height of Mod fashion was (and still is, as recent years have witnessed a big Mod revival) a long Parka jacket, short hair and a mirror-bedecked scooter. Rituals included congregating for scooter rallies all over the country, the high point of the year being August Bank Holiday when thousands of Mods converged on genteel seaside resorts—like Margate, Brighton and Bournemouth—and engaged in a mild form of gang-warfare with their arch-rivals, the Rockers. Newspaper reports tended to exaggerate their exploits and, with the fear of youth that seems endemic to this country, the older generation viewed the new cults with alarm.

Unfortunately, in the case of the Rockers, all this bad publicity dealt a terrible blow to British bike sales—in the same way that the Teddy Boys gave Edwardian-style clothing a bad image, so the Rockers made riding big capacity motor cycles an unacceptable pastime for 'respectable' people. Films like Marlon Brando's *The Wild One* were banned in some parts of the country for fear of mass-rioting, although by Hell's Angels standards the Ton-up Boys and Café Racers of Britain were mild-mannered in the extreme. The worst that most of them ever did was to bomb up and down their local bypass (this was in the days when there was no speed limit outside towns), or wake the neighbours with their reverse-cone meggas.

The Rockers of the '60s simply lived and breathed motor bikes and rode, or dreamt of riding, motor cycles that we now sigh over as classics of their time—the Triumph Bonnie, Norton Dominator and BSA Gold Star.

Production machines were rarely as fast as their manufacturers claimed them to be and a true enthusiast would go to some lengths to improve a bike's performance. In a BBC programme called 'Burning it up' a biker explained: 'If your bike is said to do 100 miles an hour and it doesn't, you're a bit unhappy about it, and fiddle about with it and try and make it do the ton. But once you've done the ton, you're—well, I don't know: it boosts you up'.

For most people, doing the ton was, and always would remain, in the realms of fantasy; getting from A to B was enough for them. And here the British industry allowed yet another lucrative market to be taken from under its nose as Japan had now entered the contest and was flooding the market with increasingly sophisticated lightweights. Government interference with hire purchase terms, not to mention the raising of purchase tax and the removal of import restrictions on foreign machines, did nothing to help motor cycle manufacturers in this country. By the end of the decade, as the '60s drew to a close, most of the great names had disappeared and the Orientals were ready to breach the gap with a new generation of superbikes.

The following machines represent a sample of the last flowering of the British motor cycle industry. Even the humblest of them is now regarded as 'classic' (though some are more classic than others) and most of them can be restored and kept running without too much trouble.

Ariel Red Hunter

Val Page joined Ariel from JAP in mid-1925, with the intention of designing a new range of models for the following season. His new engines were a 557 cc side valve and a 496 cc overhead valve, and they proved fast and reliable enough, although initially they had to be fitted into the old frames. Over the years they were developed, with the motors becoming more refined and new frames and cycle parts used. The models sold well, if not spectacularly.

Then, in 1929, young Edward Turner joined Ariel from his own shop in London. His first task was to design the Square Four (as a 500 cc overhead cam job), under Val Page's supervision and with Bert Hopwood as draughtsman—a rare trio! However, in the early 1930s, Ariel's parent company, Components Ltd, went bust and Jack Sangster bought the motor cycle company. There was some rationalization and economizing, and the upshot was that Val Page departed for Triumph, leaving Turner in charge of the design department.

The sports model ohv single had, in 1932, been given the name Red Hunter, and now Turner set about re-styling it. In what would almost become his trademark manner, he added chrome panels to the petrol tank, swept the exhaust pipes up and generally made the machine bright and attractive. His policy succeeded with the Red Hunter as it would later with the Triumph singles, and the model became very popular. A four-speed

One year before the Second World War, Ariel's Red Hunter top-of-the range sporting single looked like this. Edward Turner had restyled it in 1933, and the head and barrel were redesigned in 1938.

gearbox was adopted in 1934, and four years later the cylinder head and rocker box were redesigned, giving the now thirteen-year-old engine a new lease of life.

Ariel engineer Frank Anstey devised a form of rear suspension in 1939, which has come to be known, not surprisingly, as the Anstey link. In effect it was a sophisticated variant of the simple plunger system, and although it had all sorts of theoretical advantages, it tended to wear very quickly indeed. When Anstey left the company, Val Page returned and adapted the 350 cc ohv single for military use. The W/NG soon became popular with the Don Rs, especially for its off-road capabilities.

In 1944 Ariel was sold to BSA, which at least allowed BSA (and Sunbeam) to fit Val Page's design of telescopic fork, although immediately after the war Ariel used rigid frames and girder forks. However, in 1946 Red Hunter models (there were two, the 350 cc NH and 500 cc VH) gained tele forks and the Anstey link rear suspension. The NG and VG, which were merely de luxe models as opposed to top-of-the-range, soon followed suit.

Ariel singles were recognized as good examples of the sporting motor cycle, and they were used to great effect in grasstrack racing and scrambles. An all-alloy motor, specifically for competition use, was offered in 1949. Designated the VCH, it was essentially similar to the iron engines, and a year later it was fitted into a road model, called the VHA.

A new duplex cradle frame featuring swinging arm rear suspension was introduced in 1954, and the 500 cc VH was fitted with the cylinder head from the alloy engine. The 350 remained iron for the time being. The competition VCH (competition being used in its non-specific pre-war sense of an all-rounder) was replaced by specialist models: the HS for scrambling and the HT for trials. One of the latter, registration number GOV 132, was later to become very famous and successful indeed in the hands of Sammy Miller.

Eventually, in 1956, the 350 cc single was given the alloy head too, but by then the writing was on the wall for the venerable four-stroke singles. The end came in 1959 with the introduction of the two-stroke Ariel Leader/ Arrow range, which was popular for a time, but could not, in the end, keep the company's head above water.

The Red Hunter singles typify the solid British single-cylinder motor cycle, and are thoroughly sound machines. Spares supply is still good and prices are not ridiculously high, though the 'de luxe' models may be slightly cheaper. Genuine scrambles and trials models are quite rare, but many roadsters have been converted with varying degrees of success.

Ariel Square Four

Although the Square Four began its life in the post-vintage period (just—it was 1931), it is probably best known in its post-war incarnation. Edward Turner originally designed it as a 500 cc overhead camshaft sportster—the prototype was crammed into a lightweight 250 cc frame, and greatly impressed 'Torrens' of *The Motor Cycle* when he took it for a spin up the road. However, the production model was rather different to the prototype, having gained a lot of weight and lost a lot of zip. Nevertheless, the novelty of a four-cylinder engine with the barrels arranged in a quadrangular formation and having two crankshafts geared together guaranteed a certain level of sales.

It must have been disappointing for both manufacturer and purchaser, though, for after just one season it was bored out to 600 cc and then in 1933 the 500 was dropped altogether. After Turner had moved to Triumph, the Square Four was transformed into a completely different machine. The model that was offered in 1937, the 4G, had a capacity of 1,000 cc, overhead valves operated by pushrods, dry sump lubrication and forged crankshafts. The 'almost dangerous' bolide which had captivated Torrens had been turned into a carriage-pulling pumpkin, albeit it a very smooth and refined one. In 1939 only, a 600 cc version was offered.

The war put an end to the manufacture of the 4G, and it was not revived until 1945. The following year it gained telescopic forks, and became, according to Ariel's advertising, 'Monarch of the Multis' or 'Whispering Wildfire'—or possibly both. However, its weight had crept up to 476 lb by 1948 (which cannot have pleased Turner) and in an attempt to bring down the *avoirdupois*, Ariel introduced an all-alloy engine which saved 33 lb.

Queen Elizabeth II's coronation year was celebrated by Ariel with the introduction of the Square Four Mk II. This new Elizabethan steed featured a revised cylinder and head layout. Whereas the Mk I had had a monobloc casting, the cylinders were now separate, the idea being to promote cooling, which had always been something of a bugbear. The new engine sprouted four exhaust pipes, and is known for that reason as the four-piper. The Mk I was dropped altogether in 1954, and the Anstey link frame became

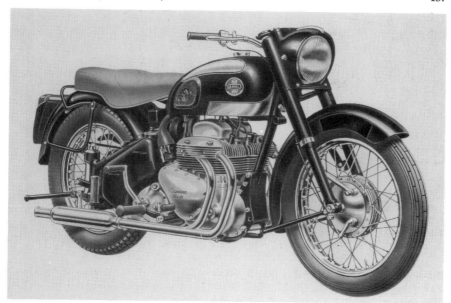

The 4G Square Four in its final form—alloy engine, four exhaust pipes and Anstey link rear suspension.

standard to the model. In this form, the machine carried on without major modification until 1959, when, like the singles, it was phased out to make way for the two-strokes.

The points which are always stressed in the Square Four's favour are that it is smooth, has good acceleration and plenty of power; on the other hand, it handles rather poorly, and can run into overheating and head gasket-blowing problems, particularly the early models. Nevertheless, it is a truly luxurious mount, and one which will always inspire a certain affection and even awe. Spares supply is not a great problem, and there can be no doubt that a good Square Four, though expensive to buy, will more than hold its value.

BSA Bantam

Like many British manufacturers who made similar claims on German designs, BSA acquired the original plans for the Bantam as part of a post-war reparation deal. It was based on the DKW RT125 but built as a mirror-image, with gearbox and gear lever on the right instead of the left-hand side. During the 1920s, DKW was the biggest manufacturer of motor cycles in the world, dealing exclusively in two-stroke engines. Despite their obvious technological superiority in this field, the RT/Bantam had faults which

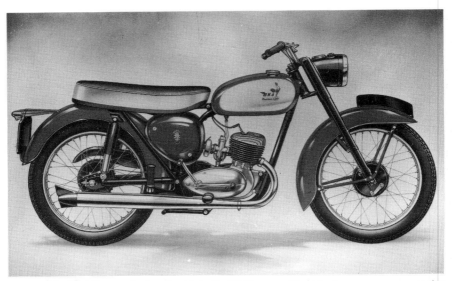

By 1960 the BSA Bantam had evolved into the D7 Super, with swinging arm rear suspension and Triumph Tiger Cub front forks. The 175 cc engine was quite reliable, putting out a lowly 7.5 bhp at 5,000 rpm.

would probably have been ironed out at the drawing-board stage had not the war intervened.

Nevertheless, the first Bantam, the D1 launched in 1948, was a very popular bike and the first in a long series of models. It was a basic machine with three speeds, a rigid frame, crude front forks and direct lighting. Nonetheless, it sold 20,000 a year, until production ceased in 1963, and compared well with the bulkier Villiers-powered machines on the market. Power output was an unspectacular 4 hp at 5,000 rpm, but the Bantam could quite happily putter along at 45 mph all day and, under the right conditions, was capable of a top speed of 55 mph. Most important of all, at an average of 100 mpg, it was economical to run.

The ride-to-work revolution brought not only an increase in the demand for cheap transport (and here the Bantam fitted the bill admirably) but also an acceleration in the pace of everyday life. Traffic increased and with it the speed of road vehicles leaving the D3, a 146 cc version introduced in 1954, in a bit of a compromising position. It had more immediate power than the D1 and could race around the inner-city congestion like nobody's business, but the gearbox and electrics had to take the brunt of an inevitable increase in rapid gearchanging and vibration.

In 1958 an updated version, the D5 or Bantam Super, appeared on the scene. It had an increased capacity of 174 cc and an Amal Monobloc carburettor, but was on the market for only a year. Its replacement, the D7, on the other hand, sported a number of improvements which made it an extremely popular bike, lasting until 1966. Instead of the rear plungers on previous models, it had swinging arm suspension and Triumph Tiger Cub front forks with a headlamp nacelle. More significantly, its designers recognized its limitations: it was a lightweight commuter bike and, despite a power increase to 7.5 bhp at 5,000 rpm, it had no sporting pretensions.

The same cannot be said for its descendants, however. To many people the D10, introduced in 1966, marks the point at which the Bantam began its steady fall into a quagmire of mechanical and electrical faults. A series of major changes, the chief one being the fixing of compression plates to the flywheel, raised the power output by 40 per cent to 10 bhp at 6,000 rpm. This increase proved to be way beyond the capacity of the modest little bike.

By the end of the year, BSA were offering the public no fewer than four D10s. They were: a three-speed economy model, the Silver Bantam; a slightly up-market four-speeder called the Supreme; the Sports Bantam, complete with racing seat, chromium-plated mudguards and high-level exhaust; and the Bushman, designed specifically for sheep-herders in the Australian outback.

The D14 Sports and Bushman models, introduced in 1968, only compounded the faults of the previous models: a large number of warranty claims were made because of the tendency for the rivets, attaching the compression plates to the flywheel, to pop out and foul up the insides of the crankcase.

One of the more interesting developments in the history of the Bantam was perpetrated by the competitions manager, Brian Martin, who used the Bushman as the basis for a trials machine. With it he won first-class awards in the 1966 Colmore and the St David's national competitions and, spurred on by this success, he entered a works team (comprising Dave Rowland, Mick Bowers and Dave Langston) in the Scottish Six Days Trial. Langston and Bowers gained firsts and Rowland finished runner-up, but the management at BSA thought it an esoteric sport and were too short-sighted to see the potential market for a trials machine.

When the day of reckoning inevitably came in 1971, Mick Bowers and Brian and Michael Martin were confident that a consortium could be formed and the Bantam continued as a trials machine. But, as with so many of the British motor cycle industry's casualties, BSA seemed to have lost all impetus and one of their most valuable customers, the GPO (who used hundreds of D1s for their telegram boys), was lost. The very numbers produced, however, mean that most Bantams are easy to keep on the road, and they can be bought quite cheaply.

BSA Golden Flash

Edward Turner's Speed Twin set the pattern for a whole host of post-war imitations but, as we know, the parallel twin was not a new idea. BSA did some serious experimental work of their own in the 1920s with a number of

An early BSA twin gets the once over—but why would the Ariel rider want to change?

twin-cylinder configurations other than the traditional V. The most prophetic of these was a 150 cc two-stroke vertical twin but it never went into production because it was considered unacceptable to a public accustomed to side-valve V-twins and singles. (This was effectively disproved some thirty years later by the Japanese.)

It wasn't until 1939 that BSA took up the challenge again, this time in response to Triumph. Most manufacturers realized immediately that an important new trend had been set and prototypes were hurriedly built, though not in time for pre-war production. The first of a pair of prototypes built at the Small Heath works was a 500 cc sports engine, designed by Val Page and developed by Joe Craig. It had the unusual feature of a single overhead camshaft driven by a shaft and two pairs of bevels on the right-hand side of the engine. Housed in a standard Silver Star frame, it was a fast machine capable of 100 mph; with further attention to cam design it might well have rivalled the Speed Twin. The 500's more sedate counterpart was a 350 cc twin with vertical valves operated by pushrods.

Both prototypes were to have been unveiled at the 1940 Earls Court Show but attention had to be quickly diverted to the all-out production of M20 WD machines, and the launch was delayed until 1946. By then Edward Turner's style was also in evidence (he was employed at Small Heath during the early part of the war) but the final design of the twin, now dubbed the Model A7, was left to chief designer Bert Hopwood with Herbert Perkins and David Munro.

The essential features—360 degree twin-cylinder format, single camshaft working pushrod-operated overhead valves, and four-speed gearbox—remained the same throughout its evolution from A7 to A10, and from A10 to the A65, until the factory's demise in 1971. In using a single, rather than twin, camshaft, BSA's unit differed markedly from most of its contemporaries; their reason for this was that it saved material and labour costs. A sports model, with a slightly higher compression ratio, was introduced in 1948 and, despite a tendency for pre-ignition, both machines were popular and continued with few changes until the introduction of a new and larger twin in 1950. The 650 cc A10 was similar in appearance to the A7 but with a number of detail improvements which made it a much more flexible, reliable machine. Finished in a striking beige-gold colour, it was christened the Golden Flash.

Like the A7, the Flash had an enormous capacity for hard work and even with a sidecar attached it could maintain a comfortable cruising speed of about 70 mph. In solo form it was one of the fastest machines on the market, with a top speed of over 100 mph. It weighed in at a modest 395 lb, and fuel consumption was 60 mpg if ridden fast and 50 mpg with a sidecar to lug around.

During the following year the plunger frame was offered, and recommended for sidecar use: handling, on solo machines at least, was improved by the introduction of pivoted-fork rear suspension. Some riders preferred the rigid frame, especially for high-speed work and on bumpy roads, as the plunger frame tended to throw the bike into a weave on poor surfaces.

A 500 cc version of the A10, also called the A7 but vastly superior to the old model, was added to the range. It had a reduced bore and stroke but many of the parts were, nevertheless, interchangeable with the 650. As on other BSA models, the rear wheel of the A7 and A10 was quickly detachable and could be removed without disturbing the rear brake, rear sprocket and chain. Both models were also equipped with 7 in diameter brakes and tyre sizes were 3.25 × 19 in and 3.50 × 19 in, respectively.

For many, the smaller machine provided a more pleasant solo ride, but it was the A10 model that was the mainstay of BSA's post-war range, remaining in production until it was superseded by the A65 in 1964.

BSA Gold Star
For a motor cycle with more than its fair share of charisma, BSA's 500 cc Gold Star had surprisingly humble origins. In 1937 BSA made it their ambition to win a Brooklands gold star—this was the special lapel badge awarded to competitors who completed a lap of the course at 100 mph and

over. It has to be remembered that in those days doing a ton was no easy task, especially as most machines had rigid frames, the minimum of front suspension and narrow tyres. But, as BSA reasoned, if Norton could win a gold star, then so could they and to this end, Len Crisp and cam expert Jack Amott went to work on the Empire Star.

When Walter Handley appeared at Brooklands that year on the specially prepared Star, BSA created the stir they had hoped for. Highly-tuned and running on a dope mixture to suit its 13:1 compression ratio, Handley won the event at an average speed of 102.27 mph and achieved the fastest lap at 107.57 mph. Naturally, the Small Heath concern capitalized on their remarkable success by naming their special competition model of 1938, the Gold Star. This was the Model M24, a sporting 500, which was based on the Empire Star but with many modifications. Fitted with an Amal TT carburettor, and with the compression ratio raised to 7.8 to 1, each of the new engines was tested to 28 bhp at 5,250 rpm. If it failed the test, the unit was reworked until it was up to standard, and in later years was sold to the customer with a copy of its power readings.

The most noticeable difference between the old and new models in a bid to increase acceleration was the exceptional lightness of the M24: the complete machine, including lights and accessories, weighed little more than 315 lb. This was achieved by making the cylinder barrel and head of aluminium, fitting the former with a steel liner and the latter with valve seat inserts. Transmission was lightened by making the gearcase out of Elektron (a magnesium alloy) and the frame of light-gauge, high-tensile steel tubing.

A road test in *Motor Cycling* found that the M24 performed well, with good road holding and general handling, concluding: '. . .the BSA company have produced a model which can fulfil the desires of the most sporting rider and at the same time one so well mannered that the inexperienced man would feel quite happy within a few 100 miles of taking delivery'. Nevertheless, public response was lukewarm, not helped by the launch of Triumph's Speed Twin at the same show, and with the onset of war the Goldie was dropped and did not reappear until the 1948 Earls Court Show.

Based on the road and competition versions of the 348 cc ohv Model B31, with bore and stroke of 71 mm × 88 mm, the post-war Gold Star was plunger sprung at the rear and retained the pre-war M24 alloy head and barrel. With a range of options for changing the engine specifics and gearing, BSA offered their new single in touring, trials, racing and scrambles form. Victory in the ACU Clubman's TT in the Isle of Man in 1949 and subsequent competition success gave the manufacturers every right to boast that 'this machine has been designed primarily for competition work and is not for the tourist who wishes to potter gently round the countryside'.

Ironically, the Goldie was too successful for its own good: it defeated the whole purpose of the Clubman's, a competition organized specifically to give non-racers the opportunity to compete on their own production machines. The idea was that it would help improve commercial models but

Above *The BSA Gold Star was a bike of many parts. Some used it for off-road sport...*

Below *...others for off-ground sport! This is one of the Hollywood Motor Rodeo performing a daring flight over four (count 'em) Ford Zephyr Zodiacs.*

because of its tremendous acceleration, almost all entrants ended up riding the BSA machine and the Clubman's TT was moved to the mainland where it became a different event altogether.

In September '49, the 500 cc Gold Star was added to the range; it was identical to the 350 except, of course, in its dimensions which were 85 mm bore and 88 mm stroke, producing 499 cc. Both models were fitted with new 8 in diameter front brakes. In 1951, the 500 (followed in '51 by the 350) was modified to improve the valve sizes and the inlet and exhaust porting; the light-alloy cylinder head and barrel were now die-cast, with separate rocker boxes. Because of a temporary shortage of nickel (world stocks being monopolized for the building of aircraft used in the Korean War) previously chromed components were now finished in matt-silver enamel.

More significant changes were made in the following year, notably the adoption of an all-welded, duplex swinging fork frame based on a design by Bill Nicholson. This could be instantly recognized by the right down tube which had a kink to accommodate a bulge in the crankcase, behind which was situated the oil pump. The swinging arm was pivoted on pressed-in, Silentbloc, rubber bushes and the large diameter Girling shock absorbers had three-position pre-load; the front forks, as before, were BSA's own telescopics with coil springs and hydraulic damping. The CB type of Gold Star engine was introduced in 1954. This was built to road racing specification: shorter con rods, improved breathing, massive finning of the head and barrel, and a swept-back exhaust pipe.

The last of the 500 cc engines was the DBD type, its most distinctive feature being the huge 1½ in Amal GP carburettor. At a top speed of 110 mph, the need to slip the clutch at anything under 30 mph and, above all, the noise, the Gold Star was an uncompromising and thoroughly anti-social machine. It set a trend for fast riding but had to be finally laid to rest (the 350 in 1962 and the 500 in 1963) when it became too expensive to produce.

The Goldie is probably best remembered as a racer, or café racer. This one has all the goodies—massive Taylor-Dow Duetto front brake, alloy petrol tank and so on.

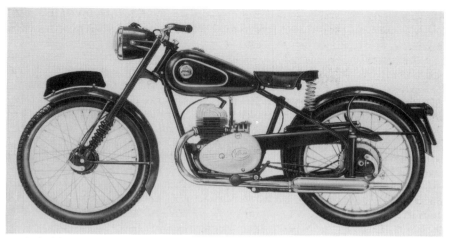

Typical of the post-war utility machine, the 150 cc James Cadet sported a Villiers engine and a minimum of equipment. Rudimentary forks and plungers must have helped ride comfort slightly.

James

The post-war years saw a host of Villiers-engined two-stroke utility machines flowing from a variety of factories. A cheap and ready supply of motors allowed makers to set up fairly easily, and though there were some unorthodox machines made—by Greeves, for example—the majority were simple, straightforward motor cycles used by men and women to get to work on. Amongst the makes which sprang up after the war to fill the demand were some with histories stretching back many years, such as Dot, Francis-Barnett, Cotton and James.

The James company was started in 1880, to make penny-farthings, and its first motor cycle was made in 1902. The business developed steadily and the range of models expanded, one of the best remembered machines being a smart 500 cc V-twin. During the Depression, however, demand for large four-stroke multis fell off, and James turned to lightweights and two-strokes using Villiers engines.

During the Second World War the James factory at Greet, Birmingham, was destroyed, but not before several thousand lightweights had been made for the military. These were designed to be dropped by parachute for use by airborne troops in enemy territory, and when the factory was re-established after the war the military model provided the basis for the first post-war civilian model, the ML.

Powered by a 122 cc 9D Villiers engine, the ML had a very simple 'vintage'-looking tubular frame and pressed-steel-blade girder forks. Over 20,000 were made over a three-year period. The ML soon evolved into the Cadet, still displacing 122 cc but with the Villiers 10D engine and slightly more substantial cycle parts. At the same time the 98 cc Comet was introduced, and also the 197 cc Captain. These names were to be associated with the same capacities throughout James production. Telescopic forks, using rubber as a suspension medium, were introduced on the Cadet and Captain models in 1950, and a new model was added to the range. This was the 98 cc Commodore, a fully weather-protected variant of the Comet.

In 1951 James was bought up by Associated Motor Cycles, but this did not affect the range of machines, which continued with improvements and refinements. Plunger suspension was introduced on the Cadet De Luxe and Captain, but this was soon superseded by a swinging arm frame.

With 98, 150, 200, and 225 cc models (the latter called the Colonel), the James range was augmented in 1957 by the new Commodore. This used the not altogether satisfactory AMC-produced engine (shared with Francis-Barnett), and eventually all the James machines save the Comet were fitted with various sizes of this power unit. Trials and scrambles competition variants (one of which was called the Commando, thus giving AMC the prerogative of attaching it to a later Norton) followed the same general pattern of development, and were campaigned with some degree of success.

The next major additions to the range were the Superswift (1962) and its sports counterpart (1963). These were fitted with the twin-cylinder Villiers 2T (and later the 4T) engine, and the Sports Superswift was a beautiful job with swoopy Italianate styling. The Comet, Cadet and Captain models continued until 1965, together with the Superswift Sports and Sports Captain, but in October 1966 James production ceased entirely.

It is not hard to find a cheap James, but it is rather harder to find a good cheap one. Villiers engine parts are relatively plentiful, but supplies for the AMC unit are not so good. Even scarcer, however, are cycle parts for these machines, but since they are quite simple it is not a hard matter to make—or have made—spares, though the question of cost relative to value is one for the owner to decide.

Early and competition models are probably more 'collectable' if only because there are fewer of them, but there is an increasing vogue for all of the post-war two-stroke cheapies. Nevertheless, they can still provide a good entree into the classic world.

Matchless G9

The post-war interest in sporting events was immense with more enthusiasts than ever competing in trials, scrambles, motocross and grass-track events. Matchless was one of the marques most heavily involved, not only in building competition machines but also in participating on the track with works-sponsored riders like Maurice Laidlow, Hugh Viney, Eddie Bessant and Jack Colver. Jack was the son of the famous Bert Colver and, like his father, he was a life-long employee of the Matchless concern.

The Matchless entry to the post-war vertical twin market was the G9 500 cc model, distinguished by its three-bearing crankshaft. The 500 was undoubtedly the sweetest of the AMC twins, with none of the problems associated with the later, bigger models.

Apart from producing civilian versions of the 348 cc and 498 cc ohv G3L and G80, one of the first of the post-war moves at the Plumstead works was to bring out a trials motor cycle based on the popular G3L WD machine. Matchless' own-make Teledraulic forks had marked an enormous improvement in front end suspension and these were retained, to great advantage, on the trials bike. The only major modifications made were to increase ground clearance and replace the standard tyres with competition ones; also, no lighting equipment was fitted. As sales grew, so Matchless (in AMC guise) were able to take over their main sporting rivals James, Francis-Barnett and Norton.

The single-cylinder G models, first introduced in 1935, marked a distinct break with the past. Sales of previous models, the V-twin Silver Hawk and Silver Arrow, had fallen drastically and something new and sporty was needed. The Clubman G3 and its trials counterpart, the Clubman Special, were just the job and rapidly became one of Matchless' most popular ranges.

At its introduction in 1948, the Phil Walker-designed G9 fulfilled much the same purpose. It gave sales a vital shot in the arm by conforming with the dominant trend of the day for vertical twins. The pressure on manufacturers to build up the country's export trade meant that the G9 was not brought on to the home market until late in 1949. However, the Super Clubman on display at the 1948 Earls Court Show gave the public a foretaste of what was to come.

The G9 was powered by a 498 cc engine with a bore and stroke of 66 mm × 72.8 mm and a compression ratio of 7 to 1. It had separate cast-iron barrels and light alloy cylinder heads with cast-in valve seats: operation of the overhead valves was by pushrod. The feature that distinguished the G9 from all other twins of that period was the one-piece crankshaft, which had a plain centre bearing in addition to the pair of roller outer bearings. As well as taking some of the load, the centre bearing provided a much more efficient distribution of oil between the two big ends. Massive twin integral flywheels were fitted, one on either side of the centre bearing, with bob-weights on the near and off-side of the assembly and gear-driven camshafts fore and aft.

Other details included wire-wound pistons, light-alloy forged con rods, dry sump lubrication and a Burman four-speed gearbox. Ignition and lighting was by Lucas magneto and carburation by Type 6 Amals. The duplex cradle frame was fitted with swinging arm rear suspension, oil-damped rear shock absorbers and Teledraulic front forks. The three-gallon petrol tank was finished in red and silver and a megaphone silencer, Dunlopillo dual-seat and twin toolboxes, containing the oil tank and battery, completed the styling.

Introduced in the same year, the AJS Model 20 Spring Twin used many of the same components as the G9 but it was the latter, with its superior traction and handling, which particularly appealed to sporting enthusiasts. At the 1950 Earl's Court Show, the G9 was one of a range of seven Matchless models and the most expensive too at £217 3s 6d. Modifications included the use of ribbed mudguards for greater rigidity, a five-spring clutch and a new suspension system, the slim rear shock absorbers being replaced with the larger diameter 'jampots'. On the new design, pressure on the oil seals was reduced by fitting the suspension springs on the outside of the main telescoping members. This also obviated the need for keeping such a critical eye on the oil content of the hydraulic mechanism, a practice which was necessary with the 'candlesticks' for maintaining efficient operation.

During the following year the shortage of nickel meant that Matchless had to modify the finish of all its machines. As a consequence, the G9 was, if anything, a more handsome machine with its black enamel tank lined in silver and red, polished light-alloy front fork sliders and 'Argenized' wheel rims.

At about this time, a tuned version of the G9 was developed by the AMC experimental workshop along the lines of a number of ideas proposed by Ike Hatch. Entered by Robin Sherry in the 1951 Senior Manx Grand Prix, the prototype came fourth at over 83 mph. This was sufficient encouragement for further work to be done; work that included extensive finning of the front rocker boxes, a six-gallon petrol tank and the same cycle parts as those used on the 7R AJS Boy Racer. Ironically, it was the latter machine which the new Matchless, ridden by Derek Farrant, beat to win the 1952 Grand Prix at an average speed of 88.65 mph and a new lap record of 89.64 mph. This was Matchless' first Isle of Man victory as an official entry since the racing activities of Harry and Charlie Collier in the 1910s.

Cashing in on this remarkable victory, a production model was on display to the public at the Motor Cycle Show of the same year. Called the G45, the pushrod-operated ohv twin differed little from Farrant's machine, with its light-alloy cylinder head, four-speed Burman gearbox and Grand Prix Amal carburettors. Over the next few years the G45 was successfully raced by many well-known riders and the press reaction was extremely positive. Of the 1954 model, *The Motor Cycle* wrote: 'Its massive, gleaming black fuel tank and heavily finned engine, equipped with twin carburettors, endow it with an extremely impressive appearance. During the racing season its performance, too, has proved to be quite impressive! Indeed the G45 has built up a reputation for high speed and reliability allied to superlative steering and roadholding. Many are the covetous glances directed at its 8 inch diameter twin-leading shoe front brake.'

Nevertheless, the G45 was not good enough to compete with the Norton Manx and was dropped in 1958 in favour of the single cylinder ohc G50. The G9 continued, in updated form, with improvements which included a new, oil-tight AMC gearbox, slim Girlings instead of jampots, and a full-cradle duplex frame. The demand for extra cubes led to the introduction of the Model G11 in 1956 with cylinders of the same stroke as the standard G9, but bored out to 72 mm to produce a capacity of 592 cc.

After a good run, the G9 was withdrawn from the range in 1961. Despite a few persistent faults, like the primary chaincase and its notorious propensity to leak, the G9 was a popular machine and represents a classic in every sense of the word.

Norton Dominator

When the Triumph Speed Twin proved to be a runaway success, the rest of the major British factories quickly made plans for their own parallel twins. Sadly, the war put an end to the possibility of production, and it was not until after 1945 that any new models could be considered. Norton did not manage to get their 500 cc twin into the showrooms until 1949.

The Model 7 Dominator, as it was called, came from the drawing board of Bert Hopwood, who had already played a part in the design and draughting of the Ariel Square Four and the Speed Twin. The new engine was plonked into the running gear of the ES2 (a 500 cc ohv single), which comprised a single down tube frame with plunger rear suspension and Roadholder telescopic front forks. The ES2 type gearbox was also used. The Dominator motor incorporated a typical Hopwood trademark in that, unlike all the other parallel twins, it used only one camshaft to open the inlet and exhaust valves. The cylinders were in a monobloc casting, though there was an air passage between them to promote cooling, and they were spigoted into the crankcase for rigidity. A single carburettor was fitted.

Norton's forte at the time was the single-cylinder engine, and the twin was not greatly promoted or developed in the first few years. However, in 1953 the company was taken over by Associated Motor Cycles (AMC), who

The Norton Dominator 88, with Bert Hopwood's engine fitted into the Featherbed frame, came on to the market in 1953 and stayed more or less the same until 1956.

already owned Matchless and AJS, and in that same year the 'garden gate' plunger frame was adapted to take a swinging arm rear end. The Model 7 continued in this form until 1956, although it gained an aluminium cylinder head in 1954.

The end of the Model 7 did not mean the end of the Dominators though, for a new line continued the name. The engine was slotted into the McCandless-designed and race-developed Featherbed frame, an extremely stiff full duplex type. Redesignated the Dominator 88 or De Luxe, it came on to the home market after 1953 (the first production runs had all gone to export markets, for this was the time of 'Export or Die'). The Featherbed soon became the standard by which all other motor cycles were judged, for it offered exceptionally good handling and steering. This encouraged spirited riding, and the Norton motor was found to be slightly fragile—or at least, not as tough as the Triumph, although it was soon strengthened.

The possibility of breakage under hard use had two consequences which stand out as important. Norton took action by making the Dominator 99, a 1956 model with a capacity of 600 cc and therefore, it was assumed, better able to satisfy the craving for speed. Owners took action by combining the best available frame (Featherbed) with the best available engine (Triumph) and making the Triton; there were also Tribsa and Norvin variants.

1956 was an important year for the Dominator range altogether, for AMC had embarked on a policy of rationalization. Several typically Norton features disappeared, including the built-up footrests (from now on they would be plain bar), the pear-shaped silencers, Armstrong rear damper units and the old-style Norton 'box. In place of the latter came the famous

AMC/Norton unit which, as the Featherbed did for frames, set new standards for gearboxes. In addition, another model was added, the 77, which featured the 600 cc motor in the old style Model 7 frame. It was intended for sidecar use, but lasted only until 1958.

The next major change came in 1961, when a full 650 cc model was announced, along with sports (SS) versions of the 88 and 99. The latter lasted only one more season, and when the 650SS came along in 1962, the 600s were dropped altogether. The 650 mutated into the 750 cc Atlas and, eventually, the Commando. Bert Hopwood's poor little 500 ended up stretched to 850 cc.

Despite the ups and downs of its bigger brethren, the 88 soldiered on until 1966, though in the last three years of its life it was available in SS form only. A production run of some fifteen years is quite remarkable and serves to emphasize the essential 'rightness' of this machine. The 88 is still a pleasant bike to ride, although it is no roadburner, and spares are still quite readily available. Some items, such as pistons, are getting a little scarce, but on the whole running or restoring a 500 cc Dominator should present no exceptional problems.

Royal Enfield Bullet
The Bullet name, chosen to denote speed and power, was first applied in the early 1930s to a range of sports machines based on Royal Enfield's standard single-cylinder models. These were specially tuned units of 250, 350 and 500 cc, the result of experimentation with different valve combinations. All three engines were constructed with pushrod tubes cast within the cylinder walls; they had chilled-iron valve guides and nitrided valve stems. The high-level exhaust and Burgess-type silencer conformed well with Royal Enfield's policy of supporting reliability and sporting trials.

The production models for 1948 were the same as the 1945 range which, in turn, was based largely on Enfield's pre-war and wartime ohv motor cycles. These were the Model RE 125 cc two-stroke, the Model G 346 cc ohv four-stroke and Model J 499 cc single-port ohv four-stroke. A fourth, the Model J2, a 499 cc twin-port ohv, was initially for export only.

The solid, stolid singles were given a good shake-up with the first appearance of the post-war Bullet in February '48 when a works team, consisting of Len Holdsworth, Charlie Rogers and Jack Plowright, rode 350 cc prototypes, with oil-damped rear suspension, in the Colmore Cup Trial. Although no cups were won, Rogers and Plowright gained first class awards and Holdsworth, a second class. The opportunity for the Bullet to show what it was really made of came in September in the ISDT. A team of riders—Tom Ellis, Vic Brittain and Charlie Rogers—took three of the prototypes to the event, held that year in Italy, and returned with the International Trophy; in addition, Brittain and Rogers won gold medals and were the only riders of 350s to do so.

The prototype engine had a cast-iron barrel deeply spigoted into the

Royal Enfield's 1956 500 cc Bullet—just a good old-fashioned plodder?

crankcase; the cylinder head was of light alloy and had fully-enclosed coil-type valve springs; and the rear wheel was quickly detachable.

By the following year a production model, the G2, with its pioneering use of swinging arm rear suspension, was on the market. The Bullet's engine layout was broadly based on that of the Model G, a notable similarity being the big end bearing, but many of its design features were completely new. Unlike the prototype, the G2 had both barrel and cylinder head made of light alloy, the former deeply spigoted into the mouth of the crankcase, the latter with cast-in iron valve seats. The valves themselves had specially hardened caps and worked within pressed-in phosphor-bronze guides. The alloy con rod and aluminium alloy piston gave a compression ratio of 6.5 to 1 and bore and stroke was 70 mm by 90 mm.

As the Bullet was built as a competition bike, emphasis was quite naturally placed on the compactness of the machine. For this reason the four-speed Albion gearbox was bolted to the back of the oil reservoir, formed, according to Royal Enfield tradition, in the crankcase. This allowed for semi unit-construction of the engine and gearbox and the use of a duplex primary chain with a slipper tensioner. The power unit was mounted in a new cradle frame with a single front down tube and swinging arm suspension at the rear. The telescopic front forks were of the standard Enfield variety and both wheels had 6 in brakes.

The 350 Bullet was a great success and public response was so positive that a road version was added to the range of trials and scrambles machines. The same basic components were used for all three models but with variations in the compression ratio, exhaust system, tyres and general equipment.

Competition work kept Enfield on their toes, with subsequent modifications implemented in their commercial machines. For example, on the 1950 Trials Bullet the compression ratio was dropped to a more suitable 6 to 1, making higher gearing possible. Petrol tank capacity was reduced to two gallons and a high-level exhaust was fitted. At a time when most manufacturers made only rigid frames for trials use, Enfield pioneered the swinging arm: in 1952 Johnny Brittain put paid to the myth that sprung frames mucked up the handling of a machine when he won the Scottish SDT on a 350 Bullet.

In 1953, a 500 cc Bullet, with a bottom end virtually identical to that of the 350 and most of the same cycle parts, was introduced. The swinging arm was specially strengthened and lugs provided for sidecar use; power output was 25 bhp at 5,250 rpm and the compression ratio 6.2 to 1; a split-skirt piston and new cam forms were adopted to reduce engine noise. *The Motor Cycle* described the 500 as having 'a lusty performance' but, in truth, it was just a good old-fashioned plodder capable of cruising at 70 mph 'and an admirable sidecar machine for high speeds or heavy loads'.

In the 1953 ISDT in Czechoslovakia, two of the new Bullets, ridden by Jack Stocker and Johnny Brittain, made up half of the International Trophy team which won without losing a single point.

Over the next few years styling changes were made to both capacity motor cycles: Enfield's famous Casquette, a cast-aluminium cowl, was fitted over the top of the forks and steering head. This contained the speedo, ammeter and switchgear, with headlamp and two small sidelights at the front. Dual-seats were adopted as standard, as were the 6 in diameter dual front brakes and qd rear wheel. A choice of finish was offered—polychromatic silver-grey, maroon or olive green.

In 1956 a new diamond style frame was introduced and, in collaboration with *The Motor Cycle*, a fairing, called Dreamliner, was designed and constructed for the 350 Bullet. In subsequent tests done by Vic Willoughby, fuel and performance were compared, with and without the fairing. The streamlined version improved the top speed by 11 per cent and fuel consumption was reduced by about a quarter.

By the time the fairing finally went into production, it had been greatly modified, the original being considered too expensive and too bizarre-looking for public taste. The Airflow, as it was called, was a dolphin-type fairing made available for the whole of the Enfield range—all, that is, except for the 350 Bullet Works Replica trials bike introduced in 1958.

Offered in celebration of the 350 Bullet's huge success in competition events (especially in the hands of Johnny Brittain), the Replica had an alloy head and barrel, Lucas magneto ignition and a small-bore Amal carburettor. Although the new model was successfully campaigned by a number of privateers, the days of the four-stroke trials machine were numbered. Britain was having to face stiffer opposition each year and by 1962 the Works Replica was replaced by a new trials model, based on the Crusader, a 250 cc overhead valver introduced in 1957. The rest of the Bullet range was also dropped in 1962 but the name lived on for a few more years in a unit-construction 350, also based on the Crusader design.

Most Royal Enfields fetch only modest prices, and the Bullet is no exception. In effect this means that the purchaser acquires a sound, working, classic bargain. There are several spares specialists, and some new parts are now being made.

Sunbeam S7 & S8

During World War Two, the Sunbeam marque was yet again the subject of a business transaction, now becoming a not particularly well-nurtured part of the BSA conglomerate. The first of only two post-war models (this is without including the dreadful scooter to which the Sunbeam name was applied) was the S7, marking a return to the founder, John Marston's original aim of offering the public 'a gentleman's motor bicycle'. The reasoning behind this move was rather more mundane, however: BSA had obtained, as part of a post-war reparation deal, the manufacturing rights to several motor cycles (the best known of these being the hugely popular Bantam) including the BMW R75, an army vehicle suitable for solo and sidecar use.

Thinking that a copy of the machine would sell well under the Sunbeam banner, BSA commissioned top engineer Erling Poppe (of White and Poppe proprietary engine fame) to draw up the necessary plans. Realizing that anti-German feeling still ran high in Britain, Poppe decided to completely redesign the engine, while retaining some of its more advanced features.

An old experimental BSA engine from the early '30s—the Line-Ahead Twin, or LAT for short—was studied for inspiration and Poppe also drew freely on his more recent experience as a designer of motor car engines. It was hardly surprising then that the first of the S7 models was rather a mish-mash of design details that were not, in all cases, particularly compatible with one another.

The S7 engine was a 487 cc unit-construction twin with chain-drive ohc and mounted with the crankshaft in line with the double cradle frame. A 'pancake' Lucas dynamo was driven off the front of the crankshaft. For some extraordinary reason the BMW's hypoid rear-drive unit was not imitated; instead, an inherently weak worm and wheel unit was used which, until the engine power was cut to 24 bhp, was easily ripped to shreds if the unit was revved too hard.

Suspension was by means of plunger springing at the rear and telescopic front forks, and both wheels had 4.75 in × 16 in tyres, although the reason for this was obscure. Although eminently suitable for a sidecar machine like the BMW, on a solo motor cycle the balloon covers could be quite dangerous in the event of a puncture. Under normal circumstances, handling was quite badly affected anyway and although a special sidecar was manufactured, the S7 was really too under-powered for haulage work.

Balloon tyres make the Sunbeam S7 easy to spot, although this example has the wrong silencer fitted (but at least it's a BSA design!).

From the start, the S7's over-riding problem was one of vibration and this was acute enough on some machines to sever all the engine mounting bolts and wear the worm drive unit to a fine bronze powder. Such a major fault should, of course, have been ironed out at the prototype stage, but the imperious management at BSA blithely disregarded the road testers' report and put the S7 into production before any modifications could be made. In 1946 a batch of machines from the first production run was sent to South Africa for the police to ride as escorts to King George VI on his official visit there. All were returned as totally unusable; only then was any serious thought given to the task of reducing vibration.

The rigid engine mountings were replaced with rubber ones and the front through-bolt mounting was fitted with rubber buffers which fitted into the crankcase and restricted sideways movement of the unit. To allow for the movement that remained, a piece of flexible tubing was added at the point where the exhaust pipe connected with the silencer. Although it required a meticulous attitude to maintenance, owners found that by ensuring that clearance of the buffers was equal all the way round, vibration was greatly reduced.

An enthusiastic roadtest in *The Motor Cycle* in 1947 noted that 'In case it might be thought that the car practice of using a flexible mounting for the engine has any disadvantage on motor cycles, it should be added that, so far as the Sunbeam is concerned, the engine movement is so well cushioned that it is in no way disturbing'.

Fully equipped, the S7 weighed 413 lb, but its bulky appearance was that of a much heavier machine and may well be the reason for the poor sales. Even in revised form (and new bilious finish in 'Mist Green') the S7 De Luxe, as it was now called, was not a raging success.

In that same year, 1949, it was decided that a sports version should be offered and the S8, utilizing standard components from the BSA range (like the decidely more elegant A10 twin's front forks and wheels), appeared. Lighter, and a much better handler than its predecessor, the S8 was offered with a black or gunmetal grey finish and proved reasonably popular, although the term 'sportster' was not quite appropriate.

Despite their obvious potential, only minor improvements were made to either of the two models; BSA was, by now, far too concerned with its own financial problems to bother about the Sunbeam. This was still the case when a promising new prototype, a 600 cc unit with hypoid shaft drive, was built in the early '50s. Instead, the S7 De Luxe and the S8 plodded on until sales were reduced to a virtual standstill and the company decided to call it a day in 1956.

Until recently, the Sunbeam twins have not fetched what might be considered a good price, but they now seem to be making reasonable money. Spares are not a problem, with Stewart Engineering of Market Harborough providing a comprehensive service.

Triumph Thunderbird

After the war the two Triumph twins (the Speed Twin and the Tiger 100) continued much as before. Telescopic forks were fitted in place of the original girders, and a smaller 350 cc model was also introduced. Edward Turner was a great believer in exporting, particularly to America, where the motor cycle had become a recreational vehicle rather than a prime means of transport. Large numbers of GIs had been trained to ride motor cycles during the war, and some had had experience of the lighter British models, perhaps leaving them slightly disillusioned with the heavyweight V-twins turned out by Indian and Harley-Davidson. These two firms, however, had the American market firmly stitched up, and neither would allow its dealers to take on other franchises. Triumph, therefore, had to build a dealer network from scratch, and to their credit they did so most effectively.

British bikes were beginning to show up well in American races, and a vogue for them was encouraged. However, with the US highway system, the bikes got far more of the throttle-wide-open treatment for longer than was possible in this country. As a result, they tended to break. Tuning for higher speeds simply increased the likelihood of a blow up—especially if the tuner was not terribly competent. Turner's answer to this, and his riposte to the other British factories who were just bringing out their own 500 cc twins, was to modify the Speed Twin engine by enlarging it to 650 cc. There was sufficient room in the crankcases to allow a stroke of 82 mm and the barrel bore was increased to 71 mm.

It has been said that anyone can make a bridge stand up, but only a brilliant engineer can make it *just* stand up. Edward Turner was always trying to make things just work, and his designs tended to be skimpy in the extreme. With the enlarged motor this had the unfortunate consequence of causing the crankshaft to break, and a lot of work was done to strengthen it. However, when this had been completed, the motor would give 34 bhp reliably, a respectable figure, and better quality petrol and a little extra tuning soon raised it too.

Turner also had a happy knack with names. We have already seen the Tigers, the Speed Twin and for the new model he brought back a North American Indian name—Thunderbird. The new model was launched in a blaze of publicity with a high-speed, long-distance run at Montlhéry racing circuit in France. H. G. Tyrell-Smith (the former Rudge and Excelsior rider), Alex Scobie, Len Bayliss and Neale Shilton were the riders, and the bikes were ridden to the circuit and ridden back again. All went to plan, more or less, and the bike became a best seller, capable of making a good profit for,

When Edward Turner enlarged the 500 cc Speed Twin to create the 650 cc Thunderbird, he set a pattern which would be copied by other British manufacturers. The early T-bird was a lovely bike, but generally, as capacities outgrew design parameters, the motor cycles suffered. In the end it showed.

while it cost little, if any, more to make than the Speed Twin, it could be sold at a premium.

The subsequent success of the 650 cc Triumphs (Tiger 110, Trophy TR6, and Bonneville) demonstrates that the concept was right, and the execution must have been, too. Spares back-up for these models is excellent, though it is worth mentioning that the pre-unit (separate gearbox) models differ in many respects from the unit models. The changeover for 650s came in October 1962, though 350 cc unit construction models had been made since early 1957, and 500s since late 1958. Prices for the 650s vary according to model with the sporting variants coming more expensive, but any of them will prove a thoroughly practical, enjoyable—and even exciting—classic.

Velocette post-war

Velocette continued with their pre-war range until 1948, when the MOV and MSS were dropped. In their place came the LE, a side-valve, horizontally-opposed, water-cooled twin of 150 cc. It featured shaft drive, hand starting and hand gear changing and the power train was suspended from a radically different monocoque, pressed steel frame. Quiet, clean and convenient, this was Veloce's attempt at making a mass-produced 'Everyman' machine. It did not catch on in the way they hoped, but ironically the MAC was in great demand.

In 1950 the LE was stretched to 192 cc and various modifications made to make the engine and transmission more robust, particularly the lubrication system and the bearings. In 1958 a four-speed, foot-change gearbox was fitted, along with a kickstarter, both items being derived from the Valiant, an air-cooled 200 cc horizontally-opposed twin introduced in 1956.

The LE is, or was, known as the 'Noddy bike', though in fact 'Ploddy bike' would have been a more appropriate sobriquet. More than fifty Police forces used the LE to help the bobby patrol his beat more efficiently. It was said that the quiet engine allowed policemen to sneak up on criminals, but a more plausible explanation is that it allowed people to call their constables without shouting too loudly.

The LE had been designed for volume production, and the Goodman family had been so optimistic that they were prepared to shut down all the other production lines to concentrate on manufacturing it. Sadly, demand never justified this, and of the bikes produced in the immediate post-war years, it was the MAC which proved most popular. It was, however, getting a bit long in the tooth, and in 1952 Charles Udall was set to work on bringing it up to date.

The first area he attended to was the engine. A new alloy cylinder head, incorporating and enclosing the rocker box, was designed and cast up, together with an Alfin alloy barrel. This was considered sufficient modification to the power plant—and there are few who would argue with that—but it was still necessary to modernize the running gear. Telescopic forks had been introduced in 1948, the Dowty Oleomatic which relied on air

So successful was the Velocette MSS that sporting variants were produced, like the Venom Clubman.

as a springing medium, but these were replaced by some of Velocette's own design.

At the rear end, the swinging fork arrangement (universally called swinging arm) held no mysteries for the factory, since they had already used such a system on pre-war racing machines. However, rather than using a one-piece fork as most other manufacturers did, Velocette used two separate arms clamped and keyed on to a spindle which pivoted on a lug attached to the seat tube. This was actually something of a bodge, but it worked. The top mountings of the suspension units made use of a patent registered by Phil Irving and Veloce Ltd: rather than a solid fixing point, the units were fitted into arcuate slots. The theory behind this was that the suspension could then be adjusted to compensate for loading—in effect more or less leverage could be exerted on the spring/damper units. In addition to the new frame, the gearbox shell was altered (and again in 1954), and new petrol and oil tanks, and a new fishtail silencer fitted.

The 350 cc MAC was a very successful machine, and demands from the USA—and doubtless from the UK too—led to the factory reintroducing a 500 cc model. This was called the MSS but it was not simply the old 81 mm × 96 mm, 495 cc engine revived, for the original unit would not fit into the new frame, being too tall. Charles Udall did the sensible thing and simply rejigged the bore and stroke dimensions to give square measurements of 86 mm by 86 mm—which also happened to accord with contemporary thinking on engine design and piston speeds.

The new MSS was used for scrambling and enduros as well as the road-ster, and in Britain in particular it found favour with clubman racers. This eventually led to the introduction in 1956 of the Venom (500) and Viper (350) sporting models. The Viper was announced first and, interestingly, its engine was derived from the new MSS unit, with the bore sleeved down to 72 mm. It was not, however, a very exciting performer until the flywheels were lightened and a hotter cam specified. The Venom, on the other hand, was a hit from the word go and soon found its metier in production racing.

So popular was it for this role that in 1960 the factory offered Clubman variants, which were more highly tuned (though later Clubman models evolved into fast roadsters rather than racers). A specially prepared machine took 12- and 24-hour endurance records in 1961—a feat which has yet to be bettered by a 500 cc motor cycle. The ultimate variant on the MSS theme came in 1964 with the Venom Thruxton. Named after the Hampshire racing circuit where a long-distance production event was held annually, the Thruxton featured a new large valve cylinder head, Amal GP carburettor, twin-leading shoe front brake, clip-on handlebars, rear-sets, and a swept-back exhaust. Not only did it look the part, but the factory claimed a power output of 44 bhp (one pure racing example was said to give 47 bhp), excellent for a 500 cc single of that time, especially a pushrod motor.

The pinnacle of the Thruxton's racing success is generally considered to have been reached in the 1967 Production TT, when Manxman Neil Kelly took a Reg Orpin-prepared machine to victory, with Keith Heckles second on another Thruxton, prepared by Geoff Dodkin. The Thruxton remains a truly 'classic' classic, but as only 1,208 genuine Thruxton engines were produced by the factory (many more have been 'Thruxtonized') a collector's chances of finding the real thing are somewhat restricted, and prices are correspondingly high.

Vincent

Phil Vincent bought the manufacturing rights to HRD motor cycles in 1928. This was primarily for the kudos of the initials which he hoped would rub off on to his own machines, but also because Howard R. Davies, founder of the short-lived HRD Motors Ltd (founded in 1925 and in liquidation by 1928), was a man whom Vincent greatly admired. Davies was a skilful rider (he won the Senior TT in 1921 on a 350 AJS and again in 1925 on his own machine) and was also respected for his technical insight. Davies' experience on the race track had taught him the importance of cutting down wind resistance, especially that of the rider, and to achieve this he lowered the saddle while keeping the petrol tank in its relatively high position. He can also be said to have started the fashion for the saddletank which, on his own machine, was carefully cut away, the lower tank rail being eliminated, to make room for the valve gear of the long-stroke engine.

In the early years Vincent used a series of proprietary engines—MAG, Villiers, JAP and Rudge—with varying degrees of success. Whatever the engine, the Vincent-HRD, like the HRD before it, was a luxury marque; several years were to pass before the number of machines built in each model range exceeded single figures and could actually be classed as a production run.

Not the most salubrious of surroundings for such a noble motor cycle—a Vincent Rapide Series B is ridden slowly past the dustbins. There is no symbolism in this!

Business really began to take off when Vincent, together with top Australian engineer Phil Irving, designed an engine of his own. Their first range included a standard, a sports, and a racing model (called the Meteor, Comet and TT Replica, respectively) and quickly gathered fame for their exceptionally good handling, brakes and acceleration. Public response was so positive that Vincent was encouraged to continue his quest for higher performance; he came up with the first of several big V-twins, a configuration with which the Vincent name would, from then on, always be associated. The Series A Rapide, with its 998 cc 47-degree V-twin engine, sold well (well, that is, for an expensive motor cycle) until production was interrupted by the war when Vincent and Irving became involved in designing marine engines for the Air Ministry.

When the opportunity arose, in 1948, for redesigning the twin, numerous improvements were incorporated to make the Series B the fastest motor cycle in the world. The Black Shadow (so named because all parts of the machine, including the aluminium alloy engine, were finished in black) had a bore and stroke of 84 mm × 90 mm, weighed only 380 lb and was capable of producing 55 bhp at 5,700 rpm, giving it a top speed of over 120 mph. The excellent braking system consisted of twin 7 in ribbed cast-iron drums front and rear. Hydraulically-damped Girdraulic front forks replaced the previously used Brampton spring variety and a self-servo drum-type clutch coped with the extreme torque of the engine. Both clutch and forks were designed by Vincent.

The Series B bristled with well-thought-out details: brake pedals, footrest, handlebars and gear lever were all adjustable, the kickstarter could be fitted to either side of the machine, both wheels were quickly detachable, and brakes and chain tension could be altered by hand, without recourse to anything more than a pair of pliers for removing the spring clip on the chain. Most outstanding feature of all was the Shadow's frame design. Nicknamed 'the boneless wonder', the inherent stiffness of the unit-construction engine was utilized to provide the main structural support between the steering head and the rear forks: shock absorption was by means of a pair of stubby spring boxes.

Without the front down tube in the way, the V-twin could be opened out to 50 degrees. Another advantage of this design was that, by resting the crankcase on a suitable support, splitting the chain and removing a few bolts, the whole of the back end of the motor cycle could be wheeled away leaving the power unit free to be worked on. A hollow sheet-steel backbone, doubling as an oil tank, was attached at one end to the bolted-on steering head and at the other to the rear cylinder head.

The first opportunity for the Black Shadow to prove its worth came in the 1948 Clubman's TT when it won first place and fastest lap. Nine out of the eleven Vincents entered completed the course, with the result that production at the small Stevenage works ran at a peak with all of thirty machines per week being built.

The Series C racing model, called Black Lightning, was the incredibly fast successor to the Shadow, making countless speed records all over the world. Best known of these were George Brown's sprinting successes on his specially prepared machines—'Gunga Din', 'Nero' and the supercharged 'Super Nero'.

Chapter 9

The European scene

With a few notable exceptions, the collecting of motor cycles made in continental Europe is not generally cultivated in the UK. Machines like the Moto-Rêve (Swiss), Griffon (French) and Minerva (Belgian) stand out at gatherings like the Pioneer or Banbury Runs because of their scarcity. They would, in any case, never have been available in such great quantities as British-built machines: there does not appear to have been much of a move to investigate the European scene more closely.

France, Belgium, Germany and Italy all had thriving motor cycle industries (the latter still does), which produced a wide variety of machines from humble clip-on-engined bicycles to sophisticated and advanced multi-cylindered racers. At the end of the vintage period, the trends in Europe were even threatening to eclipse established British principals.

The Motor Cycle was moved to comment, in an editorial of 31 October 1929: 'For sheer interest the motor cycle show in Paris is unparalleled in recent history. There are not just two or three novel exhibits, as is usually the case at the Olympia Show, but a score or more, each showing originality in conception.' The main trends at that event in Paris in 1929 were towards unit construction, shaft drive, pressed steel (or cast alloy) frames and quickly detachable wheels.

Reviewing the stands, a host of names crop up, some familiar, others not so well known. Durandal, MGC, CP Roléo, Gillet, Clément-Gladiator, Alcyon, Olympique, Labor, Monet-Goyon, Gnome-Rhône, Peugeot— were just a few of the manufacturers displaying their wares at that show. The English papers noted, however, that there were only two four-cylinder machines on show, and as these were badge-engineered variants, they really only counted as one. The French, it seems, were content with singles and twins (as, in effect, were the British), though the Motobécane/ Motoconfort side-valve 500 cc fours were singled out as, 'one of the most praiseworthy designs'.

Whilst thinking of multis, it is interesting to note that an extremely successful four-cylinder engine was laid down in 1928, in Italy. This was the four-cylinder OPRA, designed by Ing Pietro Remor, and although it was not an immediate threat to the opposition, it provided a useful test bed for

Remor. He it was who designed fours for CNA, Gilera and MV—the four-cylinder racers of the last two need no introduction.

As in this country, many continental makes went down in the 1930s, and those which survived the war turned to the production of lightweights, mopeds or autocycles (the most enduring of which must surely be the VeloSolex). There were exceptions, of course: BMW survived on its big twins; and the Italian industry is most famous for its high-performance four-strokes (though it is based firmly in the production of lightweights).

It seems probable that the most fruitful period to investigate would be the decade running from the mid-twenties to the mid-'thirties. Assuming that one can find the machines (and there are a few more appearing at British events these days), the next problem is keeping them going. Anyone used to running a vintage or veteran machine should have no trouble coping with a continental motor cycle, for the basic engineering problems are identical: if a spare part is not available, it must be made.

Post-war classics are a different matter. Spares are relatively readily available for BMWs, NSUs, Ducatis and so on, but the problem will be to find a machine at the right price for your pocket.

The following selection of continental classics is just that—a selection. Hopefully, some indication of the wealth of two-wheeled history 'over there' will be gathered from the photographs and brief marque histories. Perhaps a few holiday-makers will return to these shores with rather heavier souvenirs than they anticipated!

BMW

Granville Bradshaw's ABC may have been the first motor cycle to go into production with a horizontally-opposed transverse twin, but BMW were the first to truly succeed with the design. The first BMW motor cycle (though the company had produced engines for others) was shown in 1923 at the Paris Show. The Max Friz-designed bike owed much to aviation engineering, for BMW had been manufacturers of aeroplane power units before and during the Great War. Indeed, the famous blue and white badge represents a propeller whirring round against a blue sky.

The R32, as it was dubbed, was not a spectacular performer, but it was well engineered and made, reliable, and, with shaft drive, convenient. In 1925 production expanded to include a 250 cc (R39) single and 500 cc ohv twin, the R37 which featured fully enclosed valve gear—for the time that was sophistication indeed.

The motor cycle buying public welcomed these machines, and in 1928 two more models were added, both 750s but one was a side valve touring machine and the other an overhead valve sportster; in the system of BMW typing they were designated the R12 and R17, respectively. The latter, together with the 500 cc R37, was supercharged for racing. This, in turn, necessitated the beefing up of the frame and cycle parts, and beefing up is

Five years into motor cycle production, BMW were turning out machines like this 500 cc side-valver. Note the intriguing forks—trailing link with a leaf spring.

the correct expression, for the basic design was much as it had been except that it was now constructed from heavy duty pressed steel rather than tubes.

1935 saw the introduction of hydraulically damped telescopic forks and this is universally credited as the first use of the system on a large-scale production run. The R17 probably benefited most from this advance, as it was a very sporting mount. Producing 33 bhp from its 750 cc was considered a good specific output, but even better was the new 500 cc racer. Twin overhead cams (that's four cams in all) and a supercharger soon had the racer winning in the capable hands of such riders as Georg Meier and Jock West. The racing motor was also used in ISDT machines, presumably slightly detuned.

In 1936 the R5 500 cc ohv model set new standards for the class. A 'high cam' design (though it is less obvious as such with the engine disposed as it is), it pushed out 24 bhp at peak power, and with the four-speed gearbox this made it a formidable machine. The new powertrain was fitted into a new duplex, tubular, all-welded frame which was lighter than the previous one, but still unsuspended at the rear end. This was remedied in 1938 when production models were fitted with plunger suspension, the R5 being reclassified as the R51. Joining it in the showrooms were the 600 cc side valve R6, the 600 cc ohv R66 and the 750 cc ohv R71. The R6 was the last side valve engine BMW introduced.

During the war the German forces intially used the old 750 cc side valve R12, along with a couple of singles. The R12 retained the pressed-steel rigid frame of the civilian model, fitted with telescopic forks. It was soon joined by the famous R75, an overhead valve 750 developed in close co-operation with Zündapp, whose own KS750 greatly resembled it. Indeed, certain parts were interchangeable. Both machines were intended as sidecar haulers, and both featured sidecar wheel drive. They performed their duties extremely well.

When production of civilian models resumed in 1949, BMW's first machine was the R24, a rigid-framed 250. This was shortly joined by the R25, a plunger-framed version, and the 51/2—a revival of the pre-war 500. The next major introduction was the R67, a 600 cc variant of the R51 and then, in 1955, the R50 (500 cc) and R69 (600 cc). Both were fitted with Earles leading link forks and a revised engine, and they laid the foundation for BMW's continuing and increasing sales success. Thereafter the engine was developed to 750, 800, 900 and 1,000 cc versions, and although the forks reverted to conventional teles in 1967, the ancestry of the power unit could be clearly traced.

BMWs have always been fairly exclusive machines in this country, but pre- and immediately post-war models are rare indeed. Consequently, prices are high and spares difficult to locate. The best choice is likely to be an R69 or R50, and there is a major source of spare parts for these Earles-forked models—D. F. Dickson, Crawyn House, Killane, Ballaugh, Isle of Man, telephone 0624-897731.

Ducati
The name Ducati is, to most people's minds, synonymous with four-stroke singles and the uniquely successful use of desmodromic valve gear in motor cycles. Starting on a humble basis before the war, the Ducati factory produced radio components and later, during hostilities, military equipment. Like many businesses in post-war Italy, the Bologna-based firm ran into financial difficulties and was taken under the government's wing as part of the national reconstruction plan. It was then that the first Ducati engine was built, and a modest little affair it was.

The Cucciolo (Little Pup), designed by Aldo Farinelli, was a clip-on proprietary engine which admirably fitted the country's need for a quick remedy to the transport shortage of the immediate post-war years. The unit was a 50 cc four-stroke with overhead valves operated by pull-, rather than push-, rods and fitted with pedals for situations requiring light pedalling assistance. Capable of 300 mpg, its popularity was ensured, triggering off a boom in mopeds which has never really abated.

Encouraged by such a favourable public response, Ducati decided to produce complete motor cycles, and, for the first few years, they built lightweights using the Cucciolo engine bored out to 60 cc, with varying degrees of success. A scooter, called the Cruiser, was one of their less memorable efforts. It was too heavy, and indeed, too complex and powerful, to compete with Piaggio's simple Vespa.

Only when the company was joined by the genius of Fabio Taglioni in 1954 did the Ducati single really take off. Choosing the popular 100 cc bracket, Taglioni designed what was to be Ducati's first racing motor cycle—the Gran Sport. Even at this early stage, the little four-stroke, with its clean lines, overhead camshaft and wet sump lubrication, bore all the hallmarks of the Ducati we have since learned to know and love. The engine, with light-alloy barrel and cast-iron liner, had a bore and stroke of 49.4 mm × 52 mm, exposed hairpin valve springs, a forged three-ring piston and close-ratio four-speed gearbox. It produced 9 bhp at 9,000 rpm, later raised to 12 bhp at 10,500 rpm, and had a compression ratio of 8.5 to 1.

A programme of Grand Prix and endurance racing ensued as a means of advertising the Gran Sport: 'dustbin' streamlined versions, ridden by Mario Carini and Sandro Ciceri, broke the 100 km and 1,000 km records at Monza, averaging speeds of over 100 mph and 96 mph, respectively. 125 cc, 175 cc and eventually a 250 cc version followed and, in order to boost the power of the 125GS, Taglioni fitted a twin ohc cylinder head, raising bhp to 16 at 11,500 rpm on a 9.5 to 1 compression ratio. Still not quick enough, the Grand Prix, as it was called, was taken one step further when Taglioni put the theory of desmodromic valve control to practical use.

At high revs, valve bounce sets in because the spring-operated valves seat so rapidly that they rebound and are unable to close properly. Conventional engines have just one pair of cams to open the valves but the desmodromic system (Greek for 'controlled run') incorporates an extra pair of cams, instead of springs, for closing the valves. This means that the engine can be revved much higher, with no risk of valve float.

Taglioni was not the inventor of the system but he was the first, indeed the only, engineer to successfully apply the principle to production motor cycle engines, the first of which, the Mk IIID, appeared in 1968. The prototype desmo, the 125 cc single, had near square dimensions (55.25 mm × 52 mm bore and stroke) and produced 17 bhp at 12,500 rpm. After a hundred hours of bench-testing, as well as on the track, Ducati were confident of the engine's speed and reliability and in 1957 the desmo, ridden by Degli Antoni, made a brilliant debut as winner of the Swedish Grand Prix, with the fastest lap, as well as lapping all the other competitors. Mike Hailwood was one of the better-known racers to achieve success on the 125 desmo at this time.

A 125 cc parallel twin desmo was also produced, but this was less successful and for some years Ducati chose to concentrate on their production machines with single ohc engines with valve spring heads. These were built in a range of capacities from 124 cc to 436 cc and were renowned for their speed and superb handling. In addition, the vivid cherry-red and gold paintwork stood out like a beacon amongst the drab colours with which most motor cycles were finished in the '50s and '60s.

Despite their obvious superiority to contemporary machines, the ohc models did not sell in vast numbers outside Italy, probably because they were more expensive. In Britain, the most successful models were the 200s, based, as were all the ohc singles, on the Gran Sport. It had an all-alloy unit-

For many people the ultimate Ducati single is the 450 Desmo—this is one down, the 350 cc version, but few would spurn it.

construction engine, with forged pistons and valve gear driven by shaft and bevel gears.

Being of such a sound design, the ohc singles line stretched over a period of nearly twenty years until the end of the 1960s when problems were identified and improvements sought. These were embodied in a 350 cc single, the prototype of which was exhibited at the 1967 Motor Cycle Show in Cologne. It had a wide crankcase engine, which was to become a familiar characteristic of the Desmo, and new crankshafts. The desmodromic system operating the valve gear was similar to the one used on the early racing bikes, with the addition of light springs to assist valve closing and eliminate chatter.

Produced in 250, 350 and 450 cc form, the Desmo singles underwent a number of mainly cosmetic changes during a relatively short production period. Unfortunately, people in this country were too slow to appreciate their true value although, nowadays, demand is high for these classic examples of Taglioni's genius.

FN

'We must admit that previous to trying the machine we had the opinion that with a gear of six to one, which we believe is the standard, the speed would not be very high, but a run on the machine convinced us that the engine is capable of an extremely high number of revolutions per minute, which enables the machine to attain a speed which is quite fast enough for average British roads, and faster than is required for touring.'

Quite a sentence, that, and quite a motor cycle it was describing, for in July 1908 *The Motor Cycle* took a run on a four-cylinder FN. Although the Belgian company, famed more as an armaments manufacturer than a bike maker, was not the first to make a practical four-cylinder engine for a motor cycle, it was the first to put one into volume production.

FN's first bike was a 133 cc single-cylinder job, produced in 1902. This was soon followed by a 188 cc version and, the factory finding this sideline profitable, Paul Kelecom, already designing and making engines under his own name, was commissioned to design and develop the four. It was launched, after extensive testing, at the Paris Salon in 1905 to immediate acclaim.

Kelecom's engine, with a bore and stroke of 45 mm × 75 mm, had a well-lubricated, five main bearing crankshaft, but despite this advanced specification, the inlet valve was of the atmospheric, or automatic, type. The final drive was by shaft, but there was no clutch and no gearbox. The Americans loved it, and it is not much of an exaggeration to claim that the FN Four was responsible for all the American four-cylinder machines from the Pierce to the Indian. In 1908 a special model was made for the States, but at the British Motor Cycle Show another kind of bike altogether was announced—a single cylinder 2¼ hp, two-speed, shaft-driven number, described as 'a little gem of lightweight construction'. There was also a 1¾ hp model and, of course, the Four, the dog-clutch gearbox of which visitors

A restored FN Four type 700, made in 1914.

were advised to examine.

The following year the 2¼ hp dominated the FN stand, though it was said to be in very short supply, but there was a new, larger version of the Four with a 498 cc motor. This had been brought about by demands for more power, both for fast solo riding and for sidecar work. However, it appeared that the British required more than reliability, smoothness and power to impress them, for in 1911 *Motor Cycling* described those 'improvements on the FN machine which have brought them into closer conformity with English ideas'. What were they, you may ask, what basic fault had been ironed out, what un-English trait discarded? Well, it seemed that the handlebars had been changed, and the carrier, 'now partakes of the familiar form,' and there follows an eleven-line description.

Automatic inlet valves were obviously quite English, as well as Belgian, for they were not changed until 1913, when a new engine was displayed for the first time. With side valves in a T-shaped cylinder head, the motor displaced 748 cc, making it a 7 hp model. The main bearings were positively lubricated, but the big ends, described as 'adjustable', had to rely on splash. The crankshaft was 'big enough for a small car' and the large flywheel incorporated a multiplate clutch feeding into a three-speed gearbox in which the shafts were carried on ball bearings.

This generally up-to-date specification was rather let down by the braking arrangements—judging by the standards of hindsight. An internal expanding and an external contracting brake worked, independently, on the rear wheel—on the same drum, in fact. While this would seem to offer greater retarding exertion, the rapid build up of heat soon caused the brakes to fade.

Just before the British Show opened, R. O. Clark (who helped Levis to a famous TT win) had been breaking records on the 2½ hp, now described as a 'handy-go-anywhere mount', while the 5 hp Four was said to be well known and well appreciated for its silence and smooth running (and presumably the handlebars and carrier too!). 'It has', *The Motor Cycle* declared, 'stood the test of time, and is, moreoever, less expensive than the larger four-cylinder model'.

But time had other things in store for 1914. The FN factory was taken over by the German army, and the 750 cc Four was churned out to aid the war effort as a despatch riders' mount. After the war, the cheaper 5 hp version was not reintroduced, and the FN Four went into a slow decline. In America, home-produced fours had overtaken the Belgian machine in performance and specification, and the rest of Europe was hardly in a position to buy expensive foreign machines. A last attempt was made with a revamped, overhead valve, chain-driven model but it did not sell well, and in 1926 FN dropped the Four altogether. It was not the end of FN motor cycles, but they never produced as famous a model, despite some success with their unit-construction singles. Mention FN and most people think of the fabled Four.

Husqvarna

Husqvarna presented its first motorized velocipede to the world in 1903. This type of vehicle had already achieved unprecedented popularity in the rest of Europe and it was no great surprise that Husqvarna was the factory to launch the new type of two-wheeler in Sweden, as it had been producing push-bikes for many years.

After exhaustive tests with several foreign engines, the factory chose a Belgian-made FN 1¼ hp motor as the power unit for their first motor cycle. This was an undeniably simple construction, but it worked, and worked well, and the manufacturer could also boast of its speed. The instruction manual stated, 'On level ground the speed can be increased to three or four "mil" per hour'. This approximates to 20–25 mph, a break-neck speed for the time, considering the quality of both the roads and the brakes. The manual also taught the following in the case of the engine not starting: 'If the petrol is too cold, one can warm the carburettor by holding a burning newspaper, or other paper, underneath it. Under no circumstances should a blowlamp be used!'

After gaining experience with the first model, and following general technical developments closely, Husqvarna were able to produce their first twin-cylinder machine in 1909. The Swiss-made Moto-Rêve replaced the well-tried FN motor, while the frame and running gear were made by the Swedish factory itself.

Collaboration with Moto-Rêve lasted for ten years until 1919 but the addendum to the catalogue issued in the first year of the Great War bears witness to the fact that these were not entirely problem-free times: '*Note—* We give no guarantee on the engine, its accessories or the tyres. Our usual one-year warranty applies only to the cycle itself and all its parts'.

In 1916 Husqvarna completed its first delivery of motor cycles to the Swedish army and also made its name known, for the first time, on the competition circuit, by winning the Novemberkåsan. This was the most demanding of Sweden's reliability trials, with a pedigree stretching back to the beginning of the century.

The following testimonial from a satisfied owner of a Moto-Rêve-engined Model 75A, twin-cylinder 496 cc machine, describes how demanding competitions could be: 'I can highly recommend this machine after the Swedish Motor Cycle Club's May competition in 1915. The route was from Stockholm via Malmö and Gothenburg back to Stockholm, a stretch of 170 mil (1,060 miles). Despite exceptionally bad weather and road conditions the engine worked without complaint during the first half of the competition, and, I might add, for 36 hours without a break until the obligatory stop. The reliance and confidence one places in the machine under such conditions are well founded—Einar Sundström, Stockholm, March 1916.'

To drive such a great distance on poor roads and for 36 hours at a stretch, made great demands on both rider and motor cycle, and the May Cup was without doubt the most important long-distance race for the pioneers of Sweden. In 1922 the distance was all of 210 mil (1,312 miles), and the victor in that year rode a Husqvarna: in fact, three out of the seven penalty-free outfits were Husqvarnas—the Model 150, with the factory's own engine installed, the first one they had produced.

The Model 150 was relatively expensive, thanks to the inflation triggered off by the war. It was first shown in 1920, and the engine was a conventional unit with one-piece barrels and heads, and side valves; overhead valves were considered very special equipment and were limited to the works bikes. There was still no front brake, but a lighting system could be had as an option; either AGA's gas lamps or Bosch's electric ones.

Husqvarna's first own-make engine was rapidly followed by others of varying power and capacity. But engine production is expensive, especially when one considers the relatively small numbers of machines sold on the Swedish market, so when relations within Europe began to improve, the search began again for a manufacturer who could supply at least some of the model range with engines. In the end, JAP, and a few Sturmey-Archer, units were chosen and the British-manufacturered engines gave Husqvarna further success on the race track.

In Sweden, as in many countries, the military played its part in influencing the design and development of motor cycles. For Husqvarna, one of the best examples of this interaction resulted in the Model 500 of 1922, which superseded the army model first produced in 1916. Converted to civilian use and equipped with a sidecar, the 500 became a popular family vehicle, providing transport whilst simultaneously introducing other members of the family to the joys of motor cycling. Husqvarna was quick to see the value of offering the public a comfortable and practical sidecar, and various models were made, ranging from basic plaited cane to luxury styles in leather and aluminium. The model range always included at least one sidecar outfit, until the production of large motor cycles ceased in 1936.

Husqvarna realized that valuable publicity could be gained from racing successes and during the 1930s their competition bikes dominated domestic racing. Some impact was also made on the international scene: in 1934, *The Motor Cycle*, commenting on Gunnar Kalén (Husqvarna's star rider) and his winning lap at the Dutch Grand Prix, wrote, 'We English are no longer blind to the fact that our machines are inferior to the "Huskies" in speed'.

However, before the decade was out Husqvarna had begun an even more successful era as producers of lightweight two-strokes which later on became world-beaters in reliability trials. In 1953, one such model, by virtue of its low weight and great reliability, outshone the four-strokes which still predominated. In the Swedish Six Days Trial, a nine-man team was entered by Husqvarna on new 175 cc machines: they brought home seven gold medals and two bronze and in the ISDT of the same year, six gold, one silver and two bronze medals were achieved.

In its production form, under the name Drömbagen (Dream Bow), the

Best of the post-vintage 'Huskies' is the Model 112, of which this is a side valve variant. The 112 formed the basis of a military model, the MC42.

175 cc motor cycle was not as popular as the factory had hoped, appealing as it did to the older rider. In order to capture the younger end of the market, Husqvarna realized that what was needed was a lighter, faster model with a sportier appearance. By fulfilling these requirements, the 16- to 18-year-old market—restricted to riding smaller bikes by law—could be tapped, and the result was the Silverpil (Silver Arrow) of 1955. With a weight under the lightweight limit of 75 kg (165 lb) it was a serious alternative for prospective buyers with new driving licences. It was fast, had the unmistakable characteristics of a competition machine and soon became the most popular lightweight machine in the country. In private hands it also became very successful in motocross, where it often left its rivals in the 250 cc class behind, despite its disadvantage in cubic capacity.

The Silver Arrow was not the first or only Husqvarna to make a mark in motocross and since then gold medals and victories in international competition have ensured Husqvarna's continuing renown as a manufacturer of first class motor cycles.

Moto Guzzi

Carlo Guzzi's first motor cycle was the 500 cc Normale, which he started to build just after the Great War. It had all the recognizable points of a later Guzzi single—horizontal cylinder, external flywheel, exhaust-over-inlet valves, unit construction, dry sump lubrication and an oil bath clutch and primary drive. In short it was an advanced and reliable machine.

The engine and cycle parts were developed over the years through the

Not quite so 'classic' as the Falcone, the 250 cc Lodola might prove easier to find, and is certainly a lot of fun.

Sport (1923), GT (1928, and the first to feature Guzzi's reversed-cantilever rear suspension), Sport 14 and Sport 15. In 1934 the valve layout was changed so that both inlet and exhaust were overhead, and the gearbox became a foot change four-speeder; the new machines were known as the V series. Logically enough, the next move was to the W series, the GTC and, in 1938, the Condor, a lightweight supersports machine which was used to great effect as a pukka racer. From this were derived the famous Dondolino and Gambalunga racers.

By the beginning of the 1950s Moto Guzzi had an expensive racing model (the Dordolino) and a basic touring machine derived from the V series. The company felt that it needed a sportster to fill out the range, and the result was the Falcone, one of the most enduring machines produced anywhere. The basic 500 cc horizontal engine layout was retained, along with the external flywheel, but the crankshaft, lubrication system and overall mechanical specification were uprated. Friction damping was specified at the rear end, on the grounds that it was easily adjustable, while the front forks were an unusual—and not terribly effective—internal slider design (ie, the sliders ran into the stanchions rather than over them).

Introduced at the 1950 Italian Show, the Falcone was welcomed by 'Guzzisti' and soon became the company's staple product. In 1953 the old V series tourer (called the Astore, or Goshawk) was phased out and a new Falcone Turismo introduced to take its place. Very similar mechanically to the Sport, the Turismo reproduced some features of the Astore such as leg guards, wide handlebars and forward footrests. Though not fast either in terms of top speed or acceleration, the Falcone found favour with the authorities thanks to its reliability and stamina (it could cruise at high speed indefinitely) and many were supplied to the Police and other official bodies.

Due largely to bulk orders from such sources, the big single was kept in production until 1967. Doubtless there were many who mourned its passing.

The Moto Guzzi Falcone might not be exclusive, but it is both a classic and a good working proposition. A potential purchaser will almost certainly have to go shopping in Italy, and there is no regular supply of spares in the UK. However, the bike has a strong following in Italy, and it would not be difficult, though also not terribly convenient, to organize deliveries from its homeland. After all, what is the purpose of being in the EEC if the classic motor cyclist is to be denied the choice of continential machinery?

Motosacoche

Armand and Henry Dufaux started their business—H & A Dufaux et Cie—in Geneva, Switzerland, in 1899. The name Motosacoche, which translates as 'The motor in the tool bag', derives from a 211 cc power unit intended to clip on to bicycle frames. This was a great success, eventually being made in 241 cc and 290 cc sizes, and it led to the design and manufacture of a range of motor cycles and proprietary engines. Ranging from a 250 cc single inlet over exhaust type to 750 cc ioe V-twins, the motors were bought and used by many makers, including Royal Enfield, who fitted a Motosacoche V-twin to one of their earliest models.

A 1910 model Motosacoche. Even this basic-looking machine has front suspension.

Motosacoche engines were also made at factories in France and Italy, and some manufacturers made them under licence, too. The proprietary units were also sold under the name MAG, and became associated with many marques. Matchless, Ariel, Brough-Superior, Lea-Francis and Morgan were just a few of the British makers using the Swiss engines at some stage, and there were many continental users as well.

Motosacoche produced a large range of motor cycles under their own name, and they utilized the talents of such people as Bert Le Vack and Dougal Marchant to design new power units. Marchant developed an overhead camshaft unit which saw service in many racing machines, not just Motosacoche's own. Indeed, customers using proprietary units had more racing success than the factory itself.

Motor cycle production continued into the 1950s. The last models were a 250 cc unit construction, shaft drive single, and an overhead cam 250 cc twin. Whilst Motosacoche or MAG engines are not rare, and apparently present few problems to restorers, the motor cycles are not so common in the UK. Nevertheless, as Europe becomes more of a hunting ground for old machines, doubtless more will find their way across the Channel. All of them used conventional enough cycle parts, so renovation and running would seem to hold few, if any, pitfalls.

NSU

Like many of the pioneering British motor cycle manufacturers, NSU started off making artefacts of a very different kind—knitting machines! This expanded, as was the habit of the time, into bicycle production and thence, in 1901, into motor cycles. The first Neckarsulms (named after the town where the factory was sited) used Zedel and Minerva power units, and they sold well enough to encourage expansion.

The factory soon began to design and make its own engines, added to which was a two-speed gearbox which was incorporated into the engine pulley. Both single- and twin-cylinder motors were made, with the valves disposed inlet-over-exhaust style. Suspension was also experimented with, and a fully sprung frame was on offer during the vintage period. This featured leading link front forks, and a 'cantilever' arrangement at the rear end, similar to the system used later by Brough, Vincent and, much later, Yamaha and all the rest.

With springing and gears, the NSU seemed ideal for the Isle of Man TT races, and in the inaugural event of 1907, Geiger finished seventh on a single; in 1908 Lang repeated the result on a twin. NSU's best pre-war result was a fourth attained by Danny O'Donovan (better known as a Norton rider) in 1913.

After the First World War, motor cycle production continued apace and in great variety. Singles and V-twins in capacities from 250 cc to 1,000 cc were made, with valves disposed in side, overhead and ioe formation. All that was missing was an overhead-camshaft model, and this situation was

NSU were early users of an epicyclic gearbox, but this 1909 model has direct belt drive. The rider is priming the carburettor.

rectified in 1929, when Walter Moore was poached from Norton. He took with him his design for the CS1 Norton, and virtually repeated it in Germany. The joke at the Norton factory was that the initials NSU stood for Norton Spares Used, but they were never terribly worried by the ohc racer, for it could not match the CS1, which had been completely redesigned by Arthur Carroll.

The decade before the Second World War was, despite the world-wide depression, a good one for NSU, for their 98 cc, 200 cc and 250 cc production models sold very well. During this time the factory became one of the largest producers of motor cycles in the world. To keep the name prominent, new racers were also developed by Moore and Albert Roder—first a double overhead cam reworking of the CS1 copy and then a series of dohc twins.

Following the 1939–45 war, production was, not unnaturally, concentrated on lightweights, and a series of mopeds was developed. The most famous of these, in this country, was the Quickly. It had an advanced engine, with a hard chrome bore rather than a separate liner, and was thus lighter. It may seem strange to commend a moped as a collectable two-wheeler, but if there has to be one, the NSU Quickly is probably it.

The other outstanding post-war NSU is the 250 cc overhead cam Max and its close relation the Sportmax. They sold well in the '50s, though they were not imported in great numbers (Vincent had the franchise at one time), and some spares are still available over here. The Sportmax and Rennmax (a genuine racer rather than a sports/racer) won a good many races, including the 1955 250 cc World Championship. Ironically the factory had, by then, closed its race shop, and production of motor cycles ceased altogether in 1958.

The car side of the business continued, however, and it is interesting to note that NSU's unique method of transferring motion from the crankshaft to the overhead camshaft—coupling rods running on eccentrics—was used on the Prinz saloon car.

'And I still say we should have turned right. . .' Their transport is the sporting and de luxe 250 cc Terrot Type OSSD.

Terrot

Founded in 1901 in Dijon, Terrot soon became, for a while, the largest producer of motor cycles in France. It competed successfully in road races in the 1920s, and the range on offer to the public was very comprehensive, with models from 98 cc singles to 750 cc V-twins. Power came from engines of Terrot's own manufacture, and from proprietary units supplied by Blackburne or JAP.

One of the best known and liked Terrots is the 350 cc ohv single made in the 1930s, together with a 250 cc counterpart. A conventional construction, it had dry sump lubrication, magneto ignition, a separate hand-change gearbox and a diamond frame fitted with girder forks. A very well-styled and attractive motor cycle, it abounds in neat touches such as the cast-aluminium silencer with 'Terrot' appearing in a lozenge-shaped recess. Whilst hardly breaking new ground, a 1930's Terrot would be a novel addition to any collection, and should not present many problems to an experienced vintagent, as it is very straightforward. Contact with French enthusiasts might reveal some sources of spares.

After the war, Terrot produced a range of ohv singles in sizes up to 500 cc. These models have more of an Italian style to them, though again they appear to be very straightforward. Manufacture of Terrot motor cycles ceased in the early 1960s, after (but not necessarily because) the factory had made some technically interesting scooters.

Chapter 10

Oriental origins

The Japanese motor cycle industry began before the First World War, but in a small way only. There was more demand for transport after the war and, with the very poor, narrow roads and bridges of the era, the motor cycle proved perfect for the environment. Rather than encouraging a boom in the home industry, however, it simply fuelled demand for imported machines, mainly from America, England and Germany. Strange as it may now seem, the science of production engineering was virtually unknown in Japan at that time and it was not until Harley-Davidson, desperate for cash during the Depression, sold the manufacturing rights and the engineering drawings for their old Model UL/VL side-valve V-twins to the Sankyo company that industrial techniques became better known. Harley-Davidson also provided technical advice, helped to set up production lines, and generally put their Japanese customer on the road to success. The resulting motor cycle was called the Rikuo, or King of the Road.

Not unnaturally, the Rikuo factory became a reference point for the still small Japanese motor cycle industry, but economic control was vested in the hands of the privileged few, and it was difficult for would-be entrepreneurs or manufacturers to enter the market.

The second war changed a lot of things in Japan. The massive loss of face and the American occupation and administration (which ensured that competitive capitalism had free rein) helped to fuel an explosion of industrial expansion. At one time there were over one hundred motor cycle manufacturers or assemblers. By now the Japanese industrialists knew how to do it very well, and they lost no time in doing it! Certainly they copied European and American designs to start with, whether motor cycles, cars or consumer goods, but this phase was very soon left behind as they learned the lessons of the occident and added their own brand of oriental pragmatism.

Although it is a frequently heard complaint that the Japanese motor cycle industry destroyed the British industry by copying it, a closer examination of the most successful factories shows that they actually copied German and Italian designs. The DKW lightweight (also ripped off for BSA's Bantam), the NSU Max and Quickly, and the Adler two-stroke twin all formed patterns for successful models from Suzuki and Yamaha. Honda's concentration on four-strokes led more naturally to Italy—look at those squared-off engines and see if they recall anything else—but NSU design principles also had an important influence. German thoroughness and engineering values undoubtedly paved the way for the Japanese reputation for reliability.

Kawasaki may have taken over the BSA A10-inspired Meguro vertical twin (though it was radically reworked internally) but they soon moved on to two-stroke triples—shades of DKW again. A photograph published in the Japanese magazine *Motorcyclist*, illustrating an article on the development of the Kawasaki Z1, showed a more than passing similarity between that model's prototype and MV Agusta. In the same way, Honda four-cylinder design owed a considerable debt to Italian racers like the Benelli and Gilera fours (a debt which Benelli has since reclaimed by copying the Honda sohc engine for its own fours). Marques such as Cabton, which had copied British singles, tended not to survive the hectic evolutionary period of the Japanese industry. This comment is made without prejudice to the British single, but perhaps it does tell us something.

But the copies, whatever they were based on, were only a starting point. Japanese engineers and designers soon acquired the expertise needed to make a good motor cycle (apart, perhaps, from chassis skills, though even that is no longer true). At the end of the '50s they were given a chance to show their abilities and the results were the Suzuki Colleda, the Yamaha YD1, the Honda CB72 and, somewhat later, the Kawasaki A1.

These machines, when they reached Europe, offered both performance and refinement at a reasonable price. Not unnaturally youngsters bought them in large numbers for by comparison machines like the BSA C15, Triumph Tiger Cub and even the relatively new Ariel Arrow, seemed slow and rough. The British 250 cc learner restriction introduced in 1961 virtually handed the youth market to the Japanese on a plate. Given the choice between a CB72 or YDS1 and a ploddy old Francis-Barnett or James Superswift there was little doubt as to which was the most exciting, reliable and well-equipped machine—and it wasn't the British one. The only area where British expertise excelled was in roadholding and handling, but a novice is not necessarily going to appreciate being able to take a corner with more finesse when one bike is 20 mph faster than the other in a straight line.

The British motor cycle industry even gave up trying to compete seriously. There was not much profit for them in small bikes (despite the fact that the entire Japanese industry relied on mass sales of small motor cycles to people who welcomed them as a revolution in personal transport), and in any case the Japs would never make a big bike because they had never yet made one, and furthermore wasn't it a good idea for them to provide little bikes to get youngsters hooked on motor cycling so that they would then buy bigger British bikes?

Such a stupid, arrogant attitude is hard to credit, but it was the official line. What's more, it was firmly pushed by Edward Turner, who was in a position to know better. He had visited Japan and in his report on the major factories he had drawn attention to the new and advanced machine tools installed in these factories, and on the Japanese skill at production engineering which enabled them to turn out very fine tolerance work at a much greater rate than was possible at Meriden, Plumstead or anywhere else in the UK.

Early in 1960 Geoff Duke went to Japan and he reported back to *Motor Cycling* in a series of articles which, in retrospect, contain a host of insights to the future. The third report recounts a visit to the Honda factory or rather factories, for, 'this huge concern . . . relies upon two Tokyo factories, one for production, the other for research, built seven years ago. There is also a one-year-old windowless air conditioned unit at Hamamatsu . . . they are at present building a factory nearly 300 miles from Tokyo. They have chosen the site because of its suitability for export . . .'.

Just a few years later the exports were flowing strongly, and smear stories started to circulate. These centred on the supposed exploitation of the Japanese workforce (how else could they sell the bikes for so little?), a typical one being that workers were paid one bowl of rice a day for their labours. Needless to say the stories were not true, and Japanese workers, though living in a very different social structure, enjoyed many benefits which British employees might have appreciated, and the country as a whole had an increasingly high standard of living.

Edward Turner's theory of the Japanese building only small bikes was dealt something of a bodyblow in 1965 when the CB450 'Black Bomber' was introduced. At a time when the biggest British production machines were Royal Enfield or Norton 750s, the 450 was big indeed. And the final blow to the myth came in 1968 when the single overhead cam CB750 was shown to an astonished world. It was the first four-cylinder motor cycle to be truly mass produced, and its attractions proved irresistible. It smashed open the door to the lucrative American market, mopped up the British gravy and set the Japanese motor cycle on a course from which it has not deviated.

A final twist, and one that is producing some profit for exporters in this country, is the increasing interest in Japan in all things old. The dynamics of consumerism predicate a permanent and increasing demand for goods, and as a result there are very few industrial artefacts of any age in Japan. Last year's model is junk, so 'bin it' and buy a new one. However, as is the way of things, people do not always conform to the requirements of the economy and a certain chic is now attached to things that are really (ie, perhaps ten years!) old. Modern Yamaha or Honda singles are customized to replicate British or Italian models of the 1960s.

There is at least one businessman making a living out of exporting to Japan the sort of radiogram or record player which we junked when Pioneer and the other electronics companies offered real hi-fi at an affordable price. Similarly, there is a thriving trade in old motor cycles, and Japanese buyers are now a common sight at the major British auctions. The bikes do not have to be prestigious models and it is not vital that they are British, provided they are 'old' and 'foreign'. However, early Japanese machines are also attracting a following in their native land, where there is a large YD club for the Yamaha twins, and a 'Pioneer Run' for post-war machines. Members of the (British) Vintage Japanese Motorcycle Club and others had better grab any relics they can find here before they disappear back to the 'Land of the Rising Sun'.

Honda

The biggest manufacturer of motor cycles in the world today is that founded in 1948 by Soichiro Honda, whose career as an engineer started in pre-war years as a producer of piston rings. During the 1950s British manufacturers were still dominant but with cars becoming cheaper and motor cycles, by comparison, more expensive the market for two-wheelers was gradually being eroded.

Honda recognized the big gap that existed in the market for the small commuting bike which was easy to start, cheap to run and fast, without any of the messiness and vibration associated with bigger machines. In time, the Japanese manufacturers would also remove the stigma attached to electric starters and flashing indicators, components which are now considered essential by most people.

Developing a small engine which would run reliably was not an easy task and several manufacturers had tried, and failed, in this pursuit. Honda's involvement began in 1946 with the founding of his Technical Research Institute in Hamamatsu, rather a grand-sounding name for what was little more than a wooden shed with a handful of employees. Stocks of war surplus engines were bought, modified and fitted into ordinary bicycle frames with belt drive to the rear wheel and the fuel tank strapped on top of the crossbar.

Before long the supply had run out and Honda began building engines of their own. The first of these was little more than a copy of the army units. It had a capacity of 50 cc, developed just 1 bhp at 5,000 rpm, and was called the Model A, although its popular name was 'the chimney' because of the foul exhaust fumes it produced. It should, in all fairness, be explained that Honda's petrol substitute (petrol liberally eked out with turpentine) was much to blame for this along with twenty minutes or so of hard pedalling that was necessary for getting the engine warmed up. A later variant of the Model A, still with the same crude engine and archaic belt-drive transmission, had a much stronger, sturdier frame fitted with rocking girder front forks. It wasn't until 1948 that the Honda Motor Company was founded. The new model on offer, the Model C, was powered by a bored out version of the A engine which now had a capacity of 89 cc, developing 3 bhp at 3,000 rpm.

As the country regained its industrial strength, so the number of motor cycle manufacturers in Japan grew. All used either proprietary engines or frames or both: Honda were the first to build a complete motor cycle themselves. This was the Model D, or Dream, powered by a 98 cc two-stroke engine with square dimensions of 50 mm, a two-speed gearbox and chain final drive. The substantial frame had telescopic front forks but no rear suspension and drum brakes were fitted front and rear.

A few ups and downs were experienced over the next few years, exacerbated by the economic instability of Japan as a whole, but by the mid '50s sales had risen to an enormous level. This was encouraged by the comprehensive network of dealers and service depots which the company set up throughout the country. By this time Honda had added their first four-stroke to the range—a 146 cc single with overhead valves. The Model E was equally antiquated, by contemporary European standards, as the Model D, and was not without its faults, like poor handling and heavy oil consumption: nevertheless it was a huge commercial success.

The first of the Benly (meaning 'convenience) four-stroke models, the J, was introduced in 1953. This was an 89 cc ohv single-cylinder motor with an in-unit three-speed gearbox and an infinitely more sophisticated machine than its predecessors with its pressed-steel frame and telescopic front forks. Over the next few years, many versions of the Benly and the Dream, incorporating such refinements as swinging arm rear suspension, were produced with engines of up to 350 cc. But the greatest milestone of those busy years was marked by the arrival of the C100 Super Cub in 1958. Recognizing the need for an inexpensive, reliable, lightweight form of two-wheeled transport, Honda designed a machine that appealed to the young and old of

The C100 Super Cub, first and most successful of the step-throughs. This is a 1960 model on display at the Geneva Show.

Edward Turner's myth of the Japanese not knowing how to build big bikes was shattered by the CB450 Black Bomber, an epoch-making motor cycle if ever there was one. It was introduced in 1965 and lasted until the end of 1972. This model was tested in 1968.

both sexes by combining all the better characteristics of the moped and the scooter. The end result was what has commonly become known as the step-through, or scooterette, and without a doubt the most popular two-wheeler of all time.

The Honda Motor Company were now financially secure enough to set their sights on the outside world and on the more glamorous end of the motor cycle market. In 1959, after several years of studying what the Europeans were up to, Honda entered five machines in the Isle of Man TT. Based on the NSU 250, these were 125 cc parallel twins; the cylinders were inclined forward and each had four valves operated by twin overhead camshafts, a format which Honda used on all subsequent racing models and one which became the norm with other manufacturers of racing machines. Although the performance of the individual riders was not terribly exciting, they did win the team award and by 1961, after being dismissed so recently as a bit of a joke, Honda were winning most of the road racing titles in Europe with riders like Mike Hailwood, Tom Phillis and Jim Redman in the saddle. Their commercial success in Europe is now a matter of history.

Suzuki

Michio Suzuki, a successful spinning-loom manufacturer, built his first prototype motor cycle engine in 1937 but the war intervened and it wasn't until 1952 that the first production unit was made. Called the Power Free, Suzuki's proprietary engine was a 36 cc two-stroke single which could be clipped on to an ordinary bicycle. It was a popular unit, especially as the transmission system allowed the rider to pedal the bicycle along should the engine fail. The Suzuki company worked fast and furiously, even at this early stage, and within a few months an updated, 50 cc model was introduced, quickly followed by the 60 cc Diamond Free. The logo used was SJK, standing for Suzuki Jidosha Kogyo (Suzuki Automotive Industries) and 1954 saw the initials emblazoned on the petrol tank of their first complete motor cycle, the Colleda.

In the same year, the company changed its name to the Suzuki Motor Company Limited and the CO, with its powerful single-cylinder engine, was an instant success. Rejecting the two-stroke cycle as unreliable, Suzuki designed an entirely new engine based on the four-stroke principle and with a capacity of 90 cc developing 4 bhp at 5,000 rpm. It had an in-unit three-speed gearbox, telescopic front forks, plunger rear suspension and a choice of frames: a sturdy pressed-steel item for the tourer and a slightly more expensive tubular component for sports use.

By 1962 the Suzuki Colleda twin had evolved into the 250TB Twinace. It had a 'dynamo starter' (said the adverts) and a hydraulically actuated rear brake.

The T10 continued the 250 cc theme, though at 21 bhp/8,000 rpm it was slightly more powerful than the Twinace.

Bored out to 125 cc, the COX Colleda appeared as a more powerful alternative in the following year. But before long a completely new model, the two-stroke single-cylinder ST, was launched and for the next couple of decades Suzuki abandoned the construction of four-stroke engines completely. Better suspension and an improved lighting system were only two of the improvements incorporated in the new model: the ST engine presented a major challenge to Yamaha, the self-appointed two-stroke specialists of the day. With a capacity of 123 cc and bore and stroke of 52 mm × 58 mm, the ST engine was built in unit with the three-speed gearbox and mounted in an improved plunger frame.

The first twin in the Suzuki range appeared in 1956. This was a competition machine based on the Colleda and was powered by a 250 cc engine with in-unit four-speed gearbox and chain final drive. The Colleda TT was a high-performance motor cycle, the forerunner of a number of Suzuki models that were to dominate the TT in years to come, and with a top speed of over 80 mph. It had a pressed-steel spine frame, pivoted fork rear suspension and Earles type leading-link front forks: another unusual feature was the pair of indicators on stalks, fitted front and rear.

Like the Honda company with its Super Cub, Suzuki laid down the foundations for a secure future when they introduced their Suzumoped in 1958. The power source for this 'everyman' type of machine was the Mini-Free, a well-established 50 cc two-stroke unit which Suzuki had produced since 1954. It was mounted in a pressed-steel spine frame and, although transmission was initially by belt, this was soon changed to the more efficient chain drive. Suzuki are famous for more than just the manufacture of high-performance and commuter bikes: their range of products also includes cars, trucks, outboard motors and snowcats.

Yamaha

The history of the Yamaha motor cycle company stems back to the feudalistic days of pre-industrial Japan when Tarakusu Yamaha started work as an apprentice clockmaker and repairer of medical equipment. He was called on to repair an American reed organ and was so inspired by the instrument that he built a copy for himself. In time this led to the formation of the Yamaha Musical Instrument Company (hence the familiar logo with the three crossed tuning forks), and, in collaboration with a number of other businessmen, the founder developed his business into the biggest of its kind in the world.

During World War 2, Yahama was taken into military control and produced aeroplane components. By the early 1950s, with Japan's economic recovery well under way, it was felt at Yamaha that a new line of production should be pursued. Of the products considered—sewing machines, scooters, three-wheelers—the president of the company, Genichi Kawakami, decided on motor cycles, despite the fact that, by now, there were nearly fifty such manufacturers in Japan alone, not to mention the stiff competition posed by the older marques in Europe and America.

As was the practice in post-war Japan, Yahama selected several western models to study and emulate. The 125 cc capacity and the simplicity of the two-stroke cycle were considered particularly appealing and for this reason their final choice was an obvious one—the DKW RT125, the same model which BSA requisitioned and turned into the popular little Bantam. Yamaha's version of the two-stroke, the YA1, was almost identical to the German original, save for a few improvements which included a four-, rather than three-speed gearbox, and gear, instead of chain, primary drive. The aluminium alloy cylinder head was bolted to a cast-iron cylinder with twin transfer ports and a silicon alloy piston. Carburation was by means of a 20 mm Amal and the cradle-type frame was fitted with undamped telescopic front forks and plunger rear suspension. The rather bulky-looking styling was quite different from the DKW and the finish, in dark maroon and white, gave the YA1 its appealing nickname, the Red Dragonfly.

After rigorous testing, with over 10,000 km of reliable operation, the Dragonfly was considered fit for launching in 1954. Sales were so encouraging that a new and separate company (separate, that is, from the musical instrument side of the business) was set up in Hamamatsu. Racing successes at Mount Fuji and Asama were followed by the introduction of the

Sports models gained an S in the model specification, leading to the famous YDS-series, of which this is the YDS3—a machine which excited a lot of young riders in 1965. It stopped as well—just look at that twin-leading-shoe front brake.

YA1's 127 cc variant, the YB1 and, in 1956, the YC1, a 175 cc model based on the DKW RT of the same capacity and capable of 10 bhp at 5,000 rpm.

Attention, quite naturally, turned to the 250 cc category. This time, humiliated by Kawakami's repeated instructions to copy other manufacturers' machines, the Yamaha design team boldly demanded the opportunity to design their own motor cycle. The result was Yamaha's first twin, the YD1, which had cast-iron cylinders and vertically-split crankcases with a cast-in inlet tract. Developing 14 bhp at 6,000 rpm, the engine was suspended, by means of twin mounting lugs, from the pressed-steel frame and undamped telescopic shock absorbers were fitted front and rear.

The YD1 was an unexciting machine but a good workhorse with plenty of torque and a popular vehicle with tradesmen and families alike. Furthermore, it sold in sufficiently large numbers to enable the Yamaha motor cycle concern to expand and buy up several of its rival companies. A 20 bhp racing version was produced and won the Mount Asama race in 1957, establishing the two-stroke twin as Yamaha's special forte over other Japanese makes.

The next three years was a period of rapid production and saw the introduction in 1959 of the YDS1, the first true sports model offered by a Japanese manufacturer; kits were also available for converting the twin to road racing and motocross use. Following a brief period of economic recession, Yamaha, like all the other big motor cycle companies in Japan, sought to increase its exports market and updated versions of the YDS sports models were launched on to the US and UK markets. Despite the YDS2's numerous faults, the motor cycling press gave the 250 ecstatic write-ups and from then on, Yamaha's world sales went from strength to strength.

Kawasaki

Of the four Japanese giants, Kawasaki is the youngest motor cycle manufacturer by several years. Nevertheless its impact on the two-wheel world has been enormous.

During the early years of motor cycle production at the Kobe-based factory, Kawasaki was better known for its fighter planes than anything else. In fact, the name goes back to 1878 when Shozo Kawasaki founded a dockyard at Tsukiji in Tokyo. By the turn of the century the business was expanding at a fantastic rate to include a large number of manufacturing interests. These ranged from bridge trusses and boats to locomotives and railway coaches, yet despite its industrial importance Kawasaki Heavy Industries was not a household name and in the early 1950s it was decided that this should change. The aircraft side of the business was prosperous enough, producing aeroplane engines and fuselage components, but for some time it had been seeking new territory. What better then, than to extend its engineering expertise to the construction of proprietary motor cycle engines?

The first of these were 58 cc two-strokes, later followed by 148 cc ohv singles, which were supplied to a number of Japanese motor cycle manu-

The Kawasaki Z1 900 cc four was first seen in 1972 (and is collectable itself) but the venerable 650 was retained for a while after that. This 650-RS is a 1973 model.

Kawasaki's name is inextricably linked with high performance machinery, and if one model established that more than any other it was the 500 cc two-stroke triple Mach III H1 of 1969. At the time it was the fastest production machine in the world, and it soon spawned both 750 cc and 250 cc variants. A good early H1 is hard to find, but worth seeking out.

facturers under various brand names. One of these was their own subsidiary company, Kawasaki Meihatsu Heavy Industries, where fairly conventional utility machines, with pressed-steel spine frames and leading-link front forks, were built.

The first motor cycle to be launched under the Kawasaki banner was a single-cylinder 123 cc, two-stroke which developed 8 bhp at 6,500 rpm. It was also at this time that Kawasaki joined forces with the Meguro Manufacturing Company, the oldest motor cycle manufacturer in Japan, and began to experience financial difficulties. The agreement between the two companies gave Kawasaki the marketing rights to Meguro's ohv twins which they sold through their outlets in Japan and South East Asia.

Kawasaki's own motor cycle, the 123 cc two-stroke, was not a success but a later version, the solid B8, using the same engine suspended in a pressed-steel spine frame, sold well. The 49 cc M5 step-through moped was another commercial success at this time. However, realizing that competition from other Japanese manufacturers was strong, and that Honda, in particular, had made a secure niche for itself in the small-capacity, commuter end of the market, Kawasaki determined to make its mark with sporting machines instead. Racing and motocross versions of the B8 were produced and several works-prepared B8M machines were entered in the Japanese Motocross Championships in 1963. Kawasaki took the first six places and over the next few years the B8M achieved victories in a remarkable number of events.

Kawasaki's involvement in road racing began in 1965 with the A1R, an air-cooled twin-cylinder two-stroke based on the 246 cc road machine of the previous year called the Samurai. The 125 cc engine had disc inlet valves and a five-speed gearbox housed in a duplex frame with swinging arm rear suspension and telescopic front forks. The A1R made its debut at the Japanese Grand Prix of that year, with disappointing results but, in 1969, British rider Dave Simmonds won the World Championship on his 125 cc Kwacker and within a few short years Kawasaki's 'Green Meanies' were dominating the road racing scene all over the globe.

Chapter 11

America's big three

In February 1985 the American magazine *Cycle* published an American Memorial—a list of 143 motor cycle manufacturers 'long on history, short on survivors'. Most of the makes did not survive the Depression of the '30s, but a surprising number never got even that far. Why? The reasons lie in a man's name, a car and an industrial technique. The man was Henry Ford: the car the Model T; and the technique, mass production. In 1909 a Model T cost $850; in 1918 it cost $400. What motor cycle and sidecar could hope to compete with a cheap four-wheeler capable of carrying four or five people in considerable comfort? Even relative petrol consumption did not matter greatly, for in those days gasoline was very cheap and, thanks to Henry Ford again, wages rising. And Ford was not the only producer of cheap cars, for Chevrolet and Star soon followed his example.

Within that framework, it is not surprising to find the golden age of motorcycling in America squeezed between 1906 and 1918. Flying Merkel, with their 'cantilever' sprung frame, Cyclone with an overhead camshaft

One of the first American fours, The Pierce, made by the automobile firm. This one dates from 1909.

racer, the eight-valve Indians and Harley-Davidsons, four-cylinder models from Militaire, Pierce and Henderson—all these machines point to the technical advances which were made by American manufacturers in the early part of the century.

In 1916 *Motor Cycling* could say 'No event in history since the advent of the motor cycle has given a greater impetus to the industry in America than has the war in Europe'. It went on to say that this was not simply due to motor cycles being seen to be useful in wartime conditons, but to the general stimulation of the economy that a war provides. Munitions were required, inflation was fuelled, and the result was that more people had more money to spend—on motor cycles, the paper imagined. In addition, the campaign in Mexico against Pancho Villa, undertaken by General Pershing at, it was said, the Mexican government's request, gave proof positive of the utility of motor cycles not on some distant front, but on the USA's own border. The US Army was equipped with only three makes though, Indian, Harley-Davidson and some Excelsiors: the Big Three.

In that same year which *Motor Cyling* found so encouraging, Pope, Merkel, Thor, Dayton, Minneapolis, Feilbach, Flanders, Yale, Iver-Johnson and Schickel were either finished or on the way out. Reading Standard and Emblem survived in a small way, but neither lasted beyond 1925, so it would appear that the final sentence of *Motor Cycling*'s piece was the most prophetic, 'If the present conditions remain unchanged, the greatest fear of the American motor cycle industry is that if the prosperity of the country continues, the demand for automobiles will supersede the demand for motor cycles'.

People within the industry were not unaware of the problems surrounding them, and when Norman Shidle, editor of *Automotive Industries*, pub-

Another firm lost to motor cycling early on was Yale, one of whose 1909 models is seen here.

lished a series of articles on the importance to the car manufacturers of proper marketing and planning, more than one bike factory's publicity manager was interested in applying the same technique to motor cycles. Employees of Indian, Harley-Davidson, Reading Standard and Excelsior all contacted Shidle independently, and after some prevarication they established an informal working party. Harry Sucher summarizes their conclusions in his book, *Harley-Davidson: The Milwaukee Marvel*: ''They concluded that the industry's emphasis on the heavyweight V-twin models, together with extensive commitments to racing, had alienated the majority of potential American transportation buyers. The typical American motor cycle had grown progressively heavier, was consequently difficult to manhandle in a confined space, required much muscular energy to start, possessed an offensively loud exhaust note, and appealed almost exclusively to athletic young men whose interest was very likely to diminish with advancing age . . . the further conclusion was that a potentially vast market for low-powered low-cost utility machines, originally the target of the turn-of-the-century experimenters seeking to offer low cost transportation, had been totally ignored'. There are lessons to be learned there, even today.

The report did not change things (except that Harley-Davidson's publicity manager lost his job when he revealed what he had done), for in a November 1929 edition of *The Motor Cycle*, Herber (Bert) Le Vack, the famous Brooklands racer, recounted some of his impressions from 'Across The Pond'. 'The motor cycle', Bert reported, 'is only used by two classes of rider—the clubman and the "cop". One hardly ever sees the former riding in the city or to work, or using his machine as our boys do here. They ride mainly on club runs, long distance vacation trips, and to hill-climbs. They think nothing of riding 500 or more miles to these events . . .' and that is why they wanted large, lazy, comfortable and smooth motor cycles—like the Henderson or Indian fours. The evolution of the highway system also played a part in defining the type of bike required. Long straight roads with few tight bends or twisty sections did not make great demands on roadholding or steering, and while the torquey V-twins made travelling comfortable and lazy, it was almost luxurious on a four.

In the end, of course, they didn't even get those, and what is more, they started to buy British singles and twins which Le Vack said would never catch on. But they were bought as sports machines, and in the '40s and '50s American motor cycling appears to have split into two very separate camps. On the one hand we have the 'full dress' brigade who liked to buy every accessory on the market and add it to an already heavy machine. These people were greatly encouraged by factories (particularly Harley-Davidson) and dealers, both of whom made a nice profit out of the trade. Then on the other hand there were the outlaws and would-be outlaws who wanted a stripped down, lean, fast-looking machine. These people were not at first encouraged by any factory—indeed most Harley agents refused to work on such machines, which did wonders for the back street trade. Eventually, however, Harley-Davidson realized that it was missing out on a sizeable sector of the shrinking market, and started to offer factory customs.

Motor cycling in America has, on the whole, remained a hobby, pastime or sport. To refer to *Cycle* again, its avowed dedication is not to motor cyclists but to people who are passionate about motor cycles. Collectors in Britain seeking an American machine are most likely to come across one of the 500 cc Indians or 750 cc Harleys brought over for military use during the war (the 741 or WLA, respectively). There are others about, of course, for both of those makes were imported into this country from early days, and in later years Harley-Davidson retained a variety of concessionaires. Perhaps the most genuinely enthusiastic of these (the present importer excepted) was F. H. Warr. Fred Warr generally keeps a selection of classic Harleys in stock and his knowledge would make a visit worthwhile. Otherwise there seems to be a strong but informal Harley and Indian network, and once you find a 'member' you will be well on the way to finding a bike. Of course, you could always fly over to the States, find the motor cycle of your dreams and ship it back—some keen types have done just that.

Indian
Indian did not invent the V-twin, but by 1914 they could claim it as their own. A phenomenal expansion in the formative years of the company pro-

A very early Indian (circa 1908) at a motor cycle gathering. Faded writing on the reverse suggests that the two men are Hendee and Hedström.

vided it with a fund of capital and a reputation which would see it through the next three decades.

The business began with one of those fortuitous meetings between a businessman and an engineer who shared a common view. The businessman was George M. Hendee, a keen cyclist: so keen, in fact, that he was Amateur High Wheel champion of Arizona from 1886 to 1892, when he switched to the safety bicycle. He was also a manufacturer of cycles, and his sense of perfection was offended by the unreliability of the motorized bicycles used as pace machines in velocipede races. He began to look for a good one.

When he found it, he also found its builder, Oscar Hedström. Hedström began his career with an apprenticeship in a watch case factory where he learned to use machine tools, pattern making and foundry skills and some rudimentary metallurgy. When he got hold of a de Dion engine, he was quick to improve it and fit it into his pacing tandem.

Together Hendee and Hedström founded the Hendee Manufacturing Company in Springfield, Massachusetts, and Oscar set to work on developing a motor cycle. In 1901 it appeared, a dark blue 1¾ hp machine called the Indian, a name calculated to conjure up images of America's pioneering spirit. It had two really significant features—the transmission, which was all chain, and Hedström's own design of spray carburettor, in which the float bowl was concentric with the main jet. One cable only controlled the carb, unlike most designs of the time which required at least two for separate functions, and this made riding the Indian extremely simple.

Hendee was a good businessman, and he set about establishing the machine's reputation by entering it in reliability trials and the like. He also sent many abroad to stimulate exports. By 1903 the make was well known almost everywhere, and in 1906 the single cylinder model was enlarged to 2¼ hp. More significantly, a 3½ hp 42-degree V-twin was offered for the first time.

This new model soon proved itself, for in England the ACU 1,000 Miles Reliability Trial (later known as the International Six Days Trial) was won in 1907 by American rider Teddy Hastings on an Indian twin. He repeated his success the following year, and one of the spectators was so impressed that he immediately applied to become the official Indian importer for the United Kingdom. Hendee agreed and William H. Wells began his long association with the company.

Technical improvements continued, and of the five models offered in 1908, two had the option of mechanically operated inlet valves. The following year another landmark was achieved when G. Lee Evans came second in the Isle of Man TT, behind Harry Collier on a Matchless. A feature of the racing machine was a new loop frame (in place of the old fashioned diamond) and in 1910 this was augmented with a new, and long lived, front fork. Basically a trailing link design, it was controlled by a quarter-elliptic leaf spring which projected forwards from the steering head area. In

By 1914 Indians had gained a new type of front fork, which with the rear springing made for a comfortable ride.

addition, the standard colour was now red and a two-speed gearbox became available on the 4 hp single and 7 hp twin.

The full significance of this development came home in 1911, which was the year that the TT was run over the Isle of Man mountain circuit for the first time, and also the first time that it was divided into Senior and Junior classes. Indian entered a works team of four riders, and scored a remarkable hat trick, with Oliver Godfrey coming in first (ahead of Charlie Collier, who was later disqualified for making an unofficial fuel stop), Charles Franklin second and A. J. Moorhouse third. Jake de Rozier, Indian's own crack rider (the others were selected by Billy Wells), finished amongst the tail enders.

Meanwhile, back in the States, the Indian name was kept to the forefront by riders like Cannonball Baker, with his record-breaking long-distance runs, and oddly enough, by the Mexican revolutionary Pancho Villa. The Mexican insurrection of 1915 and 1916 spilled over the borders into the USA after Villa raided some American townships, and it was the first opportunity that the Army had had to assess the usefulness of motorized transport in combat conditions. Needless to say, the armed forces were impressed and the popularity of all motor vehicles soared: if it was good enough for the US Army, it was good enough for everyone.

The vintage period was a fruitful time for the company, which produced many famous models during this time. First of the very well known and well remembered examples was the Powerplus of 1916. Designed by Charles Gustafson, it was an advance on Hedström's original, being a 7 hp (750 cc) side valve (rather than inlet over exhaust type). *Motor Cycling* tested the first

Before the Powerplus was called Standard there was this Hedström-designed twin.

one in this country, and found it smooth, powerful and flexible. The three-speed gearbox was particularly praised. Cannonball Baker set more records on it, and by 1920 it had become so popular that it was called the Indian Standard model. Doubtless the extensive use of Indians by the US Army during the Great War—over 41,000 were supplied—helped to popularize them further, though the company did not make much money from official contracts, if any.

After the war no time was lost in introducing another enduring model, the Scout. This was a middleweight 600 cc V-twin intended to attract a completely new class of customer—people who wanted something more substantial than a lightweight but who were not prepared to wrestle with the thumping great 7 hp twins. It was a classic case of finding and filling a gap in the market. It was bought in large numbers by the authorities, and soon the speed merchants were clamouring for a faster version—perhaps to get away from the Highway Patrols! Indian responded by giving them the Chief, a 1,000 cc version of the Scout, then in 1924 the old Standard Powerplus was phased out in favour of the Big Chief, displacing 1,200 cc. Further technical improvements saw the adoption of Ricardo-type detachable cylinder heads on the Scout, the Chief and the new, small, single-cylinder Prince.

With a single and various twins, Indian needed only a four to round off the model range, and in 1927 they got one by taking over the Ace concern. Ace had a rather involved history, but the four was a Henderson design (Henderson the man, not Henderson the factory) and thoroughly dependable. Marketed at first as the Indian Ace—'The Collegiate Four'—it soon became just the Indian Four. In the same year a 45 cu in (750 cc) variant of the Scout was launched to compete with the new Excelsior 45, and shortly afterwards the 750 cc Chief was dropped.

Top of the range in 1927 was the Indian Ace Four.

In 1928 came what Harry Sucher, in his remarkably thorough history of Indian, *The Iron Redskin*, calls 'probably the best all-round machine of its time'. It was the new Scout, Model 101, and its major feature was a redesigned frame with a lower seating position. It also had a front brake,

The Four remained in production until 1940—this is a 1932, 1,200 cc model.

unlike the original model. With good performance and handling to match, the new machine soon caught on and rapidly became a racers' favourite, for it was easy to strip down and tune.

Although a 600 cc version was available, the big Scout was by far the most popular and the smaller machine was dropped in 1930. At the same time the Indian Motoplane and the Pony (later Junior) Scout were introduced. The Motoplane featured a dry sump 750 cc Scout motor in a light Prince frame, while the Pony was a 500 cc version. The dry sump theme was continued in the Sport Scout, a new-for-1934 model designed to appeal to the fast rider. To increase its appeal further, new cylinders and high compression cylinder heads, both made in light alloy, were offered for the following season. The same parts could be fitted to the Chief.

Thus the Indian Motor cycle Company, as it was now called after various takeovers, made its way through what Harry Sucher characterizes as The Great Decline. During the Second World War Indians were again used by the forces—including the British—in some numbers, but the company was on the wane. After the war it continued with the big V-twin for a time, but turned to a new type of parallel twin, the design of which turned out to be disastrously weak. The Warrior proved to be the company's downfall, and the name was sold to Brockhouse Engineering of Southport, Lancs who produced various lightweights bearing the once proud Indian motif. It has since crossed back to its native land.

Excelsior, Henderson and Ace

Ignatz Schwinn, manufacturer of safety bicycles, was looking to expand into motor cycles. He found a design by Walther Heckscher, a 500 cc de Dion-type engine in a heavy frame with leading link forks and belt drive: it was enough. In 1907 the first Excelsior was produced. It was refined and developed, and in 1910 an 800 cc V-twin was made, featuring mechanically-operated valves. It was enlarged to 1,000 cc, became a handy racing tool, and in December 1930 Lee Humiston became the first American officially to break the 100 mph barrier, which he did on a board track near Los Angeles.

Though the basic machine remained the same, the specification was updated to incorporate a three-speed gearbox and chain drive, and then a Scots immigrant, Jock McNeil, developed the Big Valve motor. At 2⅛ inches, they certainly were big, but they worked well enough to become a standard fitting. The Excelsior continued its competition and long-distance record successes, and for a brief period an overhead camshaft model was produced.

The twins took a back seat in 1917, for Schwinn then bought the Henderson concern, and started to make the Henderson Four. The Four proved more popular and production of the twins was cut back until 1924, when the 45 cu in (750 cc) Super-X took the world by surprise. That is to say, it took

The Excelsior twin as it appeared in 1911.

Harley-Davidson and Indian by surprise, although the former factory had let this very design slip through its fingers, for Arthur Constantine, the designer, had worked for Harley until they rejected his idea out of hand. Constantine resigned and took his drawings to Excelsior, who saw the potential of this unit construction, three-speed model and promptly put it into production, to their profit. A 1,000 cc version was developed from the Super-X, which brought about the demise of the original twin.

The Four has a slightly more convoluted history. Inspired by the FN Four, William Henderson designed his version of the four-cylinder motor cycle in 1910 and, with his brother Thomas, began to manufacture and sell it in some quantity. It was an immediate success, and the model developed over the years with improvements to the brakes, forks, frame and the addition of a two-speed hub gear.

In 1917 the engine was revamped, with an uprated lubrication system, three-speed gearbox and a stronger clutch. At the same time Ignatz Schwinn made an offer which the Henderson brothers could not refuse, and manufacture was transferred to the Excelsior factory. The model continued unchanged, save for an alteration to the petrol tank transfer, which incorporated the large X of Excelsior. The Four found much success with record-breaking long-distance runs, but the engine design was reaching the end of its useful life. The idea that this could be so caused a rift between the Hendersons and Schwinn, and the former left for pastures new.

Design of the new Henderson Four was entrusted to Arthur Lemon, an original Henderson employee. When launched the new model was called the K, and its main feature was positive lubrication of the main bearings, which was a first in motor cycle engineering. Fast and reliable, the K broke

Second incarnation of the Excelsior-built Henderson Four was the Model K, with an Arthur Lemon-designed motor.

many records in the capable hands of Wells Bennett. Over the years both comfort and performance were improved, culminating in 1928 with Ricardo cylinder heads to squeeze the final ounce of horsepower out of the motor.

By 1928 Arthur Lemon had left, but Excelsior had Arthur Constantine, who laid out a new four. The cylinder head configuration reverted to inlet over exhaust valves, as on William Henderson's original, but there were now five main bearings and an extremely sturdy construction throughout. Introduced as the KJ in 1929, it was soon followed by the more powerful KL.

However, the new model had a very short run, for Ignatz Schwinn brought all motor cycle production to a sudden halt in 1931. Some say he feared the worsening economic situation; others that a batch of poor quality electrical equipment fitted to Fours supplied to the Police led to too many repair claims. For whatever reason, the end of Excelsior/Henderson coincided with the end of the motor cycle as a serious force in the American transport scene.

When William Henderson left Excelsior, he immediately designed the Ace Four which, it has to be said, was technically very similar to his previous engine, though no parts were actually interchangeable. Features included the use of three main bearings, splash lubrication and a three-speed gearbox. Cannonball Baker was hired, in 1921, to break the transcontinental record which he duly did—the record had previously been held by Henderson. Disaster struck Ace in December 1922, when Henderson was killed in an accident while testing a new model, but Arthur Lemon was taken on as chief engineer. Told to produce the world's fastest motor cycle regardless of cost, Lemon built two experimental machines, one of them an extremely light special. The company found a great deal of success in hill-

William Henderson, on leaving Excelsior/Henderson, designed the Ace, which later became the Indian.

climbs using these bikes, and Red Wolverton set an unofficial world speed record of 129.61 mph.

Unfortunately, soon after that the company's financial burdens proved too great (each machine had been sold at a $50 loss due to inaccurate costing), and Michigan Motors of Detroit bought the whole concern. Arthur Lemon was retained, and asked to carry on the competition side, but he soon discovered that between the competition successes of 1923 and the new organization and recommencement of production in 1925, the opposition had caught up. Lemon had to do a lot of development work on the engine before an Ace won again, and by the time it did Michigan Motors was itself in trouble. The marque was sold off to Indian after some hard bargaining.

Indian kept the Four in production until the USA was drawn into the Second World War. It was refined slightly over the seasons, gaining plunger rear suspension at the end of its life, but it was no real match for the more recently designed Henderson K or KJ, and despite a couple of attempts to uprate the engine, Indian had to be content with second place in the performance stakes—at least until Schwinn shut down his motor cycle operation. It was an extremely expensive machine to make and sell, and it was not reintroduced after the war.

Harley-Davidson

'There is no use getting sentimental over a motorcycle. *Especially* a motorcycle. Even if it is the motorcycle I and ten million other American men have coveted all our lives, the last big-bore, honest-to-God *motorcycle*

motorcycle made in America, and the epitome of what the motorcycle dream means. Harley-Davidson'. Richard Ford, on Harley-Davidson: in *Granta 15*, Spring 1985.

Harley-Davidson have been making motor cycles in Milaukee, Wisconsin since 1903. This must make the firm, one of the world's oldest surviving manufacturers, unique, for it is difficult to think of another which has not moved at least once. Indeed, until a few years ago the original wooden shed in which Arthur Davidson and William Harley assembled their first motor cycles survived, left in place behind the dynamometer test houses of the big factory in Juneau Avenue—until a construction worker mistook it for an old store room and smashed it to matchwood with a bull-dozer. Such is the course of history.

William Harley and Arthur Davidson were soon joined by brothers William and Walter Davidson, as their 3 hp belt drive single grew in popularity. Of rugged construction, an enduring Harley-Davidson feature, it soon grew to 4 hp and in 1909, 5 hp. By then it had become known as the Silent Gray Fellow, in recognition of its colour scheme and its efficient exhaust system. On one of these machines Walter Davidson won the first official endurance run, with a perfect score, and the very next week on the very same model, the first economy run.

Someone soon had the idea of doubling up a single, and the first V-twin was born. With two sleeved down cylinders the new machine rated 7 hp

The Silent Gray Fellow—no, not the owner, but the 1912 Harley single.

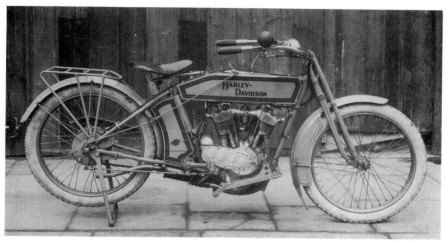

One of the first twins, an inlet-over-exhaust 7 hp model.

(1,000 cc or 61 cu in) and came with either chain or belt drive for its single-speed transmission. A two-speed hub gear followed shortly, as did a sprung seat post, for the conventional saddle offered little comfort. The new seat was given the name 'Ful-Floteing' and it played an important part in the company's advertising: 'This Harley-Davidson,' proclaimed one ad in a *Cosmopolitan Magazine* of 1912, 'Does the Work of Three Horses', and one reason why the Home Telephone Comany of Portland, Indiana expressed its unsolicited gratitude was the comfort of their new, efficient and reliable motor cycle.

With the launch in 1915 of the model J, a 1,000 cc side valve twin with three-speed transmission, the company embarked on a new phase of popularity. The racing programme, under Bill Ottaway's direction, had led to power increases in production models, giving Harleys a sporting image in place of the rather dull, plodding one held previously. Harry Ricardo, whose name crops up repeatedly in the history of American motor cycling, was called in to develop the cylinder heads, and with his help the racing model was made to give 55 bhp—a very respectable figure for the time.

After the United States entered World War 1, Harley-Davidson had, naturally, to be seen to be doing its patriotic bit and some 15,000 motor cycles were supplied to the armed forces. The management, however, did not ignore commercial chances, and when Indian committed itself almost entirely to turning out WD machines, to the detriment of the supply to civilians, Harley-Davidson were quick to make efforts to fill the vacuum. In this they had some success.

One unforeseen influence of the war was the vogue for flat twins, inspired by the fore-and-aft Douglas, which followed. Indian produced the Model

During the Second World War Harley-Davidson supplied the UK with many WLA 750s like this.

O, and Harley the 584 cc Model W Sport Twin. This proved to be a reliable machine, and successfully took several long distance records, but it never caught on in the States and its production only ran from 1919 to 1922.

A similar lifespan was enjoyed by 'The Wrecking Crew', as the works racing team soon became known. This was not because they wrecked their machines, but because they smashed the opposition almost everywhere they went. The team's demise was not due to any lack of victories, but because the management, always aware of how many pennies were going where, decided that it could no longer afford to run it.

By 1922 Harley-Davidson could claim to be the biggest producer of motor cycles in the USA, having wrested the title from Indian. Their popularity was increased by new twins with inlet over exhaust type engines in 1,000 and 1,200 cc forms. The bigger machine was particularly well thought of by bootleggers (for this was the Prohibition period) who could load up a sidecar with moonshine and still outrun the cops.

Machines of a rather different type were introduced in 1926, 350 cc singles in side or overhead valve configuration. The latter was found to be very suitable for flat track racing, and it evolved into the Peashooter, one of the most famous dirt and speedway bikes ever. With a little work by Ricardo and a weight of 215 lb the Peashooter made a reputation for itself in the States, Australia and Great Britain.

This was a prolific period for the factory, for two years later another two models were launched. One was a 500 cc side valve single very similar to the 350, the other a 750 cc side valve twin, produced in answer to Excelsior's 45, which was a great success. The Harley, however, was not as fast as the Excelsior since it shared cycle parts with the bigger twins.

The Motor Cycle of 29 August 1929 sets the scene for the next big change, 'One entirely new Harley-Davidson model, the discontinuance of the well-known 989 cc twin and big improvements to every model in the range'. The new model was a 1,200 cc side valve twin and the discontinued one was the popular Model J, first seen in 1915. Model J enthusiasts, and there were plenty of them, were not best pleased by this move, and as if to vindicate their feelings, the usurper Model VL proved rather unreliable. However, after a number of engine components had been redesigned it was found to be acceptable. Proof of its strength came in 1936, when the 1,300 cc VLH, basically an enlarged VL, went on sale. At the same time, the buddy seat was offered as an option, thus allowing riders to take their companions around with them in safety.

The year 1936 was an important one for Harley, for in June the first over-head valve twin intended for the domestic market came out. The 1,000 cc 61E was an entirely new design, with dry sump lubrication, four gears and a duplex cradle frame. Although it was fondly nicknamed the Knucklehead (from the distinctive shape of the cylinder heads) it gave considerable trouble at first, particularly with oil leaks from around the valve gear.

An interesting light is thrown on management attitudes at the factory by one incident connected with the new machine. Joe Petrali, a noted racer, was offered a bonus of $1,000 if he could reach 150 mph on the bike, and a specially streamlined model was prepared. The fairings, however, made the bike extremely unstable at high speed and it was only Petrali's great skill which saved him from being thrown off. With the streamlining removed he managed to squeeze 132 mph out of the brute, which weighed 400 lb stripped down. This constituted a new record speed but when Petrali asked Walter Davidson for half of his bonus he was refused it. Walter Davidson also refused, a little later, to supply Hollywood film studios with cheap or gratis motor cycles, on account of their financial excesses. Indian, on the other hand, managed to get a lot of screen exposure by this method. Many movie idols were enthusiastic motor cyclists, among them Clark Gable who owned several Harleys.

Still in 1936, but towards the end of it, new side valve twins appeared to replace the VL and VLH. Just to confuse matters, these were designated the UL (1,200 cc) and ULH (1,300 cc). Like the 61E (which was designated the FL or FLH) they featured dry sump lubrication. Unlike the 61E they were reliable from the outset and became a great export success. They could not maintain high speeds for long periods, however, as overheating and seizure soon set in. Speedwork was therefore left to the ohv 61E, which was soon joined by the ohv 74F (1,200 cc).

Collectors looking for Harley-Davidsons in this country are probably most likely to come across the WLA. This was a 750 cc side valve (the old DLD45) adapted for military use and supplied to the United Kingdom in the aftermath of the Coventry blitz, which flattened the Triumph factory. WLAs were also supplied to the American Army and after the war many were released on to the market at bargain prices. This suited very well the many soldiers who had been trained as motor cyclists, though it did not do much for the manufacturers.

It is by now perhaps trite to say that both world wars changed society irrevocably. One post-war phenomenon which some have traced to Service experience is that of the outlaw biker. The Harley-Davidson has become a symbol of the outlaw, despite its own respectable image, and it is interesting to follow the events that led to this association. Harry Sucher (the American motor cycle historian) dates it to July 1947, when a large club meeting of 4,000 motor cyclists at Hollister, California, was turned into a drunken riot by 500 or so outlaws. *Life* magazine used a photograph of one of these revellers on its cover, and what should he be sitting on but a stripped down UL Harley. The archetypal biker film, *The Wild One* starring Marlon Brando and Lee Marvin, was based on the Hollister episode and featured a number of Harleys, though it should be noted that Brando rode a Triumph twin. One way or another, the Harley-Davidson, stripped to its bare essentials in contrast to the ultra-respectable full dresser, had become a symbol for a section of youth culture. Looked at in a generous light, this can be seen as a rejection of the gross materialism of an older generation, but it carried with it another form of grossness—that of behaviour.

The Knucklehead motor had never really managed to keep all of its oil in the top end, and in 1948 it was replaced by the Panhead (so called from its new, saucepan-like rocker covers). Once again a new design proved to be underdeveloped, for although the new engine (in both 1,000 and 1,200 cc forms) featured clever hydraulic tappets, any reduction of pressure in the

A 1955 Panhead Model 74 (ie, 1,200 cc) on test. Massive telescopic forks make it a Hydra Glide.

The 74 cu in Panhead motor in detail.

lubrication system rendered them inoperative—and it still leaked. However, at the front end of the frame a massive pair of telescopic forks took over from the traditional leading link design. Models fitted with them were dubbed Hydra Glide, adding yet another name to the already crowded roster of Harley nomenclature.

This system of identification certainly can be confusing, for Harleys can be known by a variety of names, letters or numbers. The numbers generally refer to the capacity in cubic inches (45 cu in approximates to 750 cc; 61 to 1,000; 74 to 1,200; 80 to 1,300): the names tend to refer to a specific feature, like telescopic forks or electric start; and the letters to a particular model. Thus the side valve 45 introduced in 1929 as the D had mutated to the DL, DLD, R, RL, RLD, WL, and finally in 1955 the WLD. It was then replaced by the Model K, of the same capacity but with a fully sprung frame. However, it was much too sluggish, a trait which was not obviated by boring it out to 55 cu in (circa 883 cc) and calling it the KH. The Gordian Knot was cut by the launch of an overhead valve successor, the XL Sportster, which must be one of the best known designations ever to come out of Milwaukee. The Sportster was actually 57 cu in (just over 900 cc), which was an unusual size but it remained unaltered for sixteen years.

The traditional ruggedness of Harley-Davidson motor cycles can be evinced by the fact that even the Sportster weighed a hefty 416 lb. In order to attract different sorts of rider and to counteract the growing number of imported lightweights from England and, later, Japan, the factory began making overtures to the troubled Aermacchi concern in Varese, Italy. In 1961 Harley-Davidson purchased 50 per cent of Aermacchi's shares and began to market the sporting 250 cc horizontal single as the Spring. Later models included a 350 cc Sprint and a pair of two-stroke twins. The Italian factory was sold to Cagiva in 1978.

Above *Sportster was a name introduced in 1956: this is a classic from 1960. Note the 'Shovelhead' motor, the successor to the Panhead powerplant.*

Below *Harley-Davidson took a controlling interesting in Aermacchi, resulting in machines like this SX-350.*

Yet another name was added to the Harley lexicon in 1965 when the FL/FLH Duo-Glides (the latter indicating a fully sprung frame for the 1,200 cc ohv twins) were fitted with electric starters and christened the Electra Glides. Unfortunately this added to their already considerable weight, which necessitated more power, which overstressed the main bearings.

The problem was solved with a slight bottom end redesign. And there, with a recommendation to see the film 'Electra Glide In Blue', we can leave the Harley-Davidson model range.

As one of the few pioneering concerns still in its original line of business, it is worth following the factory's story a little further. In January 1969 the business was sold to the American Foundry and Machine Company (AFM), under whose auspices output boomed but the reputation for reliability and quality suffered. However, in 1981 Harley-Davidson was sold back to a consortium of its original owners and their successors, including Willie G. Davidson, grandson of founder William A. Davidson. Production is once again centred entirely in Juneau Avenue, Milwaukee, after a short AFM-inspired move to an assembly plant in York, Pennsylvania (though engines were still made in Milwaukee) and the company looks set to expand into other areas, including a four-cylinder engine designed by Porsche. Long may the Milwaukee Marvel continue.

Chapter 12

The best way to use it: The Classic scene

Now that you've got your classic motor cycle, what are you going to do with it? With the growth of the classic scene, there is more choice than ever, and whether your interest lies in road racing or trials, grass track or scrambles— or just taking part in runs and rallies—someone, somewhere is catering for it. Participation will almost always necessitate membership of a club, and some involve licences and suchlike.

Road racing is probably the most obvious classic sport—and they don't hang about, as the rider of this Matchless G50 demonstrates.

Vintage racing is no less exciting, and the mix of machines is more exotic. Here we see a 250 cc race—Triumph, Rudge and Excelsior.

Road racing is perhaps the most formally structured, since all circuit racing in this country is run under the aegis of the Auto Cycle Union (ACU), which requires the organizing club to conform to strict regulations. Individual competitors, too, must go through certain formalities before being allowed out into the cut and thrust of the race track. First of all, you will require a racing licence. To get one of these, you must apply to the ACU for a licence form, and in return they will send you the relevant document together with a medical certificate. This you take to your doctor, who will charge an inordinate amount for making sure that you are basically co-ordinated and physically competent, and signing it. You then send the certificate, the completed form and another sum of money back to the ACU, and they issue a licence and the current *ACU Handbook*, which contains the rules and regulations governing road racing.

You are now entitled to go racing, provided that your machine complies with both ACU and organizing club regulations, and that you have certain protective clothing—to wit, a crash helmet bearing the ACU sticker, a set of leathers, boots and gloves. These items of clothing apply to pretty well any form of motor cycle sport, and it is only sensible to buy the best that you can afford and to keep them in good condition.

The two national clubs which organize historic racing on a regular basis are the VMCC Racing Section and the Classic Racing Motorcycle Club. Normal VMCC rules apply to machine eligibility for the former (ie, a 25-year rule), while the latter has a cut-off date of 1973 (for four-strokes). Both run a series of meetings each year with various championship classes, and both are invited to other clubs' meetings and membership of one or both can give

Above *Grass tracking has a small but dedicated following. Again, the bikes are interesting in themselves—where else would you find a 1937 BSA, a 1950 AJS and a 1936 New Imperial on the same track?*

Below *This is actually a speedway race, though it looks more like dirt track. The bike is a JAP-engined Harley Peashooter.*

an active racer a busy season. The right type and age of machine will satisfy either club and give the rider an entré to the rather different vintage and classic racing scenes.

Other VMCC-organized sports include grasstrack, dirt-track, trials, hill-climbs and some speedway (though this generally takes the form of a 'demonstration'). The would-be competitor must, of course, be a member of the VMCC (or of an invited club), and the full regulations are available from that body.

A club formed fairly recently, but which has shown itself to be very active is the descriptively-named Pre-'65 Motocross Club. This organizes regular events, including the annual British Bike Bonanza which is, literally, a field day for classic off-road machines, be they trials or scrambles bikes. Two- or four-stroke bikes are eligible for club events, provided they were made before 1965, and competitors seem to fall into two distinct categories—those who want to go jolly fast, and those who want a bit of a bash-about on an old favourite. Whichever you are, the club will welcome you, and can provide technical assistance with the restoration of old competition bikes. At least one of the leading lights is actively involved in keeping historic motocross and trials motor cycles supplied with spare parts.

Away from the world of competitive sport, the classic motor cyclist—and particularly the VMCC member—has an almost confusing array of events in which to participate or spectate. After the Pioneer Run has opened the season in the spring, there are numerous runs and rallies every weekend in all

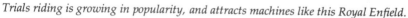

Trials riding is growing in popularity, and attracts machines like this Royal Enfield.

Left *Another popular competitive pastime is sprinting.*

Below *Road runs have always been well attended. This is the start of the 1925 London to Edinburgh Run, organized by the Motor Cycle Club. The motor cycles in the background include Royal Enfield twins and singles, a unit-construction Rover and a Beardsmore Precision.*

The 1946 Pioneer Run. Doubtless the 1913 Douglas was then the centre of attention, but now the accompanying vehicles would have a run of their own.

areas of the country. Some attract a large national (or international) entry (for example, the Banbury Run, the annual Assembly and the Festival of 1,000 Bikes), while others are strictly local. The VMCC publishes a 'fixture list' at the beginning of the season, and it is perfectly possible to combine a bit of touring or sightseeing with a road event.

The many local British or classic bike clubs which have sprung up around the country also organize their own events, as do the one-make clubs, so there need never be a dull moment for the active motor cyclist. Even ageing, or 'nouveau', rockers can indulge in a heady dose of nostalgia thanks to the Rockers Reunion Runs, which generally start in London and finish at a coastal resort.

On the other hand, some people do not want to be at all active, preferring to sit back and admire their machines, or polish them, rather than ride them. There are concours events for such, although a healthy number of concours require a motor cycle to be fully operational and, indeed, in use. However, a tradition of bringing machines to static events on a trailer survives, and it must be said that there are, in certain cases, very good arguments for doing so. It often seems, though, that a vehicle which is never used as a vehicle might as well be inside a museum.

There are old-bike enthusiasts with collections large enough to fill a very interesting museum (or two), but very few actually put their machines on public display. Any collection should be housed in a dry, preferably warmish, place. The security arrangements are up to the individual, but if the collection is properly insured, the insurance company may insist on

Above *Best known of the VMCC runs must be the Banbury, which attracts large crowds, especially at Sunrising Hill. Willing hands are always required!*

Below *A sunny day, a 1926 Royal Enfield twin (and a concours winner at that) and a chum in the sidecar. Why hide your motor cycle away when you—and others—could enjoy it?*

certain standards being met. Where there is money, or potential money, there will be rogues and it is a sad fact that an increasing number of historic machines have been stolen from private owners in recent years.

The importance of having a dry place cannot be stressed too much, for nothing acts more quickly than moisture to cause metal to deteriorate. An old dodge is to place a tray of brake fluid under a stored machine, the idea being that the fluid, which is hygroscopic (ie, it absorbs moisture), will draw the water from the atmosphere. It may work, but it is better to have little water in the first place. Regular airings and polishing will alleviate the effects of a less-than-perfect storage area, and dosing a machine with compounds like WD-40 will also help.

If it is known that a motor cycle is to be stored for some time without use, there are certain precautions that can be taken. Exposed metal can be greased or oiled, the battery removed and stored in a cool, dry place (and preferably used from time to time, even if only to power a bulb for some hours and then be gently recharged), and the machine should be raised so that both wheels are clear of the ground. This is quite important, as the tyres can develop marked flat areas if they are left in one position too long. The engine oil should be drained off, (stick a warning label to that effect in a prominent position), and the mouth(s) of the carburettor(s) or air filter(s) stuffed with oily rag, in case the inlet valve is open. Remove the spark plug(s) and squirt a little oil into the bore, then replace the plug. Before restarting the bike after the lay-off kick it over with the plugs out a couple of times—too much oil in the combustion chamber may cause a hydraulic lock and damage the motor.

Before hauling the machine out for its spring initiation (assuming it has been stored), refill all the oil you drained off and reverse all the storage procedures. Then give it the kind of check over you undertook before restoration. Finally, kick it over a few times to circulate some lubricant, tickle the carb up, cut-in the ignition and give it a long, swinging kick.

When your ankle has recovered from the kickback, try again more carefully (but with no less gusto) and old faithful will undoubtedly burst into life. Don't just stand there watching it vibrate around on the stand—get out and enjoy it: destination—fun!

240

Appendix A:

Classic motor cycle dealers

Atlantic Motor Cycles, 20 Station Rd, Twyford, Berks (0734 342266)
Bol d'Or, Limbrick Corner, Palatine Rd, Goring, Worthing, Sussex (0903 49033)
Bristol Classic Bikes, 17 Church Rd, Redfield, Bristol (0272 557762)
Ken Burgin (Italian bikes), 240 Headstone Lane, Harrow, Middx (01 428 3686)
Carolian Cars, The White House, Much Cowarne, Bromyard, Hereford (053 186 503)
Geoff Dodkin (Velocette), 346 Upper Richmond Rd West, East Sheen, London, SW14 7JS (01 876 8779)
Evesham Motorcycles, Unit 2, Hampton House Industrial Estate, School Rd, Hampton, Evesham, Worcs (0386 2937)
Michael Freeman Motors, The Camp, Stroud, Glos (028 582 297)
Honor Oak Motorcycles, 123 Brockley Rise, Forest Hill, London, SE23 (01 291 1272)
Bill Little Motorcycles, Oaksey Rd, Upper Minety, Malmesbury, Wilts (0666 860577)
Martlesham Electrical Ltd, The Old Guardroom, 19 Gloster Rd, Martlesham Industrial Estate, Ipswich, Suffolk (0473 625207)
Carl Rosner, Station Approach, Sanderstead, South Croydon (01 657 0121/2)
Starmount Motorcycles, Highgate, Hawkhurst, Kent (058 05 3506)
Brian R. Verrall & Co, 18–22 Tooting Bec Rd, London, SW17 (01 672 1144)
Fred Warr, 611 Kings Rd, Chelsea, London, SW3 (01 736 2934)
Whittox Lane Motors, Frome, Somerset (0373 66378)

Appendix B:

Spares specialists

Armours, 784 Wimbourne Rd, Bournemouth, Dorset (0202 519409): *General parts, accessories, exhausts*
A. Bennett & Son, Station St Garage, Atherston, Warks (08277 4076): *Triumph*

Autocycle, 50 Church Street, Moxley, Wednesbury, West Midlands (0902 45528): *BSA Gold Star*

Blays, 192 Heath Rd, Twickenham, Middx (01 894 2103): *BSA, Triumph, Norton, AMC*

Bri-Tie Motorcycles, 1 Armstrong St, Swindon, Wilts (0793 31518): *BSA*

Bristol Classic Bikes (see Dealers)

Burton Bike Bits, 152A Princess St, Burton-on-Trent, Staffs (0283 34130): *Royal Enfield, BSA, Norton*

C & D Autos, 1193–1199 Warwick Rd, Acocks Green, Birmingham, B11 1AW. (021 772 2062): *BSA*

Brian Carter, 76 Malvern Rd, Swindon, Wilts (0793 30653): *BSA Gold Star*

Conway Motors, 224 Tankerton Rd, Whitstable, Kent, CT5 2A7 (0227 276405): *Vincent*

Iain Cottrell, Manor Farm Buildings, Watery Lane, Weymouth, Dorset (0305 813690): *Harley-Davidson WL*

Geoff Dodkin (see Dealers)

Draganfly Motor Cycles, The Old Town Maltings, Broad St, Bungay, Suffolk, NR35 1EE (0986 4798): *Ariel*

Evesham Motor Cycles (see Dealers)

Fair Spares, 37 Albion St, Rugeley, Staffs (08894 3974): *Norton*

Ray Fisher, 185 Barrack Rd, Christchurch, Dorset (0202 483675): *BSA, Norton, Triumph*

Joe Francis Motors, 340 Footscray Rd, New Eltham, London, SE9 2ED (01 850 1373): *AMC, Norton*

A. Gagg & Sons, 106 Alfreton Rd, Nottingham (0602 786288): *AJS, Ariel, Royal Enfield, BSA, Triumph, Norton*

Gander and Gray, 594 Romford Rd, Manor Park, London E12 5AF (01 478 6062): *Royal Enfield, Norton, Triumph*

Richard Hacker Motorcycles, 18 Green Lane, London, SE20 (01 659 4045): *Triumph, AJS, Norton, BSA, Matchless*

Hamrax Motors, 328 Ladbroke Grove, North Kensington, London, W10 (01 969 5380): *AMC, Triumph*

Mick Hemmings Motorcycles, 36–42 Wellington St, Northampton (0604 38505): *Norton, Norvil*

High Gear Motorcycles, 217 Streatham Rd, Mitcham, Surrey (01 648 2900): *Triumph, Norton, BSA*

Hitchcocks Motorcycles, 28 Hemmings Rd, Washford, Redditch, Worcs (0527 25341): *Royal Enfield*

Norman Hyde, Rigby Close, Heathcote, Warks, CV34 6TL (0926 497375): *Triumph Trident*

Jacksons, Edward St, Chorley, Lancs (025 72 64151): *Triumph, BSA, Norton*

Allan Jefferies, 206 Saltaire Rd, Shipley, W. Yorks (0274 587451): *Triumph*

Kay's, 10 Bond St, London, W5 (01 567 2387)): *BSA, Triumph, Norton*

Kidderminster Motorcycles, 60–61 Blackwell St, Kidderminster, Worcs (0562 66679): *BSA, Triumph, Royal Enfield*

L&D Motors 367–369 Bath Rd, Brislington, Bristol, Avon (0272 770223): *Royal Enfield, BSA, Norton, Triumph*
Lewis & Sons, 51 Church St, Weybridge, Surrey (0932 42210): *BSA*
Bill Little (see Dealers)
Maughan & Son, 42 Townend, Wilsford, Nr Grantham, Lincs: *Vincent*
Meeten & Ward, 360 Kingston Rd, Ewell, Surrey (01 393 5193): *Villiers*
Merton Motorcycle Spares, 154 Merton Hall Rd, London, SW19 3PZ (01 542 9250): *AMC, BSA, Norton, Triumph*
Adrian Moss, Belvedere Works, St Mary Chalford, Glos (0453 883879): *Rickman Metisse*
Reg Orpin, 145–147 Goldhawk Rd, Shepherds Bush, London, W12 (01 743 1154): *Velocette*
OTJ, 10 Meadow Lane, Edenbridge, Kent (0732 862469): *BSA unit singles*
George Prew, Mill House, Barkway, Royston, Herts (0763 84763): *BSA Gold Star/RGS*
Pratts, 285 Brockley Rd, Brockley, London, SE4 2SF (01 691 3365): *Pistons*
Renovation Spares, 49 Feckenham Rd, Headless Cross, Redditch (0527 43796): *Royal Enfield*
RJ Motorcycles, 18–20 Hotel St, Coalville, Leics: *AMC, Norton*
Roebuck Motorcycles, 354 Rayners Lane, Pinner, Middx (01 868 1231/2): *Triumph*
Carl Rosner (see Dealers)
Russell Motors, 125–127 Falcon Rd, Clapham Junction, Battersea, London, SW11 2PE (01 228 1714): *AMC, BSA, Norton, Ariel*
Ralph Seymour, Hawthorn Works, Park St, Thame, Oxon (048 421 2277): *Velocette*
Shokks, 165 Malvern Rd, London, NW6 5YR (01 624 4871/01 328 8934): *Norton, Triton*
Roy Smith Motors, 116–124 Burlington Rd, New Malden, Surrey (01 949 6909/5731): *Velocette, NSU*
Stewart Engineering, PO Box 7, Market Harborough, Leics (0536 770962): *Sunbeam S7/8*
TC Motorcycles, 62 Northfield Rd, Harborne, Birmingham (021 427 6068): *Ariel, BSA, Norton, Triumph*
TMS, 92/94 Carlton Rd, Nottingham (0602 53447): *Triumph, Norton*
Tri-Supply, 2 Kemp Rd, Winton, Bournemouth (0202 514446): *Triumph*
Unity Equipe, 916 Manchester Rd, Castleton, Rochdale, Lancs (0706 32237): *Exhausts, sports items*
Vale Onslow Motorcycles, 104–116 Stratford Rd, Birmingham, B11 1AW (021 772 2062): *BSA*
Fred Warr (see Dealers)
Whittox Lane Motors (see Dealers)
L. P. Williams, Common Lane, Kenilworth, Warks, CV8 2EF (0926 54948): *Triumph Bonneville & Trident*

Appendix C:

Insurance brokers specializing in classic bikes

Clarkson Puckle
PO Box 27
Falcon House
The Minories
Dudley DY2 8PF
(0384 211011)
CJD Law and Co Ltd
3 Westgate House
Spital St
Dartford
Kent DA1 2EH
(0322 21461)
John Scott and Partners
Park Row
Farnham
Surrey GU9 7JH
(0252 725555)
Wells Brokers
FREEPOST
16A Cornhill
Bridgwater
Somerset
(0278 458913)

Schemes for VMCC members only
Short term, contact:
Mrs. A. M. Heath
Staverton House
1580 Melton Rd
Queniborough
Leics
Agreed value annual policies, contact:
J. B. Chawner and Partners
14 Market St
Altrincham
Cheshire
(061 941 4411)

Appendix D

One-make clubs

AJS & Matchless Owners
Terry Corley, c/o Trojan Finance, Dept B 13B Rowan Road, London SW16 5JF.

Ariel OMCC
P. Brocklehurst, Yew Tree Cottage, 14 Preston Old Road, Freckleton, Nr Preston PR4 1HD.
Telephone: Preston 635534.

BMW Club
Fred Secker, 64 Cavalry Drive, March, Cambs PE15 9EQ. Telephone: 03542 56276.

Benelli (Brembo Club International)
P. Rimmer, 21 Mount Pleasant, Sutton-in-Ashfield, Notts. Telephone: 0623 515736

Berkeley Enthusiast's Club
M. Rounsville-Smith, 41 Gorsewood Road, St. Johns, Woking, Surrey.

British Motorcyclists Federation Ltd
Jack Wiley House, 129 Seaforth Avenue, Motspur Park, New Malden, Surrey KT3 6JU. Telephone: 01-942 7914.

British Two-Stroke Club
Alan Abrahams, 38 Charles Drive, Cuxton, Kent ME2.

Brough Superior Club
Peter Rhodes, 15 Barnfield Road, Bollington Cross, Macclesfield, Cheshire.

BSA-Gold Star Owners Club
P. Jackson, 1 St Mary's Square, Honley, Huddersfield, W. Yorks HD7 2BA. Telephone: 0484 665931.

BSA Owners Club
Rob Jones, 37 Kilsby Close, Farnworth, Bolton, Lancs.

Classic Racing MCC
Len Haggis, 171 Brighton Road, South Croydon, Surrey. Telephone: 01-680 5244.

Cossack (and Neval) Owners
Mrs D. Dougan, 2 Cody Road, Clapham, Bedford. Telephone: 0234 63864.

DKW Rotary Owners Club
David Cameron, 17 Church Lane, North Weald Bassett, Epping, Essex CM16 6HX.

DOT
David Davies, 26 Brimble Hill, Wroughton, Swindon, Wilts.

Ducati Owners Club
Peter Fisher, 8 Waverley Road, London SE18.

Federation of British Scooter Clubs
N. F. Kerr, 73 Trowel Grove, Long Eaton, Notts. NG10 4BA.

Federation of Sidecar Clubs
Lesley Norman, 27 Longspring, Watford, Herts. Telephone: 0923 29924.

Gilera Owners Club
Gerard Gilligan, Fox House, Moor Road, Langham, Colchester CO4 5NR.

Greeves Riders Association
Peter Smith, 6 St. Georges Road, Winsford, Cheshire. Telephone: (06054) 51681.

Harley Davidson Road Crew (UK)
Harley House, Whitwood Common Lane, Whitwood, Castleford, Yorkshire WF10 5PD. Telephone: 0977 517566.

Hesketh Owners Club
C. V. R. Evans, 15 Windmill Close, Linden Village, Buckingham MK18 7BJ.

Honda OC
D. Barton, 18 Embley Close, Calmore, near Southampton, Hants. Telephone: 0703 869301.

Italian Owners Motorcycle Club GB
Chris Iredale, 36 Kingsley Drive, Adel, Leeds LS16 7PB.

James Group
Ian Telford, Four Ways, 70 Parkhill Road, Wallington, Surrey.

Jawa-CZ Owners Club
David Roberts, 31 All Saints Road, Bromsgrove, Worcs B61 0AG.

Lambretta Club of Great Britain
Kevin Wash, 8 Trent Close, Rainhill, Prescot, Merseyside L35 9LD.

Laverda-International
Andrew Vale, 8 Marney Close, Chelmsford, Essex CM2 7LR.

L.E. Velo
N. Bennett, 12 Wantage, Woodside, Telford, Shropshire TF7 5PA.

Maico Owners Club
Phil Hingston, 'No Elms', Goosey, Faringdon, Oxon SN7 8PA.
Telephone: (0367) 7408.

Morini Riders Club
Chris Webber, 24 Georgian Drive, Coxheath, Maidstone, Kent.

Moto Guzzi Club
Chris Anthony, 38 Burlington Road, New Malden, Surrey KT3 4NV.

MV Owners
Dave Kay, 26 Lichfield Road, Sandhills, Nr Walsall Wood, Staffs WS9 9PE.

MZ Riders Club
R. A. Marsh, 9 Edwards Road, Whitley Bay, Tyne & Wear, NE26 2BH.

Norton Owners Club
Pete Thistle, 30 Rose Hill Avenue, Sutton, Surrey SM1 3HG.

Panther Owners Club
Carol Mount, 90 Main Road, Duston, Northampton NN5 6RA.

Royal Enfield Owners Club
Pete Miller, 33 Eisele Close, Bulwell, Nottingham NG6 7BH.

Rudge Enthusiasts
G. W. Cox, 67 College Road, Fishponds, Bristol BS16 2HP.
Telephone: 0272 651539.

Single Cylinder Racing Register
Mark Harding, Filbet Cottage, Lower Street, Shere, Surrey.

The Scott Owners Club
The Old School House, Burton South Wirral, Cheshire L64 5TA;

Sunbeam Owners Fellowship
Joyce Tompolska, c/o Stewart Eng., PO Box 7, Market Harborough, Leics.

Suzuki Owners Club
Graham Walker, 12 Chestnut Close, Saltburn by Sea, Cleveland TS12 1PE.

The London Douglas MCC
R. G. Holmes, 48 Standish Avenue, Stoke Lodge, Patchway, Bristol, Avon.

Trail Riders Fellowship
Ian Thompson, Membership Secretary, Glebe House, St Columb Minor, Newquay, Cornwall.
Telephone: 03373 2813.

Triumph Owners MCC
Mrs E. Page, 101 Great Knightleys, Basildon, Essex SS15 5AN.

Velocette OC
9 Heather Drive, Wellington, Telford, Shropshire.

Vespa Club of Great Britain
Charles Caswell, 36 Beltinge Road, Harold Wood, Romford, Essex.

Vincent HRD OC
Phil Primmer, 17 Greenacres, Downton, Wilts. SP5 3NG.

Vintage Japanese Motorcycle Club
Dennis Lodge, 65 Greenhouse Farm Road, Palacefields, Runcorn, Cheshire.

Vintage MCC - Racing Section
Roger Kershaw, Ballacraine, 2 Mill Road, Cottingham, Market Harborough, Leics.

Vintage MCC - Road Section
Jim Hammant, Red Oaks, Mill road, Shiplake, Henley-on-Thames RG9 3LN.
Womens International Motorcycle Association
Mrs M. Hoare, 1 Chestnut Close, Waterford Park, Radstock, Avon BA3 3VY.
Telephone: 0761 33239.

Worldwide Norton Riders Club
S. O'Brien, 23 Johnson Close, Rugeley, Staffs.
Yamaha OC
Mrs M. Tuttle, 8 Telfer Road, Radford, Coventry CV6 3DD.
Telephone: 0203 597866.

Appendix E:

British museums

denotes major collection

Southern England
*Kenneth Bills Rochester Motor Cycle Museum, 144 High Street, Rochester, Kent, ME1 3UN (0634 814165)
The Brooklands Museum, Church Street, Weybridge, Surrey, KT13 8DE (0932 43573)
Totnes Motor Museum, Totnes, Devon.
The Combe Martin Motorcycle Collection, Cross Street, Combe Martin, North Devon.
Bristol City Museum, Queen's Road, Bristol, BS8 1RL (0272 299771)
Cornwall Aero Park, Culdrose Manor, Helston, Cornwall, TR13 0GA
The Warnham War Museum, main A24 Horsham to Dorking Road, near Horsham, Sussex (0403 65607)
*Sammy Miller Museum, Gore Road, New Milton, Hants.
RAF Museum, Hendon, London, NW9 5LL (01 205 2266)
*National Motor Museum, Beaulieu, Hants, SO4 7ZN (0590 612345)
Jersey Motor Museum, St Peter's Village, Jersey
Imperial War Museum, Lambeth Road, London, SE1 6HZ (01 735 8922)
Hatfield House, Tony Durose Vehicle Collection, Hatfield, Herts, AL9 5NQ (07072 62823)
The Heritage Motor Museum, Syon Park, West London (01 560 1378)
C. M. Booth Motor Museum, Falstaff Antiques, 63 High Street, Rolvenden, Kent (0580 241234)
London Science Museum, South Kensington, London, SW7 2DD (01 589 3456, ext 576)

The Midlands
*Stanford Hall Museum, Stanford Hall, Lutterworth, Leics, LE17 6DH
The Shuttleworth Collection, Old Warden Aerodrome, Biggleswade, Beds, SG18 9EP (076 727 288)
*National Motorcycle Museum, Coventry Road, Bickenhall, Solihull, West Midlands, B92 0EJ (06755 3311)
Nottingham Industrial Museum, Wollaton Park, Notts
*Museum of British Road Transport, Cook Street, Coventry, Warks
Museum of Lincolnshire Life, Burton Road, Lincoln, LN1 3LY (0522 28448)
*Midland Motor Museum, Stourbridge Road, Bridgnorth, Salop (07462 61761)
*The Geeson Brothers Motor Cycle Museum, 4 Water Lane, South Witham, Grantham, Lincs, NG33 5PH (057283 280/386)
The Donington Collection, Castle Donington, Derby, DE7 5RP (0332 810048)
*Birmingham Museum of Science and Industry, Newhall Street, Birmingham, B3 1RZ (021 236 1022)
Black Country Museum, Tipton Road, Dudley, West Midlands, DY1 4SQ (021 557 9643)

Northern England
North of England Open Air Museum, Beamish, Stanley, Durham, DH9 0RG (0207 231811)
North East Military Vehicle Museum, Exhibition Park Museum, Newcastle, NE2 4PZ
Museum of Army Transport, Flemingate, Beverley, North Humberside, HU17 0NG (0482 860445)
Automobilia, Billy Lane, Old Town, Wadsworth, Hebden Bridge, West Yorkshire, HX7 8RY (042284 4775)
*Murray's Motorcycle Museum, Bungalow Corner, Snaefell, Isle of Man (062486 719)
Lark Lane Motor Museum, 1 Hesketh Street, off Lark Lane, near Sefton Park, Liverpool (051 727 7557/2617)
*The Jack Hadwin Collection, Broughton-in-Furness, South Lakeland, Cumbria.

Scotland
*Royal Scottish Museum, Chambers Street, Edinburgh, EH1 1JF (031 2257534)
*Myreton Motor Museum, Aberlady, East Lothian (08757 288)
*Glasgow Museum of Transport, 25 Albert Drive, Glasgow, G41 2PE (041 4238000)
*Grampian Transport Museum, Alford, Aberdeenshire (0336 2292)

Northern Ireland
Belfast Transport Museum, Witham Street, Newtownards Road, Belfast
(0232 51519)
Ulster Folk and Transport Museum, Cultra Manor, Holywood, County
Down, Northern Ireland, BT18 0EU (02317 5411)

Appendix F:

European museums

Austria
Schloss Kremsegg Vintage Car Museum, 59 Kremsegger Strasse, 4550
Kremsmünster
Brandstetter Collection, Brunngasse 23, 3100 St Pölten, Niederösterreich

Belgium
Le Musée du Circuit de Spa-Francorchamps, 4878 Francorchamps
Provincial Motor Museum, Kelchterhoef, 3530 Houthalen

France
Raffaelli Motor Museum, Circuit Paul Ricard, Le Beausset 83330
Le Mans Motor Museum, Les Raineries, 72040 Le Mans-Cedex

West Germany
Bad Oeynhausen Car and Motorcycle Museum, Weserstrasse 225, 4970 Bad
Oeynhausen 13
Bad Rothenfelde Motor Museum, Parkstrasse 79, 4502 Bad Rothenfelde
Störy Small Car Museum, St Adrianplatz 5, 3205 Bockenem 12
Marxzell Transport Museum, Albstrasse 2, 7501 Marxzell
BMW Museum, Petnelring 130, 8000 München 40
German Museum, Museumsinsel, 8000 München 26
German Motorcycle Museum, Urban Strasse 11, 7107 Neckarsulm
Automuseum von Fritz B. Busch, 7962 Wolfegg
Auto und Technik Museum, D-6920 Sinsheim, Kraichgau
Daimler-Benz Museum, Mercedes Strasse, Untertürkheim, 7000 Stuttgart
60

Italy
Padiglione Cars, Autodrome Nazionale, Monza

Sweden
Helsingholm Collection, Muskotgatan 7, 800212 Berga, Helsingborg
Skokloster Motor Museum, 19060 Balsta, near Stockholm
Stockholm Technical Museum, Norra Djurgarden, 11527 Stockholm

Switzerland
Hilti Motorcycle Collection, Mirchstrasse 43, 9202 Gossau
Swiss Transport Museum, Lidostrasse 3–7, 6006 Lucerne
Edy Buhler Motorcycle Museum, Rutistrasse, 8633 Wolfhausen

Appendix G

Price guide

This guide does not constitute any kind of recommendation. Prices fluctuate according to the condition of the machine, the type of sale (auction, shop, private) and the fashionability of the marque/model. However, potential purchasers will be able to gauge roughly what their money will buy—and don't forget to haggle!

£2,000+
Manx Nortons, CSIs, Internationals
Vincent twins
Most pioneers, veterans and competition bikes

£1,000–£2,000
AJS—vintage singles
Ariel—Square Fours
BSA—Gold Stars
Douglas—pre-war twins
Norton—vintage 16H
Royal Enfield—vintage V-twins
Rudge—pre-war singles
Scott—pre-war twins
Sunbeam—pre-war singles
Triumph—Model P
         pre-war Tiger 80
Velocette—KSS
Vincent—Comet

£750–£1,000
Douglas—post-war twins
Norton—Commando
Sunbeam—S7/8
Triumph—Trophy
　　　　　Bonneville
Velocette—MSS
　　　　Venom
　　　　Viper

£500–£750
AJS—post-war singles
　　　post-war twins
Ariel—post-war Red Hunter
BSA—B33/31
　　　M20/21
　　　A10/7
　　　A65/50
Francis-Barnett—pre-war Cruiser
Matchless—post-war singles
　　　　　　twins
Norton—post-war 16H
　　　　Dominator 88/99
Panther—post-war singles
Royal Enfield—post-war 350/500 singles
　　　　　　　500/700 twins
Triumph—post-war 3T
　　　　TRW
　　　　Speed Twin
　　　　Thunderbird
Velocette—pre-war GTP
　　　　Valiant

Up to £250
Many post-war utility two-strokes
BSA—Bantam
Francis-Barnett—Falcon/Merlin

Bibliography

Marque Histories

AJS and Matchless: the post-war models, Roy Bacon (Osprey)
AJS: the history of a great motorcycle, Gregor Grant (Patrick Stephens)
Ariel: the post-war models, Roy Bacon (Osprey)
The Ariel Story, Peter Hartley (Argus)
Ariel Square Four, Roy Harper (Haynes Super Profile)
BMW R69 and R69S, Roy Harper (Haynes Super Profile)
BMW twins and singles: the postwar 250 singles and 450 to 1000 cc twins, Roy Bacon (Osprey)
Bahnstormer: the story of BMW motorcycles, L.J.K. Setright (Haynes)
The story of BMW motor cycles, Robert Croucher (Patrick Stephens)
Brough Superior: the Rolls-Royce of motor cycles, Ronald Clark (Goose and son)
The Brough Story, Ronald Clark (Goose and Son)
Brough Superior SS100, C. Simms (Haynes Super Profile)
Maintaining your Brough Superior, W. S. Gibbard (Batsford)
BSA A7 and A10 twins, O. Wright (Haynes Super Profile)
BSA Bantam, Jeff Clew (Haynes Super Profile)
The story of BSA motor cycles, Bob Holliday (Patrick Stephens)
BSA twins and triples, Roy Bacon (Osprey)
BSA Twins Restoration, Roy Bacon (Osprey)
BSA Gold Star and other singles, Roy Bacon (Osprey)
BSA: the Gold Star book, Bruce Main-Smith
The Giants of Small Heath: the history of BSA, Barry Ryerson (Haynes)
The Douglas motor cycle: the best twin, Jeff Clew (Haynes)
Douglas, Peter Carrick (Patrick Stephens)
Ducati motorcycles, Alan Cathcart (Osprey)
Ducati singles, Mick Walker (Osprey)
Harley-Davidson Motor Company: an official eighty-year history, David Wright (Patrick Stephens)
Harley-Davidson: the Milwaukee marvel, Harry V. Sucher (Haynes)
Honda, Chris Myers (Batsford)
Honda: the early classic motorcycles, Roy Bacon (Osprey)
The Story of Honda motorcycles, Peter Carrick (Patrick Stephens)
The Iron Redskin: Indian, Harry V. Sucher (Haynes)
J.A.P.: the vintage years, Jeff Clew (Haynes)
Kawasaki from sunset to Z1, Roy Bacon (Osprey)
The Story of Kawasaki motorcycles, Peter Carrick (Patrick Stephens)
The Lea-Francis Story, Barrie Price (Batsford)
Matchless: once the largest British motorcycle manufacturer, Peter Hartley (Osprey)

Matchless 350 and 500 cc heavyweight singles 1939–1965, R. Hide
Morgan sweeps the board: the three-wheeler story, Dr. J. D. Alderson and D. M. Rushton (Gentry)
Moto Guzzi: genius and sport, Mario Colombo (Albion Scott)
MV Agusta, Jeff Clew (Haynes Super Profile)
The story of MV Agusta motor cycles, Peter Carrick (Patrick Stephens)
Norton Commando, Jeff Clew (Haynes Super Profile)
The Norton story, Bob Holliday (Patrick Stephens)
Norton singles, Roy Bacon (Osprey)
International Norton, C. Simms (Haynes Super Profile)
Manx Norton, Cyril Ayton (Haynes Super Profile)
Norton twins, Roy Bacon (Osprey)
The story of Panther motorcycles, Barry Jones (Patrick Stephens)
Royal Enfield: the postwar models, Roy Bacon (Osprey)
The story of Royal Enfield motorcycles, Peter Hartley (Patrick Stephens)
The Rover Story, Graham Robson (Patrick Stephens)
Rudge, Bryan Reynolds (Haynes)
The story of Rudge motorcycles, Peter Hartley (Patrick Stephens)
The Scott motorcycle: the yowling two-stroke, Jeff Clew (Haynes)
The Sunbeam motorcycle, Robert Cordon Champ (Haynes)
Sunbeam S7 and S8, Robert Cordon Champ (Haynes Super Profile)
Sunbeam four-stroke singles 1928–1939, R. Hide
Suzuki two-strokes, Roy Bacon (Osprey)
The story of Triumph motor cycles, Harry Louis and Bob Currie (Patrick Stephens)
Triumph twins and triples, Roy Bacon (Osprey)
Triumph Twins Restoration, Roy Bacon (Osprey)
Bonnie, John Nelson (Haynes)
Triumph singles, Roy Bacon (Osprey)
It's a Triumph, Ivor Davies (Haynes)
Triumph Thunderbird, Ivor Davies (Haynes Super Profile)
Triumph Trident, Ivor Davies (Haynes Super Profile)
Velocette: a development history of the MSS, Venom, Viper, Thruxton, and scrambler models, Rod Burris (Haynes)
Always in the picture: a history of the Velocette motorcycle, R. W. Burgess and J. R. Clew (Haynes)
Velocette 1905–1971: an illustrated reference, Dave Masters
KSS Velocette, Jeff Clew (Haynes Super Profile)
Villiers singles and twins, Roy Bacon (Osprey)
Vincent HRD story, Roy Harper (Vincent Publishing Company)
Vincent vee-twins: the famous 1000 series, plus 500 singles, Roy Harper (Osprey)
Know thy beast: restoring post-war Vincents, Eddie Stevens
Vincent twins, Roy Harper (Haynes Super Profile)
Vincent HRD, Peter Carrick (Patrick Stephens)

The Yamaha Legend, Ted Macauley (Gentry)
Yamaha two-stroke twins, Colin MacKellar (Osprey)

General
The Guinness book of motorcycling facts and feats, L.J.K. Setright (Guinness)
German motorcycles of World War Two, Tony Oliver (Almark Publishing)
British motorcycles since 1950 (Volumes 1, 2 and 3), Steve Wilson (Patrick Stephens)
Motorcycle Milestones, Richard Renstrom (Classics Unlimited)
The encyclopedia of motorcycling, George Bishop (Hamlyn)
Classic motorcycles, Vic Willoughby (Hamlyn)
Motorcycles, L. J. K. Setright (Weidenfeld)
Best of British, Peter Howdle (Patrick Stephens)
The classic motorcycles, Bob Currie and Harry Louis (Patrick Stephens)
Classic motorbikes, Warren Penney and Alan Puckett (Hamlyn)
Whatever happened to the British motorcycle industry?, Bert Hopwood (Haynes)
Historic racing motorcycles, John Griffith
Motorcycles in colour, Eric E. Thompson (Blandford)
The Guinness guide to motorcycling, Peter Carrick (Guinness)
Great British bikes, (ed) Ian Ward and Laurie Caddell (Orbis)
Guide to pre-war British motorcycles, C. J. Ayton (Temple Press)
Military motorcycles, David Ansell (Batsford)
Foreign racing motorcycles, Roy Bacon (Haynes)
The Hamlyn guide to Japanese motorcycles, C. J. Ayton (Hamlyn)
The motorcycle industry: a million miles ago, Neale Shilton (G.T. Foulis)
Motorcycling in the 1930s, Bob Currie (Hamlyn)
Discovering old motorcycles, T. Crowley (Shire)
Motorcycle pioneers, M. Partridge
Roadtests republished, vol 1 1930–40, vol 2 1955–60, vol 3 1960–65, Bruce Main-Smith
Vintage roadtest journal, C. Allen
The illustrated encyclopedia of motorcycles, Erwin Tragatsch (Hamlyn)
The history of motor cycling, Cyril Ayton, Bob Holliday, Cyril Posthumus, Mike Winfield (Orbis)
Great British motor cycles of the Fifties, Bob Currie (Hamlyn)
Great British motor cycles of the Sixties, Bob Currie (Hamlyn)
Classic British motor cycles: the final years, Bob Currie (Hamlyn)
Motor Cycle cavalcade, Ixion (SR Publishers, reprint)
Reminiscences of Motor Cycling, Ixion (EP Publishing, reprint)
Motorcycles: a technical history, C. F. Caunter (HMSO)
The vintage years at Brooklands, Dr Joseph Bayley (Goose and son)
Exotic motorcycles, Vic Willoughby (Osprey)
Golden Oldies: Classic Bike roadtests, (ed) Mike Nicks (Patrick Stephens)
Classic British trials bikes: pre '65 AJS to Velocette, Don Morley (Osprey)

Classic British scramble bikes, Don Morley (Osprey)
Post-war British motorcycles, C. Ayton (Temple)
Guide to Italian motorcycles, C. Ayton (Temple)
Great Japanese motorcycles, C. Ayton (Muller)
Military motorcycles of World War Two, Roy Bacon (Osprey)
Early motorcycles: construction, operation, service, V. Pagé
Brooklands bikes in the '20s, Peter Hartley (Argus)
American racing motorcycles, Hatfield (Haynes)
Motorcycle engineering, Phil Irving (Speedsport)
Motorcycle manual, Roy Bacon
Motorcycle technicalities, Phil Irving
Restoration of vintage and thoroughbred motorcycles, Jeff Clew (Haynes)
Bikes at Brooklands in the pioneer years, Peter Hartley
Brooklands: behind the scenes, Charles Mortimer (G.T. Foulis)
Motorcycle roadracing in the '50s, Andrew McKinnon (Osprey)
British racing motorcycles, Jeff Clew (Haynes)
50 ans de motocyclettes francaises, Dominique Pascal (EPA)

Specialist Booksellers
Albion Scott Ltd, 51 York Road, Brentford, Middx, TW8 0QP (01 560 3404/5)
Bruce Main-Smith Retail Ltd, PO Box 20, Leatherhead, Surrey, KT22 8HL (0372 375615)
Chater and Scott Ltd, 8 South Street, Isleworth, Middx, TW7 7BG (01 568 9750)
Roy Harper and Company, mail order dept, 41 High Street, Spalding, Lincs (0775 68286)
Millhouse Books, The Millhouse, Eastville, Boston, Lincs, PE22 8LS (020584 377)
The Out-of-Print Book Service, 17 Fairwater Grove East, Fairwater, Cardiff, CF5 2JS (0222 569488)

Index